Parole Board hearings

law and practice

Hamish Arnott is a solicitor at Bhatt Murphy. He has been a solicitor at the Prisoners' Advice Service and the Public Law Project. He specialises in prison law and the rights of detainees. He also teaches extensively in areas related to his practice.

Simon Creighton is a solicitor and founding partner of Bhatt Murphy. He was based at the Prisoners' Advice Service between 1993 and 1998 as their first lawyer. At Bhatt Murphy he specialises in prison law, working particularly with life sentenced prisoners. He has worked on many public law challenges and applications to the European Court of Human Rights. He writes extensively on prison law and compiles the twice-yearly Update on the subject for *Legal Action*.

The Legal Action Group is a national, independent charity which campaigns for equal access to justice for all members of society. Legal Action Group:

- provides support to the practice of lawyers and advisers
- inspires developments in that practice
- campaigns for improvements in the law and the administration of justice
- stimulates debate on how services should be delivered.

Parole Board hearings

law and practice

Hamish Arnott and Simon Creighton

This edition published in Great Britain 2006
by LAG Education and Service Trust Limited
242 Pentonville Road, London N1 9UN
www.lag.org.uk

British Library Cataloguing in Publication Data
a CIP catalogue record for this book is available from the British Library.

ISBN-10 1 903307 42 2
ISBN-13 978 1 903307 42 7

Typeset by Regent Typesetting, London
Printed in Great Britain by William Clowes Ltd, Beccles, Suffolk

Foreword

In November 2005, Simon Creighton of Bhatt Murphy gave a presentation at the Parole Board's Annual Conference, whose theme was 'Working on Quality'. The workshop was aimed at increasing the appreciation of problems faced by prisoner's representatives and raising awareness of what they regard as the essential characteristics of a fair hearing. The day before that Conference, the Board ran a stakeholders' day to discuss various aspects of the Board's work and to see how they could be improved. Alongside those from the Home Office, Prison Service and Probation Service sat various representatives from firms of solicitors who specialise in representing prisoners who come before the Board. It is now unthinkable that the Board would undertake major changes in its practices without such prior consultation. It was, however, equally unthinkable back in the 1980s that this could ever happen.

Change has happened quickly. You do not have to be a grizzled veteran to recall the end of the 80s when suddenly the doors of secrecy behind which the Parole Board worked, were flung open to a curious world. Consider the principles we worked under as the 90s dawned – parole reports were written by those who knew that they would never be read by the prisoner; prisoners could make representations to the Board but had no knowledge of what the 'other side' had said about them; the Board gave a simple one-word answer to those anxiously awaiting their fate – yes or no. This left prisoners in the dark about why they had been refused release. Moreover, it left them unable to take steps to tackle whatever it was that the Board required them to do in order to have a better chance next time. These truly were the Dark Ages, and underlying all of this in respect of lifers was the ultimate power of the Home Secretary to reject Parole Board recommendations for release.

Fortunately, the courts at last recognised the unfairness of it all. Open reporting came first. Report writers could no longer rely on 'gut feelings' about prisoners, but had actively to assess and articulate why they thought a prisoner was unfit to progress. The Board actually had to *explain* why it was making its recommendations, knowing that the threat of judicial review was ever present. This was equally the case for the Home Secretary when turning down the Board's recommendations. Prisoners, moving forward from a 'knockback', knew for the first time what they needed to do to achieve a better result next time.

Inexorably, things gathered momentum. Openness led to judicial reviews, and to access to the European Court of Human Rights, establishing that decisions to release lifers should not lie with elected politicians, but rather should be taken by an independent 'court', namely the Parole Board. Recommendations for release became *directions* that were binding on the Home Secretary. Discretionary lifers came on board first, to be followed by those sentenced to Her Majesty's Pleasure and ultimately mandatory lifers. The architect of all this change was Edward Fitzgerald QC, whose name should rightly be remembered when the law on lifers is mentioned. The Convention on Human Rights was his tool and the European Court signed off the plans, but nevertheless cases took aeons to reach their final destination in Strasbourg. That was put right in 1998 when the Convention was born again under domestic law. And quite right too – after all, the UK both drafted the Convention and had been the first to sign up to it. Those who had never heard of Articles 5, 6 and 8 were forced to read and understand them. Issues of fairness and proportionality became everyday language for people who had once thought that the Parole Board should be a place of comfortable obscurity.

Perhaps more radical was the advent in 1992 of the 'oral hearing'. No more shuffling of papers in a private room for the Parole Board. Now we were out there face-to-face with prisoners and their representatives. For the first time, members and staff at the Board, who had previously communicated only by letter or phone, could converse with solicitors in person. Working relationships were built, a mutual understanding of each other's problems developed, a mutual *respect*, perhaps grudging at first, began to evolve. And solicitors began to accept that the Board was truly independent of the Government in its decision making.

It became obvious to the Parole Board that the potential of this new era of openness was enormous. Way before the advent of the Freedom of Information Act, we like to think that the Board was among the first to open up its working practices to the public and other organisations. We went on-line with our website, visitors were welcomed to our offices, and staff were encouraged to *discuss* cases with lawyers.

We even began to engage with prisoners direct. For instance, the Board now contributes to a publication written by ex-prisoners targeting that much misunderstood group of prisoners who maintain that they are innocent of their crimes; and we have written articles for 'Inside Time', a newspaper written by and for prisoners. Its editor has visited our offices and watched us at work.

It also took only a short time for another truth to hit the Parole Board. Oral hearings were good! Witness evidence assumed new importance when it complemented the written word, and not infrequently it was the deciding factor. Risk assessment – the Board's holy grail – was enhanced by the ability to see and hear from prisoners and those writing reports about them. And lawyers started to acknowledge that at last the word fairness could be applied to the process. As the Board's ability to do its job moved forward, so too did the skills of lawyers representing prisoners. Aside from the professional possibilities offered by this new gateway to judicial review, solicitors previously denied access to the courts could now develop and hone their advocacy skills, albeit in a less formal atmosphere. Those who represent prisoners in these hearings regularly are highly skilled and experienced advocates who assist the Board in doing its job. We are fortunate in having lawyers with the skills and expertise necessary in this unique and important field of law.

I wholeheartedly welcome the chance to commend this book to its audience and it is wholly appropriate that it should be Bhatt Murphy that took up the reins. Simon Creighton and Hamish Arnott are at the forefront of the law on parole and life sentences. Both Parole Board members and our staff have great respect for their professionalism and desire to engage with the Board in improving the system for all. We look forward to working with Bhatt Murphy in the future and I am certain that this book will lead to similar constructive working relationships with new firms of solicitors who are attracted to this rewarding area of the law.

And so I turn to look at the future. The experienced prison lawyers now enjoy excellent relations with the Parole Board. This means that cases are managed effectively and that hearings are able to be conducted properly. Professionalism is paramount, and this enhances the ability of both the representatives and the Board to do their respective jobs – yours to represent your client to the best of your ability; ours to protect the public within the framework of a full and fair process. There are of course lines drawn in the sand over which neither can step. However, these lines can now be regarded simply as proper boundaries – they are no longer battle lines. That is how we wish to engage with lawyers now and in the future, and I fully endorse this book as another significant step in that direction.

Sir Duncan Nichol
Chairman of the Parole Board

Preface

The idea for this book was conceived in 2004 at the time when the release arrangements for all kinds of life sentences were finally harmonised, with the Parole Board finally having the power to direct whether such prisoners are released following an oral hearing. This was a hugely significant development, which brought together the sentencing and release procedures for all life sentenced prisoners after more than a decade of divergence. It resulted from the acceptance that the European Convention on Human Rights requires a judicial body and not the executive to decide whether lifers are safe for release once they have served their punitive terms. This expansion of the Board's role as a court seemed a good opportunity to produce a guide to the law and procedures relevant to its hearings.

However, any thought that 2004 marked the end of a process following which the Board would have a period of calm during which it could adjust to its new functions was dispelled by subsequent events. Most notably these have included the decision of the House of Lords in January 2005 that recalled fixed-term prisoners were entitled to oral hearings (*Smith and West v Parole Board* [2005] UKHL 1), and the complete overhaul of how determinate sentences are administered brought about by the coming into force of the relevant parts of the Criminal Justice Act 2003 on 4 April 2005.

These events necessitated changes in the scope of this book. While the main focus is still to provide a clear guide to the law and procedures applicable to oral hearings, it also covers the Parole Board's decision-making role in other contexts, most importantly where it is deciding on the initial release of fixed-term prisoners.

The Board, as a result of these developments, now has a daunting workload. Although its remit has been extended exponentially over the past 15 years, its constitution has not materially changed and the resources available to it have failed to keep pace with its new duties. Between 1992 and 1996, the Board convened an average of 200 oral hearings a year. By 2003, the year before mandatory lifers were granted oral hearings, the enormous increase in life sentenced prisoners brought about by the Crime (Sentences) Act 1997 meant that the Board had to hold more than 1,000 hearings a year. Since the CJA 2003 and the House of Lords ruling in *Smith and West*, even though the Board has implemented new procedures to try to ensure that oral hearings are only convened where necessary, as opposed to in every case, it is anticipated that there will be more than 3,000 held each year.

Despite the Board now processing thousands of cases each year where it is required to operate as a court, it still has the same basic structure as when it was little more than an administrative arm of the Home Office. Parliament has shown no interest in assimilating the Board into the tribunals system. This book seeks to provide an in-depth guide to the decision-making practice of the Board, but also aims to look at the fault lines and areas of conflict that are likely to arise in the future.

Notwithstanding these pressures, the Parole Board has been exceptionally generous in providing practical support and encouragement for the preparation of this book. Terry McCarthy, the head of casework at the Board, has given an enormous amount of his time and has allowed us access to his own internal guidance to Board members. It would not have been possible for the book to have been completed without his help.

Christine Glenn, the Board's Chief Executive, has also been very helpful and encouraging, a reflection of her overall commitment to updating the Board and consulting with all people affected by its work. Sir Duncan Nichol, Chairman of the Board has very kindly written the Foreword.

The parts of the book dealing with the life sentence were checked by Howard Smith of LRRS. It is a testament to his professionalism that he was prepared to give up his spare time to help provide a book that is both accurate and of practical use to those working with lifers in the parole system. Paul Jackson of LRRS was also extremely helpful in providing source materials.

One practitioner who deserves a special mention in this book is Helen Jones. Helen has worked more extensively with lifers in the parole system than any other solicitor and has always shared her knowledge and expertise. Our own understanding of the oral hearings system has benefited enormously from Helen's guidance and input over the years.

No book dealing with life sentences and the parole system would be complete without mentioning the special and unique contribution made by Edward Fitzgerald QC to this area of law. Ed has been at the heart of virtually every important case for the past 20 years and his enthusiasm and commitment remain undimmed.

The book aims to encompass legal developments up to 1 October 2005. At the time of writing, new draft Parole Board rules were due to be laid before Parliament as a statutory instrument for the first time. The purpose of issuing Rules by way of secondary legislation is obviously aimed at countering suggestions that it is improper for the Board, when acting as a court, to be subject to procedures determined solely by the executive (a tension referred to in several places throughout the text). In the event, the new Rules were not brought into force before the contents of this book had to be finalised. However, the draft Rules differ from the existing Parole Board Rules 2004 only in minor respects (and even maintain the same numbering for its provisions). The proposed substantive changes are to expressly extend the Rules to cover the procedure for the recall of prisoners serving determinate sentences. The proposed changes are in fact already carried out in practice and so, if they are implemented as envisaged, it is highly unlikely to affect how hearings are managed. Changes to the Rules can be monitored by checking the Parole Board website.

Hamish Arnott
Simon Creighton
1 November 2005

Contents

APPENDICES

Table of cases

References in the right-hand column are to paragraph numbers.

Table of statutes

References in the right-hand column are to paragraph numbers.

Table of statutory instruments

References in the right-hand column are to paragraph numbers.

Abbreviations

Legislation

AJA 1999	Access to Justice Act 1999
CDA 1998	Crime and Disorder Act 1998
CJA 1967	Criminal Justice Act 1967
CJA 1991	Criminal Justice Act 1991
CJA 2003	Criminal Justice Act 2003
CJCSA 2000	Criminal Justice and Courts Services Act 2000
C(S)A 1997	Crime (Sentences) Act 1997
CPR	Civil Procedure Rules 1998
DPA 1998	Data Protection Act 1998
DVCVA 2004	Domestic Violence, Crime and Victims Act 2004
HRA 1998	Human Rights Act 1998
MHA 1983	Mental Health Act 1983
PCC(S)A 2000	Powers of the Criminal Courts (Sentencing) Act 2000

Other

ACO	Assistant Chief Officer
ACR	Automatic conditional release
ART	Aggression Replacement Therapy
AUR	Automatic unconditional release
CALM	Controlling Anger and Learning to Manage it
CARATS	Counselling, Assessment and Throughcare Services
CDS	Criminal Defence Service
CLS	Community Legal Service
CRD	Conditional Release Date
CSAP	Correctional Services Accreditation Panel
CSCP	Cognitive Self Change Programme
DCR	Discretionary conditional release
DSPD	Dangerous and Severe Personality Disorder
DTO	Detention and Training Order
ECHR	European Convention on Human Rights
ECtHR	European Court of Human Rights
ERS	Early Release Scheme
ETS	Enhanced Thinking Skills
GCC	General Criminal Contract
HCR-20	Historical, Clinical Risk Management
HDC	Home Detention Curfew

HEO	Higher Executive Officer
HMP lifer	Detained at Her Majesty's Pleasure
HRP	Healthy Relationships Programmes
HSF	Healthy Sexual Functioning
JR	Judicial review
LED	Licence expiry date
LRC	Local review committee
LRRS	Lifer Review and Recall Section
LSC	Legal Services Commission
LSP	Life sentence plan
MAPPA	Multi-agency Public Protection Arrangements
MAPPP	Multi-agency Public Protection Panel
MHRT	Mental Health Review Tribunal
NDPB	Non-Departmental Public Body
NOMS	National Offender Management Service
NPD	Non parole date
OASys	Offender Assessment System
OCPA	Office of the Commissioner for Public Appointments
OGRS	Offender Group Reconviction Scale
PAR	Parole Assessment Report
PB	Parole Board
PBR	Parole Board Rules
PC	Probation Circular
PCL-R	Psychopathy Checklist – Revised
PED	Parole eligibility date
PPG	Penile Plethysmograph
PPO	Prolific and Priority Offender
PSI	Prison Service Instruction
PSO	Prison Service Order
R&R	Reasoning and Rehabilitation
RAPt	Rehabilitation of Addicted Prisoners Trust
RM 2000	Risk Matrix 2000
ROTL	Release on Temporary Licence
RRS	Release and Recall Section
SACJ	Structured Anchored Clinical Judgment
SARN	Structured Assessment of Risk and Needs
SDS	Standard Determinate Sentence
SED	Sentence expiry date
SOTP	Sex Offender Treatment Programme
SPPU	Sentencing Policy and Penalties Unit
TC	Therapeutic community
VPS	Violence Prediction Scheme
VRAG	Violence Risk Assessment Guide

CHAPTER 1

The Parole Board

Background to the Board's creation

1.1 There have been varying kinds of early release schemes in England and Wales long before the creation of the Parole Board, although these were always at the discretion of the executive.[1] The Board itself was created by the Criminal Justice Act (CJA) 1967, at the same time as there was a comprehensive statutory regime brought in to deal with the early release of prisoners for the first time. The white paper leading to the Act[2] had proposed a system of early release for fixed-term prisoners by which those who showed 'promise or determination to reform' could earn a further period of parole of up to one-third over and above the existing automatic one-third remission. While the wording of the white paper suggests that the key reason for the introduction of a parole system was rehabilitative, there were also pressures on the prison system (overcrowding and prison discipline) that also made it attractive for managerial reasons.[3]

1.2 While there was general support for a system of selective early release, debate in parliament prior to the passing of the CJA 1967 focused on what process should be adopted to decide who should benefit. The then Labour government had proposed that the discretion should lie wholly with the Home Secretary, but this was resisted both by the Opposition and the judiciary.[4] The concerns raised in debates included the fact that if prisoners sentenced to identical terms by the courts were to be released on different dates, then something more than a purely executive decision was required. There was also concern that without some check on executive discretion, parole could be granted too readily when needed to ease the pressure of prison overcrowding.[5]

1.3 In the end the CJA 1967 created a system whereby the newly created Parole Board (along with local review committees (LRCs) located in the prisons, which were subsequently abolished by the CJA 1991) was consulted by the Home Secretary as to the suitability of prisoners for release on parole. Accordingly, the Parole Board's role in recommend-

1 For a summary of the history and philosophy behind parole and remission in England and Wales see Part 1 of *The parole system in England and Wales* Cm 532, 1988 (the Carlisle Committee Report).

2 *The adult offender* Cmnd 2852, 1965.

3 Carlisle Committee Report Part 1 para 22.

4 See Richardson, Wiedenfield and Nicolson, *Law, process and custody: prisoners and patients*, 1993 p175.

5 Carlisle Committee Report Part 1 para 22.

6 CJA 1967 s61.

ing release, including that of life sentence prisoners[6] was advisory only (although its recommendations in relation to recall cases had to be followed).[7] The Board initially consisted of 17 members, including the chair, High Court judges, recorders, psychiatrists, principal probation officers and criminologists.[8]

1.4 The procedures involved in parole applications from the creation of the Board until after the coming into force of the CJA 1991, despite the involvement of judges, were far from judicial and are unrecognisable from the procedural safeguards that have since developed. Decisions relating to initial release were all conducted on paper by panels of the Board – there was no disclosure of the material upon which the decisions were made and so no real opportunity to make representations, and no reasons were given (except in recall cases). The standard response given to fixed-term prisoners refused parole stated: 'Your case for early release on licence under the parole scheme has been has been fully and sympathetically considered but the Secretary of State regrets to have to inform you that parole has not been authorised'.[9]

Current legal framework of the Board

Constitution

1.5 The Parole Board was reconstituted by the CJA 1991 and the CJA 2003. Since 1996 it has been an executive Non-Departmental Public Body (NDPB).[10] NDPBs are designed to permit functions to be carried out at a remove from ministerial control, and so in the Parole Board case the aim was to bolster its independence from the executive (see further discussion below). The Board's overarching aim is 'protecting the public and contributing to the rehabilitation of prisoners'.[11]

1.6 The Board is not to be considered a servant or agent of the Crown[12] and as a statutory corporation it has power to do such things as are incidental or conducive to the carrying out of its functions in relation to deciding on the early release and recall of prisoners.[13]

7 CJA 1967 s62.

8 See HOC 66/68 para 4.

9 Carlisle Committee Report para 139.

10 Facilitated by an amendment to the CJA 1991 making it a corporate body – Criminal Justice and Public Order Act 1994 s149.

11 See Parole Board Business Plan 2005–6 Section 2.

12 CJA 2003 Sch 19 para 1(1).

13 CJA 2003 Sch 19 para 1(2).

1.7 The Board is to consist of a chair and no less than four other members who are appointed by the Home Secretary.[14] As an NDPB it has both a chair and a chief executive who retains overall responsibility for management. Members must include someone who has held judicial office, a psychiatrist, someone with experience of after-care services for released prisoners and someone who has made a 'study of the causes of delinquency or the treatment of offenders'.[15] The Board currently has more than 120 members, three of whom are full-time. The members include a chairman, a part-time judicial vice-chair, four full-time members and part-time judicial, psychiatrist, psychological, probation, criminologist and independent members.

1.8 Board members are appointed by the Home Secretary in accordance with guidance issued by the Office of the Commissioner for Public Appointments (OCPA). The current tenure is six years, split into two three-year terms. Re-appointment is subject to a satisfactory level of performance.[16]

1.9 The Parole Board website[17] states that in relation to part-time members:

> in order to complete the required duties, independent members and criminologists are expected to give an average commitment of two and a half days a week, probation members one day a week, psychiatrists 20–35 days a year and judges 15 days a year. A proportion of this time must clearly be during normal working hours such as attending panels and where relevant carrying out interviews. However, certain aspects such as reading dossiers and writing interview reports can be done at evenings or weekends.

1.10 The anticipated increase in workload caused by the coming into force of the relevant parts of the CJA 2003 in April 2005, and by the need to hold oral hearings for determinate sentence prisoners recalled to prison, means that the Board plans to increase its membership to nearly 200, although only three of these will be full-time salaried members.[18] The Board is serviced by a secretariat of about 58.[19] The secretariat has tended to have a very high percentage of staff on secondment from the Home Office.

1.11 In terms of case management, the Parole Board secretariat (see

14 CJA 2003 Sch 19 para 2(1).

15 CJA 2003 Sch 19 para 2(2).

16 See *Comprehensive review of lifer and parole processes*, 2001 para 5.3.

17 See www.paroleboard.gov.uk.

18 Parole Board Business Plan 2005–6 Section 3.

19 Ibid.

Appendix 10 for contact details) has a number of different teams reflecting the various aspects of the parole process. These different teams include:

- a Paper Hearings team, dealing with cases where there is no right to an oral hearing;
- a Representations Against Recall Team, which deals with the initial reviews of determinate sentence recalls;
- a Pre-Hearings Team, dealing with the paper sift process;
- an Oral Hearings Team, which deals with the administration of oral hearings; and
- a Post-Panel Team, which deals with matters arising from decisions and legal challenges.

Legal powers and duties

1.12 The Board now derives its powers from section 239 of the CJA 2003.[20] As noted above, the Board remains a corporate body.[21] It is under a duty to advise the Home Secretary 'with respect to any matter referred to it by him which is to do with the early release or recall of prisoners'.[22] There is a requirement that the Board deals with cases referred to it on consideration of all such evidence as may be adduced before it.[23]

1.13 The Home Secretary is given the power to make rules with respect to the proceedings of the Board[24] and also the power to make directions as to the matters the Board should take into account in discharging its functions.[25] Its powers in relation to its decisions as to the release of indeterminate sentence prisoners are contained in the Crime (Sentences) Act 1997, as amended; and in relation to determinate sentence prisoners in the Criminal Justice Acts 1991 and 2003.

1.14 The Board, when acting as a court-like body, remains a statutory corporation, not a court of inherent jurisdiction. As such, it can only adopt procedures expressly or impliedly authorised by the statutory framework.[26]

20 In force from 4 April 2004 – Criminal Justice Act 2003 (Commencement No 8 and Transitional and Saving Provisions) Order 2005 No 950.
21 CJA 2003 s239(1).
22 CJA 2003 s239(2).
23 CJA 2003 s239(4).
24 CJA 2003 s239(5) – see Parole Board Rules 2005.
25 CJA 2003 s239(6) – for discussion on effect of directions, see below and Chapter 10.
26 *R (on the application of Roberts) v Parole Board* [2005] UKHL 45 para 65.

Evolution of the Board's functions

1.15 The changes to the Board's legal powers and in the way it makes its decisions since its creation have been dramatic. The Board now holds oral hearings at which the prisoner is entitled to disclosure and publicly funded legal representation in all indeterminate sentence cases involving potential release on or after the expiry of the punishment phase (or 'minimum term') and in cases where extended sentence or determinate sentence prisoners are recalled to custody. When considering such cases, the Board's decision to release the prisoner is final. Where there is no right to an oral hearing, the Board's decisions are made after the prisoner has had an opportunity to make representations following disclosure of the material upon which the decision will be based, and full reasons for decisions are given.

1.16 This dramatic shift from an advisory role where decisions were made with virtually no procedural safeguards for the prisoner, to one where the Board is often acting in a judicial manner in deciding on release, has been effected primarily by numerous legal challenges by prisoners. These challenges have enhanced the standards of fairness in parole proceedings both by reference to the requirements of the European Convention on Human Rights (ECHR), and to what is required under common law standards.

Administration of sentences and the ECHR

Article 5

1.17 The major impact on the development of the Board's role, especially in the right to oral hearings, has been brought about in cases involving breaches of the ECHR. The key article that has been invoked in order to enhance the fairness of Parole Board decision making is article 5 (see below), which prohibits arbitrary detention.

Article 5

1. Everyone has the right to liberty and security of person. No one shall be deprived of his liberty save in the following cases and in accordance with a procedure prescribed by law:
   (a) the lawful detention of a person after conviction by a competent court;
   (b) the lawful arrest or detention of a person for non-compliance with the lawful order of a court or in order to secure the fulfilment of any obligation prescribed by law;
   (c) the lawful arrest or detention of a person effected for the

purpose of bringing him before the competent legal authority of reasonable suspicion of having committed and offence or when it is reasonably considered necessary to prevent his committing an offence or fleeing after having done so;

(d) the detention of a minor by lawful order for the purpose of educational supervision or his lawful detention for the purpose of bringing him before the competent legal authority;

(e) the lawful detention of persons for the prevention of the spreading of infectious diseases, of persons of unsound mind, alcoholics or drug addicts, or vagrants;

(f) the lawful arrest or detention of a person to prevent his effecting an unauthorised entry into the country or of a person against whom action is being taken with a view to deportation or extradition.

2. Everyone who is arrested shall be informed promptly, in a language which he understands, of the reasons for his arrest and the charge against him.
3. Everyone arrested or detained in accordance with the provisions of paragraph 1(c) of this article shall be brought promptly before a judge or other officer authorised by law to exercise judicial power and shall be entitled to trial within a reasonable time or to release pending trial. Release may be conditioned by guarantees to appear for trial.
4. Everyone who is deprived of his liberty by arrest or detention shall be entitled to take proceedings by which the lawfulness of his detention shall be decided speedily by a court and his release ordered if the detention is not lawful.
5. Everyone who has been the victim of arrest or detention in contravention of the provisions of this article shall have an enforceable right to compensation.

1.18 The two relevant parts of article 5 are 5(1)(a) and 5(4). Prisoners serving sentences imposed by criminal courts are clearly lawfully detained within 5(1)(a), so when does 5(4) require access to a further review process to decide whether detention remains lawful?

> At first sight, the wording of Article 5(4) might make one think that it guarantees the right of the detainee always to have supervised by a court the lawfulness of a previous decision which has deprived him of his liberty ... Where [this] decision ... is one taken by an administrative body, there is no doubt that Article 5(4) obliges the Contracting States to make available to the person detained a right of recourse to a court; but there is nothing to indicate that the same applies when the decision is made by a court at the close of judicial proceedings. In the latter case the supervision required by Article 5(4) is incorporated in the

decision; this is so, for example, where a sentence of imprisonment is pronounced after 'conviction by a competent court' (Article 5(1)(a) of the Convention).[27]

1.19 This principle applies where detention remains for the purpose contemplated by the sentencing court. So, where a normal determinate sentence is imposed by a criminal court as punishment, the review required by article 5(4) is already incorporated by the imposition of the sentence. Detention cannot become arbitrary for the purposes of article 5 because, at any time during such a sentence, it remains justified as what the court thought appropriate for punishment and as such satisfies article 5(1)(a).[28]

1.20 It follows that if, in the case of the gravest murders, the sentence is genuinely one of lifelong detention as punishment, article 5(1)(a) will be satisfied for the whole of the prisoner's life.[29]

Article 5 and indeterminate sentences

1.21 In 1983 the then Home Secretary issued a ministerial statement[30] that clarified how he intended to exercise his discretion in releasing life sentence prisoners. The life sentence was effectively divided into two: the 'tariff' phase, that is the punitive term which the lifer has to serve for reasons of retribution and deterrence; and the post-tariff phase, when detention is based on whether the lifer is deemed to pose a risk to the public. In setting the tariff the Home Secretary consulted the judiciary, and in deciding to release the Home Secretary consulted the Parole Board. This statement applied to all lifers.

1.22 The European Court of Human Rights (ECtHR) in Strasbourg court first analysed the discretionary life sentence when a prisoner, who had been released and recalled before the procedures for tariff setting were clarified, challenged the procedures relating to his recall to custody.[31] The court noted that the discretionary life sentence was only imposed under domestic law where the offender was assessed as being dangerous and unstable, and these characteristics were by their very nature susceptible to change.[32] Therefore, after release, re-

27 *De Wilde, Ooms and Versyp v Netherlands* 1 EHRR 438.

28 *R (on the application of Giles) v Parole Board* [2004] 1 AC paras 51–52, *R (on the application of Smith) v Parole Board* [2005] UKHL 1 para 36.

29 *Wynne v UK* (1995) 19 EHRR 333, and such sentences can now be imposed under the criteria contained in CJA 2003 Sch 21.

30 30 November 1983.

31 *Weeks v UK* (1988) 10 EHRR 293.

32 Ibid para 46.

detention required a review under article 5(4) to confirm that there was a 'causal link' with the objectives of the sentencing court.[33] The sentencing court could not predict whether an offender needed to be detained when the punitive phase of the sentence expired, and so a further judicial assessment was required at that stage to avoid detention no longer being justified under 5(1)(a).

1.23 There followed a number of domestic challenges that confirmed that for discretionary life sentence prisoners, as dangerousness was the criterion for imposition of the sentence, detention after the tariff (or punitive phase) required an assessment of dangerousness.[34] The requirement under article 5(4) for this assessment to be carried out by a court-like body, even for the initial release of those sentenced to life imprisonment for very serious crimes, was subsequently confirmed by the ECtHR.[35]

1.24 These decisions led to a divergence in the way that the different life sentences were administered. For example, the ECtHR initially accepted the government's argument that, although the 1983 statement applied to all lifers, the mandatory life sentence for murder, imposed automatically irrespective of dangerousness, was in reality a sentence of lifelong punitive detention[36] and so any release mechanisms could properly remain in the hands of the executive.[37]

1.25 Notwithstanding these comments, the ECtHR later decided that the mandatory indeterminate sentence for those convicted of murder when under 18 (the HMP life sentence) (see para 7.2) required an article 5(4) hearing to determine detention after the tariff phase on the basis that the sentence (which involved considerations of the offender's welfare) could only justify this following a finding of dangerousness.[38] Eventually the ECtHR accepted that its earlier finding that the sentence for adults convicted of murder was one of lifelong punitive detention could no longer be sustained as the domestic arrangements had clearly divided the sentence up into two phases as with any other life sentence, with dangerousness being the key to detention in the post-tariff phase.

33 Ibid paras 42 and 58.

34 *R v Secretary of State for the Home Department, ex p Benson* [1989] COD 329, *R v Secretary of State for the Home Department, ex p Bradley* [1991] 1 WLR 134.

35 *Thynne, Wilson and Gunnell v UK* (1991) 13 EHRR 666.

36 Statement of Angela Rumbold 16 July 1991.

37 *Wynne v UK* 19 EHRR 333.

38 *Singh and Hussain v UK* (1996) 22 EHRR.

> The Government maintained that the mandatory life sentence was nonetheless an indeterminate sentence which was not based on any individual characteristic of the offender, such as youth and dangerousness, and therefore there was no question of any change in the relevant circumstances of the offender that might raise lawfulness issues concerning the basis for his continued detention. However, the Court is not convinced by this argument. Once the punishment element of the sentence (as reflected in the tariff) has been satisfied, the grounds for the continued detention, as in discretionary life and juvenile murderer cases, must be considerations of risk and dangerousness.[39]

1.26 Accordingly, mandatory lifers became entitled to article 5(4) compliant reviews on tariff expiry. The whole process of life sentences moving from being wholly administered by the executive, to being judicially controlled, therefore took about 20 years. Release arrangements for all indeterminate sentences were eventually harmonised by the coming into force of the relevant parts of the CJA 2003 in January 2004.

1.27 Although the position for determinate sentences and article 5 is generally as set out above, extended sentences (that is, sentences comprising a punitive 'custodial term' together with an 'extension period' of supervision in the community imposed to protect the public) are different. Although not indeterminate, similar considerations as for life sentences apply to detention during the extension period. As the extension period is not imposed punitively, but to protect the public, whether detention is necessary for this purpose requires examination under article 5(4).[40]

Article 6

1.28 It has been decided that when considering whether it is appropriate to release a prisoner that the Parole Board is not determining a 'criminal charge' within the meaning of article 6 of the ECHR (even when considering a recall based on further misconduct).[41] Whether article 6 applies insofar as liberty is a 'civil right' remains undecided,[42] although in cases where article 5 applies it is difficult to see what article 6 in its 'civil right' aspect would add in terms of fair procedure.

39 *Stafford v UK* [2002] 35 EHRR 32.

40 *R (on the application of Sim) v Parole Board* [2003] EWCA Civ 1845.

41 *R (on the application of Smith) v Parole Board* [2005] UKHL 1.

42 Ibid.

Consequences of the applicability of article 5

1.29 Article 5(4) requires review of the legality of detention by a 'court'. However, the court referred to in 5(4):

- does not necessarily have to be a court of law of the classic kind integrated within the standard judicial machinery of the country;
- but must be independent of the executive and any parties to the case;
- and needs to provide a judicial procedure appropriate to the kind of deprivation of liberty in question;
- and must have the power to direct, not only advise on, release.[43]

1.30 The need for the review to be 'wide enough to bear on those conditions which, under the ECHR, are essential for the lawful detention of a person in the situation of the particular detainee'[44] necessitates the reviewing body to be fact-sensitive and rule on the essential question of risk to the public. Accordingly, the availability of judicial review of a non-ECHR compliant parole procedure does not remedy the breach of article 5(4), as the grounds for judicial review are too narrow.[45] The Parole Board, as an expert quasi-judicial body set up to examine risk, was clearly suited to the task of carrying out such reviews, subject to amendments to its powers and procedures.

Oral hearings, disclosure and the power to release

1.31 At the time of the first case in which article 5 was held to apply to the administration of discretionary life sentences by the ECtHR, the Board did not have directive powers of release in periodic reviews, and even in recall cases the procedure adopted did not provide for full disclosure of any adverse material. Accordingly, article 5(4) was held to have been breached without consideration as to whether an oral hearing was required.[46] However, when the CJA 1991 introduced procedures to consider the post-tariff release and recall of discretionary lifers, and gave the Board the power to direct release, procedures for disclosure and the holding of oral hearings were also introduced into the parole process for the first time.[47]

1.32 The necessity for oral hearings was examined when the ECtHR

43 *Weeks v UK* paras 59 and 61.

44 *R (on the application of Smith) v Parole Board* [2005] UKHL para 37.

45 *Weeks v UK* para 69.

46 *Weeks v UK* paras 63–68.

47 The Parole Board Rules 1992.

confirmed that an article 5(4) review was necessary to review the post-tariff release of HMP lifers:

> The Court is of the view that, in a situation such as that of the applicant, where a substantial term of imprisonment may be at stake and where characteristics pertaining to his personality and level of maturity are of importance in deciding on his dangerousness, Article 5 para 4 requires an oral hearing in the context of an adversarial procedure involving legal representation and the possibility of calling and questioning witnesses.[48]

1.33 As the scope of article 5(4) widened to include all kinds of indeterminate sentences, and extended sentences for recall during the extension period, the statutory framework has been amended to give the Board directive powers, and the Rules governing hearings have been amended to increase the scope of oral hearings.[49]

1.34 Despite the administrative burden they create for the Board, there are obvious advantages both for the prisoner and for the Board in holding an oral hearing. Home Office research conducted into decision making by panels of the Board identified the following reasons:

- information in the dossier can give a one-sided view of the prisoner and the level of risk;
- legal representation can assist the prisoner in putting his/her case;
- the procedure is seen to be fair;
- risk assessments are 'human judgements';
- hearings allow direct communication between the prisoner and the Board.[50]

1.35 The courts have also recognised in the absence of an oral hearing:

> assumptions based on general knowledge and experience tend to favour the official version as against that which the prisoner wishes to put forward. Denying the prisoner of the opportunity to put forward his own case may lead to a lack of focus on him as an individual. This can result in unfairness to him, however much care panel members may take to avoid this.[51]

48 *Hussain and Singh v UK* (1996) 22 EHRR 1 para 60.

49 The Parole Board Rules 1997 were introduced to cater for HMP and automatic lifers, and the Parole Board Rules 2004 for mandatory lifers and extended sentence prisoners. See Chapter 10 for a discussion on the degree to which Parole Board hearings are 'adversarial'.

50 Padfield, Liebling and Arnold, *An Exploration of decision-making at discretionary lifer panels*, Home Office Research Study 213, December 2000.

51 *R (on the application of Smith) v Parole Board* [2005] UKHL 1 para 66.

Independence of the executive

1.36 The ECtHR, even at a time when the Board's powers and procedures were insufficient to meet the requirements of article 5(4), considered that it was sufficiently independent and impartial:

> The Parole Board sits in small panels, each of which in the case of life prisoners includes a High Court judge and a psychiatrist. The manner of the appointment of the Board's members does not, in the Court's opinion, establish a lack of independence on the part of the members. Furthermore, the Court is satisfied that the judge member and the other members of the Board remain wholly independent of the executive and impartial in the performance of their duties.
>
> There remains the question whether the Board presents an appearance of independence, notably to persons whose liberty it considers. On this point, as the Government stated, the functions of the Board do not bring it into contact with officials of the prisons or of the Home Office in such a way as to identify it with the administration of the prison or of the Home Office.[52]

1.37 While the first paragraph of the above quote in relation to the performance of Board members remains unquestioned, albeit that it is now rare for High Court judges to chair panels, there are concerns about the Board's structural independence from the Home Office, notwithstanding its NDPB status since 1996. The Board remains sponsored by the Release and Recall Section (RRS) of the Home Office. When the issue of sponsorship was reviewed in 2001, the primary purposes of sponsorship were identified as:

- providing ministers with advice on the overall efficiency and effectiveness of the Parole Board and its usefulness as an instrument of government policy;
- supplying the Board with funds and managing the system of appointing members and the chairman;
- monitoring the Board's performance and providing support and advice and, if necessary, imposing sanctions to ensure efficient and effective delivery of required services;
- advising the Board and ministers of issues relating to NDPD status, and conducting quinquennial reviews of the Board.[53]

1.38 Although the review identified sponsorship as a potential problem in relation to perceived independence, it stated that it was 'unclear how far public or prisoner concerns about the Board's independence

52 *Weeks v UK* para 62.

53 *Comprehensive review of parole and lifer processes*, October 2001 para 5.4.3.

are a problem in practice, rather than theory',[54] and the conclusion was that the Board could remain sponsored by a department whose decisions it was required to review. Furthermore, the Board was until recently located in the same building as the National Offender Management Service (NOMS) departments making early release and recall decisions, and shares seconded staff with them. These facts do raise issues of perceived independence when the Board is increasingly required to act as a court-like body in its decision making, and it remains to be seen whether its current relationship with the Home Office is sustainable.[54a]

1.39 One issue in relation to independence that has recently been examined in the courts is the degree to which the Board is required to act in accordance with directions issued by the Home Secretary when acting as a court-like body. When the procedures to provide discretionary lifers with article 5(4) compliant reviews were introduced in 1992, the Home Secretary accepted that it was not appropriate to issue directions to the Board. This was on the basis that it was the Board's responsibility, in acting as an independent court, to apply the appropriate test for release.

1.40 However, when release procedures for indeterminate sentence prisoners were harmonised in 2004, the Home Secretary's view changed.[55] He issued directions as to matters the Board was required to take into account. These were subsequently held not to be binding on the Board, as it would be incompatible with article 5(4) for the executive to determine how a judicial function should be carried out.[56] Accordingly, the Board is required to follow directions only when it is not required to act as a court-like body by article 5.

Common law standards of fairness

1.41 As demonstrated above, the primary engine of enhancing fairness in Parole Board decision making has been through the application of

54 Ibid para 5.4.5.

54a Although a complaint to the ECtHR raising these issues was ruled inadmissible in 2000 (*Hirst v UK* [2001] CLR 919).

55 Perhaps in response to the Comprehensive Review of Parole and Lifer Processes which reported in 2001, which suggested that it would not be unlawful for directions to be issued in relation to the release of lifers.

56 *Girling v Parole Board* [2005] EWHC 546 (QBD) – the Parole Board Rules are in a different category, being essentially procedural and now having been issued by statutory instrument.

the ECHR. Domestic courts, by contrast, when first asked to examine a procedure whereby the liberty of prisoners was determined by a secretive process, did not consider that common law requirements of fairness aided the prisoner. When holding that a mandatory lifer was not even entitled to the reasons as to why release was being refused, Lord Denning stated:

> But, so far as I can judge of the matter, I should think that in the interests of the man himself, as a human being facing indefinite detention, it would be better for him to be told the reasons. But, in the interests of society at large, including the due administration of the parole system, it would be best not to give them.[57]

1.42 The justification for what now seems like an astonishing assertion was rooted in the notion of early release being a privilege, not a right, and the spurious assumption that for prisoners to know the reasons for decisions would both inhibit the candour of reports and lead to unmeritorious litigation by prisoners. Nevertheless, the judgment bound the courts for many years in relation to how natural justice was held to apply to parole processes. It took another ten years until a discretionary lifer finally managed to obtain an order to disclose parole reports under common law standards of fairness,[58] by which time the article 5 cases had achieved the same result. *Payne* was eventually overruled when the House of Lords decided that in the tariff setting process for mandatory lifers (which at the time remained an executive decision of the Home Secretary) fairness required disclosure sufficient to make meaningful representations, and also reasons for the decision.[59] In relation to determinate sentence prisoners, the Carlisle Committee Report that led to the changes brought in by the CJA 1991 recommended that there should be disclosure of the dossier and reasons given for decisions and this became practice after the Act came into force in 1992.

1.43 However, the increasing judicial role of the Board necessitated by the need to carry out article 5(4) compliant reviews has impacted on how the courts now view the Board's duties to act fairly in accordance with the common law. When two determinate sentence prisoners challenged the refusal of the Board to hold oral hearings to determine whether they had been correctly recalled, the House of Lords decided there was a right to an oral hearing in such circumstances,

57 *Payne v Lord Harris of Greenwich and another* [1981] 2 All ER 842.

58 *R v Parole Board, ex p Wilson* [1992] 1 QB 740.

59 *R v Secretary of State for the Home Department, ex p Doody* [1994] 1 AC 531.

even though article 5 was not directly engaged.[60] The decision was surprising, as in terms of what the common law requires it marked a significant shift from *Doody*.[61]

1.44 What brought about this shift was a recognition that the Board was a judicial body, and that the recall context was one where, notwithstanding the direct applicability of article 5, there was a factual loss of liberty, the review of which required the highest standards of fairness. Also influential in the decision was the evidence put before the court that in many other common law jurisdictions it is the norm that when a prisoner is recalled an oral hearing is convened.[62] A further factor was that although the Board claimed to have a policy that oral hearings were held where fairness required it, by the time the House of Lords heard the cases, the evidence was that in the previous 19 months the Board had only held an oral hearing for a recalled determinate sentence prisoner in four cases out of 1,945. This must have raised concerns over whether the Board was properly exercising its discretion.

1.45 The Lords' finding that the Parole Board was required to act judicially when considering the recall of determinate sentences led to the confusing finding that if the Board breached the common law duty of fairness in not holding an oral hearing, then there was also a breach of article 5(4). As four out of five of the Lords did not consider that article 5(1) could be breached by the recall of a determinate sentence prisoner, it is at first sight hard to see how article 5(4) can be breached by the deficiencies in the procedures adopted. The rationale appears to be that if the Board is acting judicially when deciding a question of liberty, then the procedural guarantees have to be informed by ECHR standards.

60 *R (on the application of Smith) v Parole Board* [2005] UKHL 1 – although the Lords stated that the right was not absolute, the circumstances in which it was considered hearings should be allowed were so wide that it is difficult to see how a hearing cannot be held when requested by the prisoner. Accordingly, the practice adopted after this case was to offer hearings in all cases where an initial paper review did not result in release.

61 See above.

62 See, for example, the decision of the US Supreme Court in *Morrissey v Brewer* 408 US 471 (1972).

CHAPTER 2

Other agencies involved in the parole process

2.1 Beyond the individual prisoner and the Parole Board there are a number of other agencies involved in the policy, administration and decision-making in parole processes.

The National Offender Management Service (NOMS)

2.2 NOMS[1] is an agency within the Home Office that now has responsibility for the management of both the Prison and Probation Services. It was created in 2004 following the publication of the Carter Review *Managing offenders, reducing crime* which recommended greater integration between the agencies dealing with offenders. The creation of NOMS has not been without criticism, as there was little consultation before the effective merger of the services was carried out, and there are also concerns that the move was made as a means of facilitating the privatisation of services (the principle of 'contestability').[2]

Lifer Review and Recall Section (LRRS)

2.3 This is a department in the Sentencing Policy and Penalties Unit (SPPU) of NOMS and is therefore part of the Home Office. It has casework responsibility for Parole Board reviews for those serving life and indeterminate sentences. This includes making decisions on behalf of the Home Secretary on Parole Board recommendations for transfer to open conditions, co-ordinating release on life licence, preparation of the licence for issue to the prisoner on release, consideration of whether the supervision element of a licence may be cancelled and making decisions as to whether lifers should be recalled. This department has been renamed on a number of occasions (it was for a long time known as Lifer Unit) and has in the past been moved between the Prison Service and the Home Office.

Release and Recall Section (RRS)

2.4 This is also a department within the SPPU of NOMS and performs a similar function in relation to determinate sentenced prisoners as

1 See www.homeoffice.gov.uk/inside/org/dob/direct/noms.html.

2 See NAPO briefing for MPs December 2004, Nick Davies 'A system in chaos' *Guardian* 23 June 2005.

LRRS does for lifers. It has overall responsibility for parole policy and procedures, including offering support to parole clerks in individual prisons where necessary.[3] It accordingly makes decisions on behalf of the Home Secretary on matters where the Parole Board does not have the final say (such as the initial release of prisoners liable to removal, or those recommended for parole who are serving sentences of 15 years or more for offences committed before 4 April 2005). It also makes decisions as to the recall of those serving determinate sentences on licence, including extended sentences, and has casework responsibility for the recall hearings.

The Prison Service

2.5 The Prison Service is an executive agency managed by a Director General within the Home Office under the NOMS umbrella. The Prison Service issues policy guidance in the form of Prison Service Instructions (PSIs) and Prison Service Orders (PSOs). Individual prisons are subject to supervision by Area Managers and Prison Service Headquarters retains policy responsibility for matters such as offending behaviour programmes and management of Category A prisoners.

2.6 The governor of the prison holding the prisoner retains responsibility for issuing the licence in relation to determinate sentence prisoners. Prisons will also have a parole clerk who is responsible for collating reports for parole reviews in determinate cases and disclosing the dossier to the prisoner and forwarding it to the Board.[4]

2.7 Prisons holding lifers will usually have a Lifer Manager and Lifer Clerk. The lifer departments of individual prisons have responsibility for the transfer of prisoners (except where the move involves category A prisoners, or is a move to open conditions which can only be authorised by LRRS following a Parole Board recommendation).[5] Contact details for all prisons in England and Wales can be found on the Prison Service website, as can copies of most PSIs and PSOs.[6]

3 PSO 6000 para 5.4.1.

4 PSO 6000 para 5.2.1.

5 PSI 8/2004.

6 See www.hmprisonservice.gov.uk/prisoninformation.

The Probation Service

2.8 Although managed under NOMS, the National Probation Service[7] remains a separate statutory body (created by the Criminal Justice and Courts Services Act (CJCSA) 2000). The National Service has a director general, and the directorate is responsible for the issuing of policy guidance in the form of Probation Circulars (PCs).

2.9 The Service is further divided into local probation boards that now cover the same geographical area as police areas.[8] This was made to facilitate the multi-agency public protection arrangements now required by sections 325–326 of the Criminal Justice Act (CJA) 2003 (see below). The Service's functions include providing for the supervision and rehabilitation of offenders, including primary supervision of those released on licence.[9]

2.10 Offenders sentenced to custody are appointed a probation officer (now termed 'offender manager' in the Probation Service's National Standards[10]) by the local probation board for where they were sentenced. This officer is usually called the home or field probation officer. The officer should co-operate with the prison in developing a sentence plan, and when released on licence will be responsible for supervising the licence. The local probation officer will be responsible for preparing reports for parole hearings giving a view as to risk to the public, but also assessments of any release plan and any suggested extra licence conditions.

2.11 Individual prisons also have probation departments staffed by probation officers seconded from local areas. They will also be responsible for writing reports for Parole Board reviews so that dossiers will normally contain two probation reports.

Multi-agency Public Protection Arrangements (MAPPA)

2.12 Sections 325–326 of the CJA 2003 place a joint duty on the area chief police officer, the local probation board and the Prison Service to establish arrangements to assess and manage the risks posed by, broadly, serious sexual and violent offenders. In practice each area operates

7 See www.probation.homeoffice.gov.uk.

8 CJCSA 2000 s4.

9 CJCSA 2000 s1.

10 See PC 15/2005.

under detailed MAPPA guidance issued in PC 54/2004. The Prison Service has issued its own guidance in relation to its responsibilities in PSO 4745. These arrangements help determine how offenders are to be managed, and may involve recommendations being made as to, for example, additional licence conditions to deal with specific concerns.

2.13 Identified offenders are categorised as posing either a low, medium, high or very high risk of harm.[11] Each area must operate management of the risk of such offenders at three levels.[12] Level 1 is 'ordinary risk management' which will normally be appropriate for low or medium risk offenders and is appropriate where management is possible by one agency without active participation of other agencies. Level 2 is 'local inter agency risk management' which is appropriate where the active involvement of more than one agency is required, but where the risk is not so serious as to warrant referral to level 3.

2.14 Level 3 is the 'Multi-agency Public Protection Panel', which is responsible for the management of the 'critical few'.[13] The guidance defines the 'critical few' as those assessed to be at high or very high risk of harm who present risks that can only be managed by a plan that requires close supervision at a senior level, or exceptionally high profile cases (even where the risk of harm is not assessed as high) where management issues may impact on public confidence in the criminal justice system.

2.15 Although the MAPPA do not have a formal role in the parole process, the guidance states that any risk assessments that may have a bearing on the appropriateness of release should be disclosed to the Home Office and the Parole Board.[14] The guidance further notes that as such assessments may impact on the prospects of the offenders' liberty, fairness requires 'as full a disclosure as possible' to the prisoner.[15] Clearly the MAPPA guidance cannot detract from the general duty of disclosure to prisoners.[16]

11 PC 54/2004 para 99.
12 PC 54/2004 para 109.
13 PC 54/2004 para 116.
14 PC 54/2004 para 91.
15 PC 54/2004 para 92.
16 See PSO 6000 for determinate sentence prisoners and the Parole Board Rules 2004 in relation to oral hearings.

CHAPTER 3

Public funding

3.1 Prison law as a category is funded by the Legal Services Commission (LSC) as part of the Criminal Defence Service (CDS) that was established together with the Community Legal Service (CLS) by the Access to Justice Act (AJA) 1999.[1] Firms can have either a general criminal contract (to cover general police station advice and criminal defence work) under which they can take on prison law cases, or a 'stand alone' prison law contract if the firm does not do normal criminal defence work. For a 'stand alone' contract the supervisor standard includes having carried out 350 hours prison law work in each of the preceding three years.[2]

3.2 There are currently proposals regarding competitive tendering for CDS contracts. As these are based on duty solicitor slots at magistrates' courts, there is no obvious manner for accounting for prison law in these proposals, particularly for firms that only have a specialist prison law contract and do not undertake routine criminal defence work.

Scope of prison law

3.3 Regulation 4 of the Criminal Defence Service (General) (No 2) Regulations 2001[3] confirms that the LSC will provide funding, which in practice is provided through contracts with approved firms, to any individual who:

> (f) requires advice and assistance regarding his treatment or discipline in prison (other than in respect of actual or contemplated proceedings regarding personal injury, death or damage to property);
> (g) is the subject of proceedings before the Parole Board;
> (h) requires advice and assistance regarding representations to the Home Office in relation to a mandatory life sentence or other parole review; ...

3.4 The General Criminal Contract (GCC), by which individual firms are bound by when carrying out work under the CDS, determines the circumstances in which Advice and Assistance and Advocacy Assistance can be given. This[4] is now somewhat outdated as the specification has not managed to keep up with the changes in the law, such

1 AJA s12.
2 See LSC Manual, 2B-138.
3 SI No 1437.
4 See Contract Specification, Part A 5.2.

as the harmonisation of early release procedures for lifers. However, the specification explicitly permits advice and assistance and advocacy assistance to be provided to prisoners within all Parole Board procedures.

3.5 The current eligibility limits set out on the CDS Keycard No 41a(2), issued October 2005, are:

- Advocacy Assistance is available where weekly disposable income does not exceed £194 and disposable capital does not exceed £3,000 (for those with no dependants; £3,335 for those with one dependant, £3,535 for those with two dependants with a £100 increase in the limit for each further dependant).
- Advice and Assistance is available where weekly disposable income does not exceed £92 and disposable capital does not exceed £1,000 (for those with no dependants; £1,335 for those with one dependant, £1,535 for those with two dependants with a £100 increase in the limit for each further dependant).

3.6 Evidence of capital is accepted as being the prisoner's certification by signing the form. In terms of income, prisoners will not be able to supply pay slips (as prison work is not contractual) or proof of benefits (not being eligible), and so usually the only evidence of what income they are receiving will be what they certify on the CDS 2 or 3.[5]

3.7 Although prisoners are separated from their spouses/partners by the fact of imprisonment, this does not necessarily prevent the aggregation of means. Regulations require the aggregation of the means of the prisoner and his/her partner (defined as 'a person with whom the person concerned lives as a couple, and includes a person with whom the person concerned is not living but from whom he is not living separate and apart'),[6] unless the partner has a contrary interest in the matter or where 'in all the circumstances of the case it would be inequitable or impractical to do so'.[7] The guidance from the LSC on this issue confirms that the fact that one partner is in prison does not mean that the couple are living 'separate and apart'. For this definition to be satisfied there must be a breakdown in the relationship, so at least one of them needs to regard it as at an end.[8] Prisoners serving long or life sentences may have someone with whom they intend to live with eventually, but might be required to reside in a hostel rather

5 Contract Specification, Part B 2.6.

6 Criminal Defence Service (General) (No 2) Regulations 2001 Sch 1 para 1.

7 Criminal Defence Service (General) (No 2) Regulations 2001 Sch 1 para 6.

8 LSC Manual 4E-004.

than a home address on release. In these circumstances there is a strong argument that they should not be treated as having a partner for the purpose of aggregation of means.

Advice and assistance

3.8 This is the kind of funding that will be used where there is either no oral hearing, or at the initial stages of a case where it is unclear whether there will be one. The forms that must be completed are CDS 1 and CDS 2. The forms can be completed by post as the solicitor can exercise a devolved power to accept a postal application where there is 'good reason' to do so,[9] which the guidance in the contract states will include where the client is in prison. Similarly a claim for telephone advice prior to the signing of the form can be claimed for where there is good reason.[10]

3.9 As with other kinds of CDS advice and assistance, there is a sufficient benefit test:

> Advice and Assistance may only be provided on legal issues concerning English law and where there is sufficient benefit to the Client, having regard to the circumstances of the Matter, including the personal circumstances of the Client, to justify work or further work being carried out.[11]

3.10 The payment rates for advice and assistance are:[12]

	National	*London*
Preparation and attendance	£46.90 per hour	£49.70 per hour
Travel and waiting	£26.30 per hour	£26.30 per hour
Letters and phone calls	£3.70 per item	£3.85 per item

3.11 The upper limit of the amount of work that can be undertaken without applying for an extension is £300.[13] Beyond this limit, prior authority to carry out further work can be applied for from the relevant area office on form CDS 5. If authority is granted further work 'actually and reasonable carried out in accordance with the Sufficient Benefit test' can be claimed for up to the maximum agreed extension.[14]

9 Contract Specification, Part B 2.1.
10 Contract Specification, Part B 2.3.
11 See Contract Specification, Parts A 5.3 and Part B 2.5.
12 See Contract Specification, Part E 2.1.
13 Contract Specification, Part B 5.5.
14 Contract Specification, Part B 2.8.

3.12 As noted above, a case may start as an advice and assistance matter at a stage at which it is unclear as to whether there will be an oral hearing (for example, where representations are made to the single member in the 'sift' process for lifers), but then proceed to an oral hearing. In these circumstances the matter proceeds as a single case but the solicitor can grant advocacy assistance as long as the applicable benefit test is met (see below), and the limit on the work that can be carried out will be the higher of either the initial advocacy assistance limit, or any extension to the advice and assistance limit obtained on CDS 5. When the matter concludes, it should be reported as an advocacy assistance matter and all work can be claimed at advocacy assistance rates. This is so even where the Parole Board decides to convene an oral hearing but that hearing does not subsequently take place, provided that the relevant qualifying criteria were met.[15]

Advocacy assistance

3.13 This is the type of public funding used in relation to the preparation for, and advocacy at, oral hearings. The forms that have to be used are CDS 1 and CDS 3, although if there has already been provision of advice and assistance in the matter (see above) only a CDS 3 needs to be signed by the client. The solicitor can then grant advocacy assistance under devolved powers. As with advice and assistance, it is possible to accept a postal application for advocacy assistance where there is good reason and to claim for prior telephone advice.[16]

3.14 In relation to Parole Board applications and hearings, the applicable merits test is that advocacy assistance may not be provided if 'it appears unreasonable that approval should be granted in the particular circumstances of the case'.[17] This is clearly not dependent on the prospects of success, which reflects the fact that Parole Board hearings are the way in which the state is satisfying the duty to have detention based on a perceived risk to the public reviewed in accordance with article 5 of the European Convention on Human Rights (ECHR). There may also be many reasons that it may be in the interests of the prisoner for representation to be provided where there is no prospect of release.

15 See guidance in *Focus* on CDS LSC, issue 11, April 2003.

16 Contract Specification, Part B 4.1.

17 Contract Specification, Part B 4.3.

18 Contract Specification, Part E 5.2.

3.15 The payment rates for work carried out as advocacy assistance are:[18]

	National	*London*
Preparation and attendance	£56.15 per hour	£60.00 per hour
Advocacy	£68.25 per hour	£68.25 per hour
Travel and waiting	£26.30 per hour	£26.30 per hour
Letters and phone calls	£4.05 per item	£4.05 per item

3.16 The upper limit of the amount of work that can be undertaken without applying for an extension is £1,500.[19] As with advice and assistance beyond this limit, prior authority on form CDS 5 can be applied for from the relevant area office, and the same rules as for advice and assistance apply for claiming for work carried out under an extension. Extensions will nearly always be needed where an expert report – for example, from an independent psychologist – is obtained, especially where the expert is to attend the hearing to give evidence.

3.17 Counsel can be instructed to represent the prisoner at the hearing under devolved powers, although counsel can only be paid at the same rates that apply to solicitors.[20] If counsel is instructed, the Contract Specification states that the solicitor cannot claim for any time spent at, or traveling to and from, the hearing to accompany counsel (although the LSC have conceded that there may be very exceptional cases where payment in these circumstances would be appropriate – where, for example, this might be necessary for 'equality of arms'; however, prior authority for this should be sought).

Limits on allowed work

3.18 Unlike with police station or criminal defence work in the courts, there is very little guidance on what the LSC will consider as an appropriate amount of time for specified units of work (the Contract Specification contains no guidance on specific units of work in relation to parole applications or hearings). Clearly it is extremely important to ensure that attendances on the file justify the amount of time recorded for any work claimed for.[21]

3.19 In relation to travel time to visit prisoners, the contract suggests that travel time of up to three hours one way may be justified to visit a prisoner if the solicitor is already acting and either:

19 Contract Specification, Part B 5.5.

20 Contract Specification, Part B 4.8.

21 See LSC Manual 4H-019.

- there is no other local contactor available (including, if necessary, at short notice); or
- the client's problem is so specialised that, in the solicitor's reasonable view, there is no more local contractor with the expertise to deal with the case; or
- the solicitor has significant previous knowledge of the case or dealings with the client in relation to the issues raised by the case so as to justify renewed involvement even though the client is at a distance.[22]

Judicial review

3.20 Public funding for judicial review applications arising from any matter within the prison law category can be carried out as Associated CLS Work under crime contracts.[23] Initial work can be carried out as Legal Help, but Public Funding certificates need to be applied for to issue judicial review claims on form CLS App 1 and the appropriate means form (usually MEANS 1 as the prisoner will not be on benefits). Financial eligibility for full representation under the CLS is more complicated (as certificates can be granted subject to contributions). However, a prisoner with disposable capital of £3,000 or below and disposable income of less than £268 will be financially eligible with no contribution.

3.21 The merits test is set out in part 7 of the Funding Code. Full representation may be refused if the prospects of successfully obtain the result sought are poor or unclear. If the prospects of success are borderline, funding will be refused unless there is a significant wider public interest, or overwhelming importance to the client, or significant human rights issues in the case.[24] Furthermore, even where the prospects of success are good, in terms of cost benefit analysis the likely benefits of the proceedings should justify the costs, having regard to the prospects of success and all other circumstances.[25]

22 Contract Specification, Part B 7.9.
23 Contract Specification, Part F 1.1.
24 Funding Code, para 7.4.5.
25 Funding Code, para 7.4.6.

CHAPTER 4

Assessment of risk

continued

Introduction

4.1 The Parole Board is required to undertake a risk assessment in each case that it considers. Indeed, the task of evaluating and assessing risk is the key to the entire review process. The Board's duty was described in the following manner in one case:

> assessing a risk is not the same as reaching a conclusion about a factual event. A risk, as Lord Diplock observed,[1] is a noumenon. If I may have the temerity to amplify, a noumenon is the opposite of a phenomenon, it is an object of intellectual intuition, not something which may be observed.[2]

4.2 A fuller discussion of the legal issues around the appropriate test for release and the manner in which the Board must approach that test follows in Chapter 9 below. This section aims to explore the methods by which the Board will seek to arrive at an assessment of risk.

An overview of risk assessment[3]

4.3 There is no empirically tested, scientific method of assessing risk and there is no definitive psychological consensus on how risk can be controlled and managed. With this background in mind, it is not uncommon for prisoners to complain that the offending behaviour programmes run by the Prison Service are untested, ineffective or that they are based largely upon evidence obtained from the US and Canada where offending behaviour programmes are delivered in a different manner and environment. These arguments may well have some validity and it may be possible to find psychologists who support these views. By way of illustration, the research findings that the main thinking skills programmes run by the Probation Service appeared to have the effect of increasing re-offending rates[4] received a great deal of media coverage.

1 See *Attorney-General v English* [1983] 1 AC 116.

2 *R (on the application of Hirst) v Parole Board and Home Secretary* [2002] EWHC 1592 (Admin) para 83.

3 Most of the information in this section is taken from Hazel Kemshall, *Risk management of serious and violent offenders*, 2002, prepared for the Scottish Executive and available on their website; Hazel Kemshall, *Risk assessment and management of known sexual and violent offenders*, Home Office Police Research series, Paper 140, 2001; and Harper and Chitty (eds) *The impact of corrections on re-offending: a review of what works*, Home Office Research Study 291, 2005.

4 Harper and Chitty, p xiii.

4.4 However, it is mistaken to assume that the decision taken by the Prison Service to use cognitive offending behaviour programmes as the key tool in risk assessment does not have a respectable academic and well-researched basis. One comprehensive Home Office study provides an overview of the difficulties that arise in researching and monitoring the effectiveness of these programmes – not least due to the lack of reliable long-term evidence from this country – but concludes that:

> International evidence from systematic reviews of practice on reducing re-offending tends to support the use of cognitive-behavioural offending programmes and interventions with offenders.[5]

4.5 As no risk assessment can ever be truly scientific, there will inevitably be a subjective element. Given that there is no way for a risk assessment ever to be 'proven' to be correct or incorrect, the Parole Board are entitled to rely upon the overall approach taken by the Prison Service with its very strong reliance on prisoners attending accredited offending behaviour programmes in custody.

4.6 The current policy has been made with the full knowledge that despite the 'robust' evidence from around the world about the effectiveness of these programmes, 'in Britain the evidence is mixed and limited'.[6] The aim of the policy is to draw on the international evidence and domestic research to try to ensure that interventions and programmes can be more effective in identifying and targeting the needs of individuals. As there is a recognition that risk assessment is 'highly fallible', the emphasis has tended to focus on whether it is defensible, being the extent to which decisions can be considered reasonable based on an understanding and evaluation of decisions where there has been a negative outcome.[7] The courts have approved the view of the Prison Service that it is reasonable to rely on the cognitive behavioural method of risk assessment. In one case where there was a strong divergence between a prison and independent psychologist about whether a particular risk assessment tool should be relied upon, the court ruled in the following terms:

> The position may be summarised in this way. There clearly is a body of professional opinion that has grave reservations about the utility of SARN [Structured Assessment of Risk and Need]. On the other hand, there is another body of professional opinion which does not share those reservations, and which considers it to be a useful tool, not of course

5 Harper and Chitty, p xii.

6 Harper and Chitty, p 77.

7 Kemshall, 2001, p 21.

the be all and end all, but a useful exercise. There is also a respectable body of professional opinion, with which the defendant was entitled to agree, that it would be of advantage for the claimant to undertake the SARN. Against this background, the claimant's challenge comes nowhere near surmounting the irrationality threshold.[8]

4.7 In the light of this background, it is highly unlikely that it will assist a prisoner's application for parole to seek to undermine the principles that underpin this method of risk assessment. As a very general guide, in cases where a prisoner has valid reasons for believing that the conventional risk assessment and treatment programmes used by the Prison Service are not suitable in his or her particular case, it will usually be more productive to concentrate on the specific features of the individual which might justify a different type of approach. One of the more common examples of where this might arise will include cases where conventional Prison Service intervention might cause further psychological or psychiatric damage to an individual as a result of their past experiences. In all such cases, independent expert evidence will be essential. It should also be remembered that although the completion of courses and the level of risk given by psychological assessment tools is influential with the Board, they are not conclusive. The Board's duty is always to consider the totality of the evidence before it.

Methods of risk assessment

4.8 Risk assessment requires a calculation of the frequency or likelihood of re-offending and the impact that any re-offending will have on potential victims.[9] The aim is therefore not just to try to predict whether someone will re-offend, but also if they do, the types of offence that will be committed. This is an important component of the assessment process and has particular application to lifers as it is necessary to distinguish between offending that causes serious harm to the public and other possible non-violent or sexual offending.[10]

4.9 The two main approaches to the assessment of risk are:

- actuarial risk assessment;
- clinical risk assessment.

8 *R (on the application of Bealey) v Home Secretary* [2005] EWHC 1618 (Admin) 27.

9 Kemshall, 2002, para 3.1

10 The test for release is whether the lifer still poses a risk to the safety of the public – see Chapter 9 below.

4.10 Home Office research indicates that the actuarial method is the most accurate, but that there are significant limits to the extent that it is possible to apply general information to an individual. Consequently, the advice is that:

> The combined use of clinical and actuarial methods in an holistic approach to risk assessment is now advocated as the approach most likely to enhance both the predictive accuracy and usefulness of risk assessments or sexual and dangerous offenders.[11]

Actuarial risk assessment

4.11 Actuarial risk assessment is based upon the statistical probability that people will re-offend. The factors that are used to make this actuarial assessment are usually referred to as static risk factors. They are static as they are the features pertaining to the individual that are not susceptible to change with treatment. The types of features that are analysed to arrive at the static risk assessment are:

- date of birth;
- previous convictions;
- current conviction (often referred to as the 'index offence' in life sentence cases);
- employment history;
- relationship history.

4.12 The static risk assessment will usually identify an individual as being either a low, medium or high risk of future offending. The predicted likelihood of future offending will then inform the extent to which intervention is necessary through offending behaviour programmes.

Clinical risk assessment

4.13 Clinical risk assessment is a far more subjective method of assessing risk and is based much more on the traditional medical and mental health diagnostic techniques:

> It is based upon detailed interviewing and observation by the clinician in order to collect information on the social, environmental, behavioural and personality factors that have resulted in harmful behaviour(s) in the past.[12]

11 Kemshall, 2001, p 60.
12 Kemshall, 2002, para 3.25.

4.14 The clinical assessment will assist in the identification of the dynamic risk factors, those factors which are susceptible to change with treatment or over the passage of time. Within the OASys, now the main risk predicting tool utilised by the NOMS and which is discussed further below, dynamic risk factors are referred to as 'criminogenic needs'. These will encompass the following features:

- employment;
- drug and alcohol misuse;
- education;
- social networks;
- pro-criminal associations;
- poor emotional management;
- mental health issues.

4.15 The identification of these factors is intended to enable treatment needs to be focused more effectively, such as through housing and employment support or drug and alcohol work. For violent offenders, the ageing process itself will often be a key dynamic risk factor, as a major dynamic risk factor in violent offending is the existence of anti-social attitudes which are very often higher in young people.

4.16 When assessing sex offenders, a number of further and more focused dynamic risk factors have been identified as follows:

- impaired relationships with adults;
- lack of victim empathy;
- extent and nature of anger, particularly whether instrumental or expressive;
- cognitive distortions and rationalisations for offending;
- sexual fantasy and deviant sexual arousal;
- anti-social personality;
- impulsivity.[13]

4.17 The dynamic features will not all be present in every case.

Risk assessment tools

4.18 A number of assessments are utilised by the Prison and Probation Services to undertake the assessment of risk. The key tools are as follows.

13 Kemshall, 2001 pp20–21.

OASys

4.19 This is the joint Prison/Probation Service Offender Assessment System[14] and is now the key risk assessment tool for the purposes of sentence management. It is designed to provide continuity in identifying and treating risk from conviction through to release and should be updated annually. It is based on both documentary records and interview with the prisoner and is designed to identify static risk factors and the progress through treatment of dynamic risk factors. A similar system known as ASSET is used for those under 18 years of age. It is a computer-based system which will structure sentence planning and resettlement plans. OASys has not replaced all other risk assessment tools and once broad areas of risk are identified, other more specific risk assessment methods will still be utilised.

4.20 PSO 2205 states that the key aims of OASys are to:

- assess how likely an offender is to be reconvicted;
- identify and classify offending-related needs;
- assess risk of harm (to self and others);
- assist with management of risk of harm;
- link assessments, supervision and sentence plans;
- indicate any need for further specialist assessments;
- measure how an offender changes during the period of supervision/sentence.

4.21 The levels of risk of harm used in OASys are:

- *Low* – No significant, current indicators of risk of harm.
- *Medium* – There are identifiable indicators of risk of harm. The offender has the potential to cause harm but is unlikely to do so unless there is a change in circumstances, for example, failure to take medication, loss of accommodation, relationship breakdown, drug or alcohol misuse.
- *High* – There are identifiable indicators of risk of harm. The potential event could happen at any time and the impact would be serious.
- *Very high* – There is an imminent risk of harm. The potential event is more likely than not to happen imminently and the impact would be serious.

4.22 As the OASys is designed to be used both at the very start of the prison sentence and then annually thereafter, the initial OASys assessment is likely to be used as a starting point to help determine whether more

14 See PSO 2205.

focused risk assessment is necessary. As the prisoner progresses through the sentence, or where other risk assessment tools are available, they will be incorporated into the OASys report.

Offender Group Reconviction Scale (OGRS)

4.23 This predicts, from a number of criminal history and demographic factors (ie, purely 'static' factors), the probability that an offender will be reconvicted within two years of release from custody or the start of a community sentence. It is often used as a starting point for risk assessment for programmes such as FOCUS (see below) to help guide the level of intervention that will be necessary.

Violent Risk Assessment Guide (VRAG)

4.24 This is the most widely used actuarial tool for assessing violent recidivism and will assign people to one of nine risk categories for future offending. It is limited to the extent that it does not contain any assessment of the nature, severity or frequency of future violence. It involves analysing features ranging from the age at the time of the index offence, performance at school and the history of substance abuse through to existence of psychopathy and personality disorders. There is a more refined version of VRAG designed to address the levels of dangerousness in high risk men called the Violence Prediction Scheme (VPS).

HCR-20

4.25 Historical, Clinical Risk Management which takes into account 20 items[15] and is a tool for assessing risk of future violent re-offending that does take into account both static and dynamic factors. It will measure an individual's motivation to change and coping mechanisms, and although it was originally developed as a case management tool, it is increasingly seen as an accurate predictor of future violent behaviour.

Psychopathy Checklist – Revised[16]

4.26 The major method used to assess the level of psychopathy as a distinct personality disorder. It has 20 items which are rated on a three-point

15 These can be found in Kemshall, 2001, pp11–12.
16 PCL-R, or Hare's psychopathy checklist.

scale, and a high score (above 30) may suggest that the offender's risk will not be reduced by normal accredited offending behaviour programmes. A high score may mean a prisoner is assessed by the Dangerous and Severe Personality Disorder Unit (DSPD).

Risk Matrix 2000

4.27 An actuarial-based assessment of future risk of sexual and violent offending which has been developed from the Structured Anchored Clinical Judgment (SACJ) which is based on empirical research into recidivism amongst sex offenders. While the SACJ contained an extensive clinical assessment, the Risk Matrix 2000 was developed from a shortened version concentrating on static risk factors which had been developed to address those situations where the necessary dynamic and clinical data were not available. Although this risk assessment tool can be used for both sexual and violent offenders, it is used far more extensively for sex offenders.

Structured Assessment of Risk and Need (SARN)

4.28 More akin to clinical assessment, SARN has been developed by Dr David Thornton of the Prison Service and combines the actuarial assessment of risk with the SACJ. This is an instrument that is currently being used within the national prison Sex Offenders Treatment Programme (SOTP), and which is described in the SOTP Accreditation documentation. In brief, four 'risk domains' are considered, relating to sexual interests, distorted attitudes, socio-affective functioning and self-management. It is used to set treatment targets and to determine the level of intervention required. It does have acknowledged limitations as it cannot quantify changes in static risk and is restricted to covering variables that have been identified in research to date, leaving open the possibility that there are further unidentified predictors.

Penile Plethysmograph (PPG)

4.29 This is used to assess deviant sexual interests and is the only risk assessment tool that requires a degree of physical intrusion. It measures physical arousal to different images as a method for assessing whether there is arousal to deviant images so that treatment can be focused on specific areas and problems.

Offending behaviour programmes

4.30 The courses provided by the Prison Service are almost exclusively cognitive offending behaviour programmes that are intended to direct criminal attitudes and beliefs by addressing deficits in thinking and behaviour. Courses are now accredited through the Correctional Services Accreditation Panel (CSAP), which is designed to ensure that the principles underpinning effective practice are implemented.[17] Since 1999 there has been an increased focus on establishing programmes that can also be run in the community by the Probation Service.

4.31 Attendance on offending behaviour programmes is always voluntary. The courts have upheld decisions to refuse prisoners enhanced privilege status as a result of sentence planning reviews that set attendance on these courses as targets. This has been upheld even for prisoners who maintain their innocence, the court being of the view that it was appropriate for the Prison Service to encourage prisoners to address their offending.[18]

4.32 The Prison Service currently runs 19 fully or provisionally accredited programmes and the Probation Service has 16 programmes. Accredited programmes were available in 112 out of 137 prisons as of 1 April 2004.[19] The key programmes that are available are as follows.[20]

Enhanced Thinking Skills (ETS)

4.33 The programme addresses thinking and behaviour associated with offending. It targets the following cognitive deficits: impulse control, cognitive style, social perspective taking, values/moral reasoning, critical reasoning and interpersonal problem solving. The programme employs a sequenced series of structured exercises designed to teach interpersonal problem solving skills, impulse control and improve perspective taking ability. It is targeted at male and female medium to medium-high risk offenders, and can be sequenced with another programme (such as SOTP, CALM and the CSCP).

17 CSAP was put in place in 2002, replacing the General Accreditation Panel which had been in operation since 1996.

18 See, eg, *R v Home Secretary ex p Hepworth* [1998] COD 146.

19 Harper and Chitty, 2005, pp33–34.

20 These summaries are mainly taken from Annex to Reducing re-offending – national action plan July 2004.

Reasoning and Rehabilitation (R&R)

4.34 As with ETS, R&R teaches offenders a range of social and cognitive skills and provides a sequenced series of structured sessions designed to teach interpersonal problem solving. It is targeted at male and female high-risk offenders and can be sequenced with other programmes. This course was phased out during 2004, being wholly replaced by the ETS.

Think First

4.35 The Probation Service's community-based equivalent of the ETS.

Cognitive Skills Booster

4.36 This, as the title suggests, is a programme designed for those who have already completed a course such as the R&R or ETS to refresh and put into practice the skills that have been learned. It is available both in prison (usually in open conditions) and through the Probation Service.

Controlling Anger and Learning to Manage it (CALM)

4.37 This programme is aimed at those whose anger or poor emotional control lead to a criminal offence. All participants must meet the criteria of a current or previous offence precipitated by anger or poor emotional control. Any offence type may be included. Not all violent offenders will be suitable for CALM. Offenders whose use of aggression is only instrumental (ie, to achieve another goal) are not suitable for the programme. This may include, for example, armed robbers. The course has replaced the ad hoc anger management programmes which were previously run by many prisons, and is also now run by many probation areas.

Aggression Replacement Training (ART)

4.38 A Probation Service programme designed to reduce aggressive behaviour by improving social skills, anger management and moral reasoning.

Cognitive Self-Change Programme (CSCP)

4.39 Using a rolling format, this intensive programme aims to reduce instrumental violence and related offending behaviour in adult men defined as being at high risk of reconviction. The programme addresses the individual's anti-social thinking patterns, violent fantasy, lack of insight into violent behaviour, poor management of increased arousal or anger and socio-cognitive skills deficit. It is aimed at those with a pattern of convicted and unconvicted violence throughout their life span and whose violence is not resultant of substance misuse alone. The core elements of the programme take approximately one year to complete but is dependent on an individual's progress though treatment. CSCP continues post completion, where skills are practiced and maintained, for the remainder of the individual's time in custody and on licence.

Sex Offender Treatment Programmes (SOTP)

4.40 The main focus on SOTP is for it to be completed in prison in closed conditions. However, on completion the course can continue through refresher programmes in open conditions and in the community. All probation areas now run some form of the SOTP.

- *Core Programme*: The treatment goals of this programme include helping offenders develop an understanding of how and why sexual offences were committed to increase awareness of victim harm issues, and to develop meaningful life goals as part of a relapsed prevention plan. The programme is targeted at male medium and high risk sex offenders, and challenges thinking patterns, develops victim empathy and relapse prevention skills.
- *Extended Programme*: A supplementary programme for high-risk offenders covering five treatment need areas: dysfunctional thinking styles; emotion management; offence-related sexual fantasy; intimacy skills; and inadequate relapse prevention plans. It is targeted at male high and very high risk sex offenders.
- *Adapted Programme*: Treatment goals are similar to the core programme, but treatment methods are adapted to suit learning-disabled sex offenders across all risk levels. The programme is designed to increase sexual knowledge, modify offence-justifying thinking, develop ability to recognise feelings in themselves and others and to gain an understanding of victim harm, and develop relapse prevention skills.
- *Rolling Programme*: This programme covers the same topics as the core programme but with less emphasis on obtaining an adequate offence account, and more emphasis on relationship skills and attachment deficits. It is targeted at male low and medium

risk sex offenders, but sex offenders who have completed primary treatment programmes and who are serving long sentences can attend as a 'top up' programme.

- *Booster Programme*: This programme is designed to provide an opportunity for offenders to refresh their learning in treatment and to prepare for additional relapse prevention and release work.

Healthy Sexual Functioning (HSF)

4.41 The programme is designed to complement the SOTP for those prisoners considered to have disordered or deviant arousal patterns. It has four modules: understanding sexuality, patterns in sexual arousal, promoting sexual healthy interest and relapse prevention.

Healthy Relationships Programmes (HRP)

4.42 This intervention is designed for male offenders who demonstrate a risk of being violent to an intimate female partner. High risk offenders receive a high intensity programme, while lower risk offenders receive a moderate intensity programme. Both programmes target attitudes supporting or condoning domestic violence, poor emotional control, skills deficits and motivational issues.

Victim empathy

4.43 As is self-evident from the title, these programmes are intended to address deficits in victim empathy and to encourage more understanding of the experiences of victims of crime. Many of the programmes listed above will have components which address victim empathy. Where specific victim empathy courses are not available, prison chaplaincies may provide a non-accredited programme designed to encourage greater victim empathy called the Sycamore Tree Trust programme.

Substance abuse programmes

4.44 As well as the accredited offending behaviour programmes, the National Drugs Programme Delivery Unit manages a number of interventions designed to address problems related to drug and alcohol abuse and offending. The key courses and treatments available in prison are the following.

Rehabilitation of Addicted Prisoners Trust (RAPt)

4.45 RAPt is run though a charitable foundation in association with the Prison Service in a number of prisons and aims to treat drug and alcohol addiction through a version of the 12-step programme.

Counselling, Assessment and Throughcare Services (CARATS)

4.46 This is designed to address problems of addiction to drugs and alcohol through a mixture of assessment and counselling and seeks to provide continuity of treatment through to the community by establishing links with probation and community based addiction services. It is a service which is available to prisoners throughout their sentences who have completed other drug interventions.

FOCUS and PASRO

4.47 These are courses designed to address the lifestyle and behavioural choices that underpin drug use and addiction and which seek to explore the link between substance abuse and offending.

Therapeutic communities

4.48 The only current alternative to the accredited cognitive behavioural courses is through admission to a therapeutic community (TC).[21] There are currently five democratic therapeutic communities for men and one for women. The most well known and the longest established is HMP Grendon. It has 235 places for Category B and Category C prisoners. It has five 'communities' and an assessment unit. Grendon is also able to offer the SOTP, a move designed to prevent prisoners engaged in therapy having to be moved on to different prisons to address this treatment need. The others are:

- HMP Dovegate (near Uttoxeter) has 200 places for Category B prisoners – four communities, an assessment unit and a high intensity programme unit.
- HMP Gartree (near Market Harborough) has one community offering 23 places for Category B lifers.

21 See PSO 2400 – Democratic Therapeutic Communities.

- HMP Aylesbury has a young offender institution, part of which contains 22 therapeutic places for young offenders.
- HMP Blundeston (near Lowestoft in Suffolk) opened a therapeutic community in 2004 providing 40 places for Category C prisoners.
- HMP Send, which in 2004 opened a 40-place therapeutic community for women.

4.49 The special status of TCs is reflected in the admission procedures, which are normally through a referral from the medical officer, although an application for a transfer can also be made directly to Prison Service headquarters.[22] They are described as democratic communities as they are based on an egalitarian model with the community – which includes prisoners, prison staff, probation officers and the psychiatric and psychological teams – setting the boundaries of acceptable behaviour both within therapy and in the general prison environment. This can be difficult, given the very obvious hierarchy that has to exist within any prison.

4.50 Although the communities are very staunchly defended by those who have participated in them, it is often the case that prison psychologists will place greater emphasis on the accredited programmes and will consider that prisoners who have successfully completed their therapy should still attend the accredited programmes. Historically, this often created a major problem for lifers who had successfully completed their therapy at Grendon, which is a Category B prison. They would often find that there was enormous reluctance from the Prison Service and Home Secretary to accept that they should move directly from Grendon to open prison conditions. Grendon is now able to hold Category C prisoners who have completed therapy so that in appropriate cases, they can be considered for transfer directly to open conditions without having to return to the mainstream prison estate.

Dangerous and Severe Personality Disorder Units (DSPDs)

4.51 These are relatively new units that are designed to fill the lacuna in the provision of treatment to dangerous prisoners whose dangerousness is linked to a personality disorder. As these prisoners will invariably have a high PCL-R score (see above), they will be deemed unsuitable

22 See PSO 2400.

or unable to benefit from the accredited offending behaviour programmes available. The diagnosis of this condition posed particular problems for the Prison Service, as it had previously been deemed to be untreatable. The consequence of this was that special hospitals could decline to accept people with severe personality disorders on the grounds that no effective treatment could be offered leaving the Prison Service to attempt to address their treatment and progress.

4.52 Although the units were set up in 2002 in Whitemoor and Frankland, two high security prisons (alongside similar units in Rampton and Broadmoor), the provision of services and the undertaking of assessments has been painfully slow and it is still impossible to assess how the units will work in practice and how long treatment is likely to last. A specially designed course called Chromis, intended to reduce violence in offenders whose psychopathy disrupts their ability to engage in normal offending behaviour courses, is in operation. Prisoners are not required to consent to a transfer to a DSPD, but are not under any compulsion to agree to participate in the assessments or treatment once a transfer has taken place.

Prisoners who maintain their innocence

4.53 There has always been a particular problem for prisoners who maintain their innocence to establish that they have satisfactorily addressed their offending behaviour.[23] This need not, however, be an insuperable barrier to attending accredited courses as part of the progress through the life sentence.

4.54 Prisoners convicted of sexual offences, or with a sexual element to their offence, are in the most difficult position, as attendance on the SOTP requires that an active account is given of the offence. Where the prisoner cannot give this account, then it will usually lead to an assessment that they are unsuitable for the programme. This will not mean that they can progress without completing the SOTP, as the Prison Service and the Parole Board find it very difficult to accept that there is any other method of safely assessing risk. Various attempts have been made to allow prisoners to attend versions of the SOTP (for example, in cases where one sexual offence is admitted and another denied), but the trend has been away from this, as it is felt that it is

23 The legal implications are discussed in Chapter 14 on remedies, below; this section is designed to look at the impact on attending offending behaviour courses.

not possible to provide an accurate assessment of risk and progress in treatment while any sexual offences are still denied.

4.55 For other courses, it may still be possible for prisoners who maintain their innocence to be considered acceptable for attendance. The various cognitive skills programmes, such as the ETS, are not offence-specific, which gives wider scope for attendance. Prisoners can examine aspects of their choices and thinking that resulted in previous convictions or their general lifestyles at the time of the current conviction through these programmes. Prisoners convicted of murder who consider that a manslaughter conviction was more appropriate should also be able to attend this type of course.

4.56 Drug and alcohol treatment courses are not dependent on a prisoner admitting guilt of a particular offence. Any prisoner who admits to a substance abuse problem is eligible. As prisoners often develop drug problems, or more severe drug problems, in custody, there is no need for these courses to be linked to convictions.

4.57 In general, other courses will usually be available to prisoners who have previous convictions even if they deny their index offence. It is possible to explore issues such as anger management in relation to an earlier conviction or behaviour even if guilt is not admitted for the current offence.

4.58 The Parole Board is very anxious to assure prisoners who maintain their innocence that this is not a barrier to release and has even devoted part of its website to this issue. Their figures for 2003 reproduced on the website show that the success rate for all parole applications is more than 50 per cent lower for prisoners who maintain their innocence. The Board accepts that in cases involving sexual offending, parole refusal rates are like to be at their highest. The Board did conduct a survey of 50 mandatory lifers who maintained their innocence and yet achieved release. It was noted that they had all spent lengthy periods of time in open conditions and the majority had undertaken offending behaviour work into areas such as anger management, thinking skills and assertiveness.

CHAPTER 5

Determinate sentences: an overview

continued

Introduction

5.1 A detailed examination of sentencing principles and provisions is outside the scope of this book, as is any comprehensive consideration of early release mechanisms that do not involve the Parole Board.[1] However, an overview is necessary in order to understand the relevant functions of the Parole Board. This chapter deals with the various kinds of fixed term, or determinate, sentences that can be imposed by the courts, and the relevant early release schemes that apply to them.

How determinate sentences are served

5.2 After sentence, prisoners will generally be sent to the nearest local prison that holds a remand population. Then, depending upon the length and seriousness of their offence, they will be placed in one of a number of security categories (ranging from Category A for those deemed to pose a high risk to the public, to Category D for those considered to be suitable for open prisons). Prisoners will then be allocated to a prison with conditions of security appropriate to their category. Security category is reviewed at regular intervals to enable prisoners to progress to less secure prisons when appropriate. Guidance on initial and subsequent categorisation and allocation is contained in PSO 0900.

5.3 Prisoners will also be subject to sentence planning with a view to identifying risk factors and appropriate offending behaviour work aimed at reducing the assessed risk to the public.[2] For those prisoners whose initial release is not automatic, but depends on the Parole Board assessing the risk to the public as being acceptable for release, the degree to which a prisoner has progressed through the prison system and is seen as having addressed the relevant risk factors through offending behaviour work will clearly be very important.

1 See Creighton, King and Arnott, *Prisoners and the law* 3rd edn, Tottel Publishing, 2005.

2 See PSO 2205 and Chapter 4.

Summary of release arrangements and the Parole Board role

5.4 How determinate sentences are administered depends on two factors. First the length of the sentence, and second when it was imposed.

Summary of early release arrangements for determinate sentence prisoners

Sentence length	*Offence committed*	*Release dates*	*Parole Board involved*	*Oral Hearing*	*Oral hearing possible if recalled*
Fewer than 12 months – AUR scheme	Sentenced on or after 1 October 1992	Automatically at halfway – no licence	No	No	N/a – no licence
12 months to under four years – ACR scheme	Before 4 April 2005	Automatically at halfway – on licence	No	No	Yes
Four years and more – DCR scheme	Before 4 April 2005	Eligible at half point of sentence (automatic at two-thirds) – on licence	Yes	No	Yes
12 months and more – SDS	On or after 4 April 2005	Automatically at half point – on licence	No	No	Yes
Extended sentence – custodial term under four years	Before 4 April 2005	Automatically at half point of custodial term (automatic at two-thirds) – on licence	No	No	Yes
Extended sentence – custodial term more than four years	Before 4 April 2005	Eligible at half point of custodial term (automatic at two-thirds) – on licence	Yes	No	Yes
Extended sentence – any length of custodial term	On or after 4 April 2005	Eligible at half point of custodial term (automatic at end of custodial term) – on licence	Yes	No	Yes

5.5 There are now three generations of release arrangements for determinate sentences, under the Criminal Justice Acts (CJAs) 1967, 1991 and 2003, respectively. In summary, the Parole Board is only involved in the following situations:

- Considering the suitability for release on parole licence of prisoners serving sentences of four years or more (including extended sentences with custodial terms of four years or more) where the offence was committed before 4 April 2005. Parole eligibility is at the halfway point, except for those sentenced before 1 October 1992 where it is at the one-third point. The Parole Board will decide suitability for release by considering the case only on the papers although in exceptional circumstances fairness may require an oral hearing.
- Considering the suitability for release on licence of extended sentence prisoners serving sentences for offences committed on or after 4 April 2005. Again this will be a paper review except for exceptional cases.
- Deciding whether recalled determinate sentence prisoners should be re-released on licence whenever the offence was committed. If on an initial consideration of the case on the papers the Board does not direct release the prisoner will have a right to an oral hearing before the Board.
- Advising the Home Secretary, where circumstances make it practicable, as to whether the power to release a prisoner early on compassionate grounds should be exercised.

The CJA 1967

5.6 The arrangements under the CJA 1967 apply to prisoners who were sentenced prior to the coming into force of the CJA 1991 on 1 October 1992 (referred to in this book as 'CJA 1967 cases'). Accordingly, they apply to an ever decreasing number of prisoners. Eligibility for release on parole licence, if recommended by the Parole Board, is set at one-third of the sentence for these prisoners. Unconditional release (with no licence supervision) is set at two-thirds. The coming into force of the CJA 1991 did not affect the administration of these sentences, as transitional arrangements preserved the eligibility dates.[3]

The CJA 1991

5.7 The CJA 1991 came into force on 1 October 1992 and applies to all those sentenced on or after that date, up until the coming into force

3 CJA 1991 Sch 12 para 8.

of the CJA 2003 (and still applies for those sentenced to under 12 months). For sentences of 12 months and over, the CJA 1991 applies except for sentences in relation of offences committed on or after 4 April 2005, the date of commencement of the relevant parts of the CJA 2003.[4]

5.8 The commencement of the CJA 1991 on 1 October 1992 was anomalous in that the early release provisions it introduced were applied to prisoners *sentenced* after their coming into force, whenever the offences were committed. This risked offenders, who may have committed similar offences on the same day, being subjected to different release regimes purely on the basis of the date on which the court disposed of their case. By contrast, the amendments brought in by the CDA 1998 and the CJA 2003 apply only to offences *committed* after the relevant commencement dates.

Release schemes under the CJA 1991

5.9 The CJA 1991 introduced three release schemes administered according to the length of sentence. Those serving fewer than four years are defined as 'short-term prisoners' under the Act, and those four years or more as 'long-term prisoners':[5]

- *Automatic unconditional release (AUR)* – Short-term prisoners serving less than 12 months are released unconditionally at the halfway point.[6]
- *Automatic conditional release (ACR)* – Short-term prisoners serving sentences of 12 months to less than four years are released under licence supervision automatically at the halfway point.[7] Licence supervision continues, subject to recall, to the three-quarter point, the licence expiry date (LED).[8]
- *Discretionary conditional release (DCR)* – Long-term prisoners, those serving four or more years, become eligible for release on parole licence at the halfway point (the parole eligibility date, or

4 The Criminal Justice Act 2003 (Commencement No 8 and Transitional and Saving Provisions) Order 2005 SI 2005 No 950 – initial release dates under the CJA 1991 were preserved in relation to sentences imposed for offences committed before 4 April 2005 by para 19.

5 CJA 1991 s33(5).

6 CJA 1991 s33(1)(a).

7 CJA 1991 s33(1)(b).

8 CJA 1991 s37(1).

PED) if recommended by the Parole Board[10] and are in any event released automatically on licence at the two-thirds point (the non-parole date, or NPD),[11] the licence expiring, subject to recall, at the three-quarter point.

- *The 'at risk provisions'* – After release if offenders are convicted of a further offence committed before sentence expiry date (SED) they can be ordered to return to prison by the court sentencing for the new offence. The period of the order to return cannot exceed the length of time between the commission of the new offence and sentence expiry of the original offence.[12] If the return to custody term together with any new sentence is less than 12 months, the prisoner is not released unconditionally at the halfway point but on a three-month licence.[13]

Further provisions for sexual and violent offences under the CJA 1991

Extended licences

5.10 For offences committed up until 30 September 1998[14] the sentencing court can direct, in the case of sexual offences, that the offender be subject to licence supervision for the whole of the sentence.[15]

Extended sentences

5.11 For offences committed on or after 30 September 1998, but before 4 April 2005[16] the sentencing court can, for certain sexual or violent offences, impose an extended sentence.[17] This combines a custodial term, commensurate with what would have been imposed for the offence had an extended sentence not been appropriate, together with a further period of licence supervision in the community. The length of the custodial term determines the initial release date.[18] Extended sentence prisoners are not eligible for release on HDC (see below).

10 CJA 1991 s35(1).
11 CJA 1991 s33(2).
12 Powers of Criminal Courts (Sentencing) Act (PCC(S)A) 2000 s116.
13 CJA 1991 s40A.
14 The date of the coming into force of the relevant parts of the Crime and Disorder Act 1998.
15 The power is now under PCC(S)A 2000 s86.
16 The date of the coming into force of the relevant parts of the CJA 2003.
17 Now under PCC(S)A 2000 s85.
18 CJA 1991 s44.

Principles of sentence calculation under the CJA 1991

5.12 The way in which multiple and overlapping sentences imposed for offences committed before 4 April 2005 are calculated is complicated and has been the subject of repeated judicial criticism. Individual prison governors as legal custodians of prisoners have a duty to work out release dates correctly. PSO 6650 contains very detailed guidance on this area.

5.13 In summary, the CJA 1991[19] requires multiple and overlapping determinate sentences to be treated as a 'single term' for the purposes of working out which is the applicable release scheme. Accordingly, where the court imposes consecutive sentences, the single term is the aggregate period of all such sentences – so, for example, two consecutive sentences of two years would result in a four-year single term and the application of the DCR scheme. For concurrent, overlapping sentences, the single term starts with the date of imposition of the first sentence and ends with the sentence expiry date of the last such sentence to be imposed. So if a prisoner, when he/she had served one year of a three-year sentence, was given a further three-year sentence, the result would be a single term of four years.[20]

5.14 In relation to sentences imposed after 30 September 1998, section 51(2) of the CJA 1991 (as amended) confirms that sentences will not be single-termed with any earlier sentence if the prisoner has been released from any of the earlier sentences. This change was brought in to avoid the complications in working out the single term that arose where prisoners who had been recalled to custody received further sentences.

5.15 Under the CJA 1991 the prison is responsible for determining how much remand time falls to be deducted from the sentence.[21]

The CJA 2003

5.16 For determinate sentence prisoners, the main provisions of the 2003 Act came into force on 4 April 2005.[22] The transitional provisions state that the Act's provisions in relation to release only come into force in relation to offences committed on or after 4 April 2005.[23]

19 CJA 1991 s51.

20 See *R v Home Secretary ex p Francois* [1999] 1 AC 43.

21 CJA 1967 s67 (as amended) – see the guidance in Chapter 4 PSO 6650.

22 See the Criminal Justice Act 2003 (Commencement No 8 and Transitional and Saving Provisions) Order 2005 SI 2005 No 950.

23 Ibid Sch 2 para 4.

5.17 The 2003 Act's provisions in relation to sentences of under 12 months (the 'custody plus' sentence) were not brought into force in April 2005, although there have been pilots in place since January 2004[24] of the 'intermittent custody' sentence,[25] which was designed to allow offenders to maintain employment and family ties while serving a custodial sentence at, for example, weekends. The current pilots relate to courts within the catchment area of two 'intermittent custody centres' at HMP Kirkham for men, and HMP Morton Hall for women.

Release arrangements under the CJA 2003

5.18 The 2003 Act has, to an extent, simplified release arrangements for determinate sentence prisoners, as the distinction between long-term and short-term prisoners is removed and all offenders (except extended sentence prisoners) will now be released automatically at the halfway point. In summary, the position for those sentenced for offences committed on or after 4 April 2005 is that:

- Those sentenced to less than 12 months (unless in an intermittent custody pilot area) are still dealt with under the AUR arrangements (see above) of the CJA 1991 including the 'at risk' provisions.[26]
- Those sentenced to 12 months or more (now referred to as the 'Standard Determinate Sentence' (SDS) are released automatically on licence at the halfway point (the conditional release date, or CRD)[27] and the licence will remain in force until the SED.[28] For SDS prisoners released on licence there are no 'at risk' provisions.
- Where an offender commits a specified sexual or violent offence[29] which has a maximum sentence of less than ten years, and where the court considers the offender at significant risk of causing serious harm by the commission of further such offences, the court is required to impose an extended sentence.[30] As with extended sentences administered under the CJA 1991, this comprises

24 Criminal Justice Act 2003 (Commencement No 2 and Saving Provisions) Order 2004 SI No 81.

25 CJA 2003 s183.

26 Criminal Justice Act 2003 (Commencement No 8 and Transitional and Saving Provisions) Order 2005 SI No 950 Sch 2 paras 14 and 29.

27 CJA 2003 s244(3)(a).

28 CJA 2003 s249(1).

29 Listed in CJA 2003 Sch 15.

30 CJA 2003 ss227 and 228.

a custodial term, commensurate with the seriousness of the offence, and an extension period to be served on licence, imposed to protect the public. Those serving extended sentences under the 2003 Act are eligible for release halfway through the custodial term if the Parole Board directs,[31] and are only automatically released once the custodial term has been served in full.[32] The offender remains under licence supervision until the end of the entire extended sentence.

Sentence calculation under the CJA 2003

5.19 Under the CJA 2003[33] sentences imposed for offences committed on or after 4 April 2005 that are wholly or partly concurrent have their release dates calculated separately. The offender will not be released until the latest release date and will remain on licence until the latest sentence expiry date.[34]

5.20 Sentences imposed consecutively are aggregated so that, for example, where an offender receives two SDSs of three years to run consecutively, the automatic release date will be three years after the imposition of the sentences.[35]

5.21 Under the CJA 2003, remand time is not calculated by the prison but rather the sentencing court makes a direction specifying the amount of remand time to be deducted from the sentence.[36] The court does not need to make a direction if it considers it just in all the circumstances not to do so.[37]

Effect of additional days added as punishment

5.22 If prisoners are given additional days as punishment by adjudicators in the prison disciplinary process[38] then both under the CJA 1991[39] and CJA 2003[40] the additional days must be served in full. The relevant

31 CJA 2003 s247(2).
32 CJA 2003 s247(4).
33 See Chapter 18 of PSO 6650 for guidance.
34 CJA 2003 s263.
35 CJA 2003 s264.
36 CJA 2003 s240.
37 CJA 2003 s240(4)(b).
38 For detailed examination see Creighton, King and Arnott, *Prisoners and the law* 3rd edn, Tottel Publishing, 2005 Chapter 9.

release dates, licence expiry and sentence expiry dates are put back by the total number of days given as punishment.

Young and child offenders

Detention and Training Orders (DTOs)

5.23 For those under 18 the normal determinate sentence will be a DTO imposed under section 100 of the PCC(S)A 2000. The maximum sentence is 24 months and generally half is served in custody and half in the community.

5.24 If during the supervision period of the DTO the offender fails to comply with the requirements of supervision, the court may order the offender to be detained.[41] The Parole Board does not play any part in the release or recall of those serving DTOs.

Other sentences

5.25 If the offence is sufficiently serious, those under 18 at the time of its commission can receive a determinate sentence imposed under section 91 of the PCC(S)A 2000. For those aged 18 and above but under 21, the sentence of detention in a Young Offender Institution can be imposed.[42] There is no restriction (except the available maximum for the offence) on the length of such sentences. These sentences are administered in the same way as determinate sentences for adults. Release dates and liability to recall will depend on the length of sentence and when it was imposed.

5.26 Those serving these sentences who are released before they are 22 years old are subject to a minimum three months' licence supervision.[43] This does not just apply to sentences of under 12 months where otherwise there would be no supervision, but may require the offender to remain on licence beyond the expiry date of the sentence imposed by the court (if not released until sentence expiry because of, for example, the imposition of additional days). This possibility of supervision beyond the SED has been held not to breach article 5

39 CJA 1991 s42.
40 CJA 2003 s257.
41 PCC(S)A 2000 s104.
42 PCC(S)A 2000 s96.
43 CJA 1991 s65.

of the European Convention on Human Rights, on the basis that it constitutes a restriction on, not a deprivation of, liberty.[44]

5.27 Section 228 of the CJA 2003 allows the court to impose an extended sentence on those under 18 on conviction for offences committed after 4 April 2005.

Effect of transfer under the Mental Health Act 1983

5.28 Prisoners may be transferred from prison to hospital at any stage in their sentence under the Mental Health Act 1983.[45] Transfer does not affect automatic release dates for determinate sentence prisoners. So for ACR and SDS prisoners the prison remains responsible for issuing a licence at the appropriate time, the conditions of which are amended to take into account the fact that the person is detained under the Mental Health Act 1983.[46]

5.29 Cases where the Parole Board are responsible for the initial release decision are different, as those detained in hospitals are not eligible for review by the Parole Board. However, if a prisoner is parole eligible and the hospital, or a Mental Health Review Tribunal (MHRT), advises the Home Office Mental Health Unit that treatment is no longer required (or that no effective treatment can be given), then a parole application can be made.[47] The RRS is responsible for preparing a dossier for the Board rather than the prison. If release is at the NPD, then the RRS takes responsibility for issuing the licence.[48]

Other mechanisms of early release

Home Detention Curfew (HDC)

5.30 Also introduced by the Crime and Disorder Act 1998 was the possibility of early release on electronic tag.[49] This provides that most short-term prisoners (those serving less than four years) serving

44 *R (Davies) v Home Secretary* [2005] EWCA Civ 461. It is of note that breach of this licence cannot result in executive recall but is punishable on conviction by the courts: see CJA 1991 s65(6).

45 Mental Health Act 1983 s47.

46 See guidance in PSO 6000 Chapter 11.

47 Mental Health Act 1983 s50; PSO 6000 para 11.3.

48 PSO 6000 para 11.4.

49 CJA 1991 s34A (as amended).

three months or more can be released earlier than the halfway point of the sentence on a curfew condition. The curfew remains in force until what would have been the automatic release date.[50] Those serving extended sentences are excluded from the scheme.[51]

5.31 This scheme is known as Home Detention Curfew and is generally at the discretion of the governor of the prison.[52] The scheme is complex although, broadly, those serving sentences for sexual or violent offences are excluded. If the curfew condition is breached prisoners can be recalled, and any representations against recall for this reason will be considered by the RRS on behalf of the Home Secretary.[53] The Parole Board has no role to play in granting HDC or reviewing recall for breach of the curfew condition. If the recall is upheld on review the prisoner will then be released automatically on licence at the halfway point of the sentence.[54]

5.32 For those sentenced for offences committed on or after 4 April 2005 the CJA 2003 re-enacts entitlement to consideration for early release on HDC.[55] The maximum period remains 135 days and the guidance in PSO 6700 and related PSIs will continue to be relevant. Although the Act has removed the distinction between short-term and long-term prisoners, guidance has been issued[56] to the effect that those serving four years or more (who were not eligible for HDC under CJA 1991) will be 'presumed unsuitable' for HDC, and will only be released under the scheme in exceptional circumstances.

The Early Release Scheme (ERS)

5.33 Prisoners who are 'liable to removal' from the UK within the meaning of section 46(3) of the CJA 1991, or section 259 of the CJA 2003 for those whose offences were committed on or after 4 April 2005[57] may qualify for the ERS.

50 CJA 1991 s37A(3).

51 CJA 1991 s34A(1).

52 See PSO 6700, PSI 9/2001, PSI 19/2002, PSI 39/2002 and PSI 31/2003 for guidance on the scheme.

53 CJA 1991 s38A(4).

54 CJA 1991 s33A.

55 CJA 2003 s246.

56 Note from the Chief Executive of NOMS, April 2005.

57 Those liable to removal are where there has been a decision or court recommendation to deport, a refusal of leave to enter, illegal entry, or those liable to administrative removal because of, for example, overstaying of leave to remain.

5.34 Prisoners liable to removal are not eligible for HDC, but the ERS provides for early release up to 135 days before what would otherwise be the earliest date of release. Guidance on the scheme is contained in PSI 27/2004 and Chapter 9 of PSO 6000. There is a presumption in favour of release, except for those serving more than four years for specified sexual or violent offences.[58] Decision making is primarily delegated to individual governors by PSI 27/2004 and the Parole Board does not play any role in this. Unlike with HDC, the length of sentence does not affect eligibility.

Compassionate release

5.35 CJA 1991 s36 and CJA 2003 s248 contain power for the Home Secretary to release determinate sentence prisoners early on compassionate grounds where there exist 'exceptional circumstances'.

5.36 Detailed guidance on the circumstances in which the power will be exercised is contained in Chapter 13 of PSO 6000. The policy makes clear that the exceptional circumstances test is a stringent one (for example, terminal illness where death is likely to occur soon[59]). In CJA 1991 cases, the Home Secretary is expected to consult the Parole Board before releasing long-term prisoners unless circumstances make such consultation impracticable[60] and a similar proviso applies under the CJA 2003 for post 4 April 2005 offences in relation to those serving extended sentences.[61] Such consultation will be on the papers and the Board's remit will essentially be related to consideration as to whether there is any ongoing risk to the public.

Special Remission

5.37 Part 13 of PSO 6650 contains the policy of when Special Remission will be granted. This is where the Royal Prerogative of Mercy is used to reduce a sentence because of the prisoner's meritorious conduct, or where a prisoner has been persistently misled to his/her disadvantage as to his/her correct release date. This again is a power that is exercised rarely, as it requires the granting of a royal warrant to effect the sentence reduction.[62] The Parole Board plays no part in the process.

58 See PSI 27/2004 Annex A.
59 PSO 6000 para 13.4.
60 CJA 1991 s36(2).
61 CJA 2003 s248(2).
62 PSO 6000 para 13.1.6.

Temporary release

5.38 Prisoners can request release on temporary licence (ROTL) for certain purposes including resettlement.[63] Such periods of temporary release do not impact on the prisoners' actual release dates and it is for the governors of individual prisons to carry out the necessary risk assessments and grant the licences. The Parole Board plays no role in this process.

63 Prison Rules 1999 r9, and guidance in Instructions to Governors 36/1995 as amended: see Creighton, King and Arnott, *Prisoners and the law* 3rd edn, Tottel Publishing, 2005 Chapter 10.

CHAPTER 6

The release of determinate sentence prisoners

Introduction

6.1 The only circumstances in which the Parole Board is required to consider the initial release of determinate sentenced prisoners is for those sentenced prior to 1 October 1992; Criminal Justice Act (CJA) 1991 discretionary conditional release (DCR) and extended sentence cases where the custodial term is four years; and all CJA 2003 extended sentence cases. Other determinate sentence prisoners are released automatically at the halfway point.

6.2 Extensive guidance on the arrangements for such parole reviews is contained in PSO 6000 Chapter 5, which has been extensively revised to coincide with the coming into force of relevant parts of the CJA 2003 on 4 April 2005.

Parole eligibility dates

6.3 In summary the parole eligibility date (PED) is:

- At one-third of sentence for CJA 1967 cases ('existing prisoners' sentenced prior to 1 October 1992) who, if not released on parole licence are released unconditionally at the two-thirds point.
- At one-half of sentence for CJA 1991 DCR cases (including those whose sentenced to multiple sentences for offences committed before 4 April 2005 where the resulting 'single term' is four or more years). If not released on parole licence this category of prisoner is automatically released on licence at the two-thirds point (the 'non-parole date', or NPD).
- At one-half of the custodial term for CJA 1991 extended sentences (for offences committed between 30 September 1998 and 3 April 2005) where the custodial term is four or more years. If not released on the Board's recommendation the prisoner is released automatically on licence at the two-thirds point.
- At one-half of the sentence for CJA 2003 extended sentences (for offences committed on or after 4 April 2005). If not released on the Board's recommendation the prisoner is released at the end of the custodial term for CJA 2003 extended sentences.

6.4 When the main relevant provisions of the CJA 2003 were brought into force on 4 April 2005, the existing release dates under the CJA 1991 for those serving sentences for offences committed prior to that date were preserved.[1] The position on release dates for this class of

1 Criminal Justice Act 2003 (Commencement No 8 and Transitional and Saving Provisions) Order 2005 SI No 950 Sch 2 para 19.

prisoner following recall after 4 April 2005 is more complicated (see paras 12.35–40).

The review process

6.5 The parole review process is essentially the same in all the above cases.[2] The timetable for consideration of cases is set out in Appendix B to PSO 6000 Chapter 5 (see below).

Beginning of the parole process

6.6 The parole review process begins 26 weeks before the first PED or subsequent anniversaries, as PSO 6000 confirms that for those serving long enough sentences (or custodial terms in the case of extended sentences) that there is a right to an annual review of parole eligibility.[3] The timetable starts with the prisoner applying for parole on a prescribed form.[4] The prisoner is able to opt out of the process if he/she does not wish to apply for parole.[5]

6.7 The prison holding the prisoner is responsible for preparing the dossier.[6] In order to avoid disruption to the parole process, prisoners whose parole process is underway should not be transferred to another prison before their dossier is completed unless there are exceptional circumstances, such as where a move is required on the grounds of security, good order or discipline, health or other compassionate factors, or to avoid severe overcrowding.[7] Where such a transfer does take place, responsibility for compilation of the dossier rests with the prison with 'the greater knowledge of the prisoner' and such responsibility should be agreed at the time of the transfer.[8]

The dossier

6.8 If the prisoner applies for parole it is the responsibility of the parole clerk to request reports from prison staff and outside agencies including the Parole Assessment Report (PAR) from the home or

2 See PSO 6000 para 8.4.5.
3 PSO 6000 para 5.9.2.
4 At PSO 6000 Chapter 5 Appendix C.
5 PSO 6000 para 5.13.
6 PSO 6000 para 5.14.1.
7 PSO 6000 para 5.11.1.
8 PSO 6000 para 5.11.2.

Timetable for determinate sentence parole review (PSO 6000 Chapter 5 Appendix B)

Week 26
Parole clerk issues parole application to prisoner.

↓

Week 25
Parole clerk requests parole reports.

↓

Week 17
Reports completed.
Dossier and disclosure form disclosed to prisoner.

↓

Week 13
Representations and disclosure form received from prisoner.
Dossier checked and signed off by governor.

↓

Week 12
Deadline for dossier to be received by Parole Board.

↓

Week 7
Dossier considered by panel of Parole Board.

↓

Week 6
Parole Board decision issued (either parole awarded, refused or decision deferred).
Prison notified of decision and prisoner informed.

↓

Weeks 2–3
If applicable, the prison checks that release arrangements are in place with the Probation Service.

↓

Week 1
If applicable, the prison prepares release licence.

↓

Week 0
If applicable, the prisoner is released at parole eligibility date (or anniversary if subsequent review).

supervising probation officer. These are then compiled into a dossier, and form the basis of the material upon which the Parole Board will make its assessment of risk to the public. What the dossier should contain is outlined in Appendix F of PSO 6000 Chapter 5 (see box on p74 below).

Disclosure of the dossier

6.9 The reports in the dossier should be written with a view to open reporting.[9] Before the dossier is sent to the Parole Board the prisoner must be given access to a copy of the dossier (subject to the restrictions on disclosure set out below) so that he/she has the opportunity to make representations on the contents of the dossier. The prisoner is not given a copy of the dossier, although copies can be obtained by the prisoner or his/her legal representative on payment of the administrative charges involved in the copying.[10]

6.10 When instructed in relation to parole reviews, legal representatives can provide advice and assistance under the CDS General Criminal Contract. It is important to obtain a copy of the dossier as soon as it is available so that instructions on its contents can be obtained and representations forwarded to the parole clerk for inclusion prior to its being sent to the Board. However, the dossier is often disclosed much later than the timetable prescribes, and sometimes only after it has been forwarded to the Parole Board with the prisoner's own representations. In these circumstances further representations can be made directly to the Parole Board. However, if the dossier has been sent to the Board it is important to contact the Board to ascertain when a panel is due to consider the case to ensure any further representations are received in time.

6.11 PSO 6000 makes clear that 'in the interests of fairness, the presumption must be that all reports are disclosed'.[11] However, it also sets out five grounds upon which, exceptionally, reports may be withheld from the prisoner.[12] These are:

- in the interests of national security;
- for the prevention of disorder or crime – this includes information relevant to prison security;
- for the protection of information that may put a third party at risk;

9 PSO 6000 para 5.15.1.
10 PSO 6000 para 5.15.1.
11 PSO 6000 para 5.16.
12 PSO 6000 para 5.16.1.

- where, on medical and/or psychiatric grounds, it is felt necessary to withhold information where the mental and/or physical health of the prisoner could be impaired; and
- where the source of the information is a victim, and disclosure without their consent would breach any duty of confidence owed to that victim, or would generally prejudice the future supply of such information.

6.12 The decisions on withholding information should be made by the governor or a nominated senior officer[13] and the relevant decision maker is encouraged to seek guidance from RRS on such decisions. If a request is made to not disclose any material the governor or nominated senior officer must:

- consider whether the information is relevant;
- if it is relevant, consider whether it could be re-written to exclude information which is not disclosable without reducing its impact. Any decision on re-writing such documents should be made in consultation with the author of the material;.
- if re-writing is not possible, consider whether a gist of the document can be produced. If it is not possible to produce a gist, consider whether it meets the criteria for non disclosure (see above).[14]

6.13 When it has been decided that a document is not for disclosure, the prisoner must be informed that information has been withheld on a disclosure form, and under which limb of the non-disclosure criteria, but must not be given any information about the non-disclosed material itself.[15] Where there has been a request for non-disclosure of relevant information, where the non-disclosure criteria are not met then it should not be included in the dossier unless the author or source agrees it may be disclosed.[16]

6.14 The policy notes that it will only be in 'rare' cases that information is so sensitive that no part of it can be disclosed on application of the non-disclosure criteria. In these circumstances the prisoner must be advised and 'his representative (recognised barrister or solicitor) may apply to have sight of the information. Permission would normally be given only after having first received a written undertaking that they will not disclose the information, in full or in part, to the prisoner'.

13 PSO 6000 para 5.16.2.
14 PSO 6000 para 5.16.3.
15 PSO 6000 para 5.16.5.
16 PSO 6000 para 5.16.6.

A request by the representative should only be refused after consultation with RRS.[17]

6.15 The potential unfairness of partial or non-disclosure of material that may be relevant to the Board's assessment is obvious, as the prisoner's right to make meaningful representations will be affected. There are also potential ethical problems in a legal representative receiving material that is not disclosed to the client (although this course can be adopted if the client agrees).

6.16 The provisions in the determinate parole process now largely mirror those in the Parole Board Rules (PBR) 2004 and comments on disclosure issues under the PBR[18] are relevant (although in relation to the release of a prisoner early during the currency of the sentence imposed as punishment article 5 of the European Convention on Human Rights is not directly engaged). Accordingly, as in cases under the PBR, once disclosure of material is made to a representative it would be open to the representative to make further representations to the governor and/or RRS as to further disclosure to the prisoner. There has been at least one case in relation to a determinate sentence prisoner, where there has been non-disclosure both to the prisoner and the legal representative that the Administrative Court has ordered that fairness requires the use of a special advocate, who has no contact with the prisoner after receiving the material, but who can make representations in relation to it to the Board in closed session.[19]

Contents of the dossier

6.17 Further guidance on the dossier contents is contained in Appendix G to PSO 6000 Chapter 5. This guidance confirms that it is important that the summary of the offence accurately reflects the sentencing court's findings. The guidance states that, where possible, a report should be obtained from the police as soon as possible after sentence, but that material that may not reflect the findings of the sentencing court, such as pre-trial prosecution evidence, bail summaries and witness statements 'must not be included in the dossier as they do not necessarily set out the circumstances of the offence as established in

17 PSO 6000 para 5.16.10.

18 See para 10.30.

19 *R (Patel) v Home Secretary and Parole Board* CO/2588/2004 Order 15 June 2004, a model approved by the House of Lords in lifer cases in *R (on the application of Roberts) v Parole Board; sub nom Roberts v Parole Board* [2005] UKHL 45.

court: they are liable to challenge by the prisoner and could mislead the Parole Board'.[20]

6.18 This is a common problem, and if there is such erroneous and prejudicial material in the dossier representations should be made to the parole clerk to have it removed before the dossier is sent to the Board. If the parole clerk is unwilling to do so then the matter can be referred to RRS. The Board is under a duty to consider any documents provided to it in the dossier[21] and it has been held that this means that it is unable to remove such material itself.[22] In cases where there are only minor errors or concerns in the dossier it may be simpler, rather than entering into time-consuming correspondence about what the dossier should contain, to deal with the issues in the representations submitted to the Board. PSO 6000 confirms that complaints about the contents of the dossier can be made through the normal prison complaints procedure[23] but that consideration by the Board will not normally be deferred pending the complaint's investigation.

The key reports

6.19 As the Board's focus will be on the risk the offender poses to the public, the key reports will be from those from the probation officers and any psychology report completed during the sentence (a psychology report compiled in the prison is not mandatory and will only be completed if the prisoner has had contact with a psychologist[24]).

6.20 Detailed guidance has been given to probation officers as to what needs to be included in reports prepared for determinate sentence prisoners.[25] This guidance recognises that the prison probation officer and home probation officer should provide complimentary but distinct assessments of the prisoner.[26] In relation to the prison probation report, the guidance specifies the matters that should be evident from the prison probation officer's report:

- An interpretation and analysis of prison behaviour, including sentence plan, adjudications, impact of offending behaviour work and other relevant risk reduction work such as literacy and vocational qualifications.

20 PSO 6000 Chapter 5 Appendix G para 2.
21 See CJA 2003 s239(3)(a).
22 *R v Parole Board ex p Harris* [1998] COD 223.
23 PSO 6000 para 5.15.3.
24 See PSO 6000 Chapter 5 Appendix G para 14.
25 Appended to PC 34/2004.
26 PC 34/2004 para 5.1.

- An analysis of the offender's motivation to change and sustain an offence-free lifestyle upon release. This assessment must be based not only on prisoner's stated intent but should include some analysis of his/her ability to achieve this.
- An assessment of whether licence conditions might strengthen and sustain a prisoner's motivation to change.[27]

6.21 In relation to the home probation officer's report the guidance states that it should contain:

- Previous convictions and offending history, including any evidence of patterns of offending and any previous relevant history/ personal background that informs the reasons for offending.
- A list of offending-related factors (such as problematic drink or drug use) that provides a full understanding of all triggers to offending behaviour. In particular, instances of violence, and the targeting of certain types of victim, should be mentioned.
- Offence analysis, ie a full account of the offence(s), including any mitigating and aggravating factors.
- Responses to previous custody/supervision, and attitude to authority (including the relationship with the supervising officer).
- Victim awareness/empathy (understanding the impact of the offence on the victim or his/her family) and any future risk to the victim, family and friends.
- An assessment of the offender's motivation to change and sustain an offence-free lifestyle upon release. This assessment must be based not only upon a prisoner's stated intent but should include a realistic analysis of his/her ability to achieve this.
- The content of the resettlement plan, including a risk management plan and supervision plan and appropriate licence conditions reflecting, where appropriate, the wishes of the victim.[28]

6.22 The Prison Parole Assessment is completed either by the prisoner's personal officer, or an officer with personal knowledge of the prisoner. The report should be completed following an interview with the prisoner, consultation with other relevant members of staff and consideration of the prisoner's records.[29]

27 PC 34/2004 para 6.2.
28 PC 34/2004 para 7.3.
29 PSO 6000 Chapter 5 Appendix G para 10.

PSO 6000 Chapter 5 Appendix F

Parole dossiers must include (where applicable)

	Contents of Parole Dossier	*Source*
1.	Front cover sheet and index	Parole Clerk
2.	Summary of offence from *one* or all of the following sources • Police report • Pre-sentence report (probation) • Pre-sentence psychiatric report • Court transcription of sentencing remarks	RRS
3.	Court papers (including Form 5089 & 5035) (including, if the offender has appealed, *the appeal papers must be included*)	Sentencing Court/Court of Appeal
4.	Court transcription of sentencing remarks	Prison/RRS
5.	List of previous convictions	Police/Court/Probation
6.	Pre-sentence medical, psychological or psychiatric reports (if applicable)	Probation/Healthcare/ prison psychology
7.	Copy of previous parole dossiers (if applicable)	Parole Clerk
8.	Copy of previous parole refusal notice(s) (if applicable)	Parole Clerk
9.	Sentence Planning and OASys documentation	Prison/Probation
10.	Adjudications and ADAs (if applicable)	Prison
11.	Prison parole assessment	Prison
12.	Seconded Probation Officer's report	Seconded Probation Officer
13.	Report(s) on offence related work (if any)	Prison
14.	Prison medical/psychiatric/psychological reports (if applicable)	Prison/other
15.	Post Sentence psychology report (if any)	Prison Psychology
16.	Category A Review report (if applicable)	Category A Clerk
17.	Security Report	Security Manager
18.	Victim Personal Statement (if available)	Field Probation Officer/ police
19.	Parole assessment report	Field Probation Officer
20.	Prisoner's disclosure form/representations	Prison
21.	Parole Board Member interview report (if carried out)	Parole Board Member
22.	Disclosure form/representations	Prisoner/legal Representative

The Parole Clerk must check that dossiers contain these reports.

The Secretariat WILL return dossiers to establishments if they do not contain the reports.

The dossier may also contain other relevant information such as pre-sentence reports, Prison Chaplain's report or job offers or letters of support. Letters/Other Papers – these may be included in the dossier but none of these documents are essential for the parole review.

Representations

6.23 The disclosure form that the prisoner is invited to sign when a copy of the dossier is given to him/her includes a section upon which the prisoner can write his/her own representations or comments on the dossier. There is no set format for representations submitted by legal representatives. As noted above, to ensure that representations are considered by the Board they should be sent to the parole clerk so that they are attached to the dossier prior to its being forwarded to the Board. However, if time constraints make this impossible representations can be forwarded to the Board. If this is done it is sensible to confirm their receipt and obtain an assurance from the Board that the representations will be forwarded to the panel considering the prisoner's case.

Contents of representations

6.24 The content of representations will obviously depend upon the contents of the dossier. If there are disputed facts in the dossier and these have not been amended in correspondence with the prison and/or RRS prior to representations being submitted, a further statement from the prisoner can be included together with other evidence of the true facts. Prior authority can be obtained from the LSC on form CDS 5 to obtain independent expert reports (such as from an independent psychologist) if necessary. Other common issues that may need to be addressed in representations are:

- providing background information on matters such as disciplinary findings of guilt, and custodial history;
- providing information about offending behaviour programmes or other activities in prison that have not been dealt with, or dealt with sufficiently, in the reports contained in the dossier;
- further information about release plan (supporting statements/ letters from family, those providing a release address/job offers) especially if the home probation officer's report is not particularly detailed;
- details of outside activities that prisoners have been allowed (such as town visits, community work or periods of resettlement leave).

6.25 Representations should focus on risk to the public, and the directions the Board have to consider (see below) provide a guide as to the issues upon which the Board will focus.[30]

30 See also para 10.59 on written representations in lifer cases, as many of the points raised there will also be relevant to determinate sentence parole reviews.

Parole Board member's interview

6.26 Up until 1 April 2004 DCR prisoners were interviewed by a Parole Board member as part of the parole process. When this was first introduced after the coming into force of the CJA 1991, it was seen as a way of ensuring that prisoners, in the absence of oral parole hearings, had an opportunity to meet a representative of the body that would be making the decision as to whether they should be released.

6.27 In fact the interviewing member's role was never particularly clear. The joint Prison Service/Probation Service Comprehensive Review of Parole and Lifer Processes, which reported in 2001, noted that it was not clear whether the purpose was to enhance procedural fairness for the prisoner, or to allow the Board better to assess the risk to the public. Accordingly, from April 2004[31] the Parole Board only carry out an interview (which the prisoner cannot be compelled to attend) where it considers that without one there is insufficient information to make a decision. The interviewing member used to advise on whether the panel considering the prisoner's case should include a psychiatrist. This role in the absence of an interview is delegated to the governor.

Decision making

Procedure

6.28 The Parole Board consider DCR release cases on the papers. However, it has been held that even where the prisoner has no statutory right to an oral hearing the Board retains a discretion to hold one where fairness requires this.[32] It is only in very exceptional cases that the Board will consider that fairness requires an oral hearing in a DCR release case.[33]

6.29 The Parole Board indicated, before the House of Lords confirmed that oral hearings should be the norm in determinate sentence recall cases, that the test applied when considering whether a hearing was needed in recall cases was 'where there is a disputed issue of fact which is central to the Board's assessment and which cannot fairly

31 See PSI 29/2004 and PSO 6000 para 5.17.

32 Under CJA 1991 s32(3); see *R v Parole Board ex p Davies* HC, 27/11/96 unreported; CJA 2003 s239(3) is in the same terms.

33 The Board agreed to hold one in the *Patel* case referred to above, but this was in the context of the Administrative Court ordering that a special advocate should be appointed to deal with withheld material.

be resolved without hearing oral evidence'.[35] While this should not be seen as a conclusive statement of when oral hearings should be held (clearly there may be cases where disputes of opinion can only be resolved at an oral hearing) it provides a guide as to how the Board will approach requests for hearings. If a prisoner contends that the decision on release requires a hearing, this should be made clear in the representations to the Board.

6.30 If the Board, in the normal way, considers release on the papers this will be done by a panel of three Parole Board members. When the Parole Board consider cases on the papers a panel of three will generally consider 24 cases in a session. The members should have the dossier three or four weeks prior to the date of consideration and take turns in leading the discussion of cases (so each member will be required to prepare in detail eight cases per session).[36]

The test for release

6.31 As noted above, this section is dealing with the initial release of determinate sentence prisoners, where such a decision is subject to a Parole Board decision. This therefore includes DCR prisoners, CJA 1991 extended sentence prisoners where the custodial term is four or more years and CJA 2003 extended sentence prisoners. As the purposes of each of these sentences is different, it is necessary to look at them separately when considering the relevant test for release.

CJA 1991 DCR cases

6.32 DCR prisoners have been sentenced to a term of imprisonment that is commensurate with the seriousness of the offence.[37] As the sentencing court has decided that the whole of the term should be imposed as punishment, no fresh issues as to the legality of detention pursuant to the sentence can arise under article 5 of the European Convention on Human Rights.[38] Accordingly, within the statutory scheme, initial release is at the discretion of the executive.[39] In practice the Home

35 See *R (Smith) v Parole Board* [2005] UKHL 1 para 34.
36 Information from the Parole Board's website: www.paroleboard.gov.uk.
37 Powers of Criminal Courts (Sentencing) Act (PCC(S)A) 2000 s80(2)(a).
38 See *R (on the application of Giles)* [2004] 1 AC paras 51–52.
39 CJA 1991 s35(1) states that after a DCR prisoner has served half the sentence 'the Secretary of State may, if recommended by the Board, release him on licence'.

Secretary has delegated the final decision on DCR release cases to the Board for all prisoners serving sentences of less than 15 years.[40] The Home Secretary's retention of the right to make the final decision in relation to those serving 15 or more years has been held to be lawful by the Court of Appeal on the basis that this difference in treatment is justified, given that this category of prisoner will have been convicted of very serious offences.[41] This is despite the recognition that a fixed cut-off point will inevitably operate arbitrarily in some cases.

6.33 This framework means that when it comes to the test for release of DCR prisoners, the Home Secretary is entitled to issue directions[42] to the Board as to matters it should take into account.[43] The most recent directions came into force on 1 May 2004.[44] The directions include great detail as to the matters the Board should take into account when coming to their decision (and as such can provide a guide as to matters to deal with in written representations).

6.34 The Board is directed to consider 'primarily' whether

> the risk to the public of a further offence being committed at a time when the offender would otherwise be in prison and whether such risk is unacceptable. This must be balanced against the benefit, both to the public and the offender, of early release back into the community under a degree of supervision which might help rehabilitation and so lessen the risk of re-offending in the future.[45]

It is not necessarily the risk of the similar kind of offending that led to the imposition of the sentence that will justify the refusal of parole.

CJA long-term extended sentences

6.35 Those sentenced to an extended sentence for an offence committed between 30 September 1998 and 4 April 2005, where the custodial term is four or more years, are eligible for release at the halfway point of the custodial term.[46] As the custodial term will be the same as the

40 Parole Board (Transfer of Functions) Order 1998.

41 *R (on the application of Clift) v Secretary of State for the Home Department* [2004] EWCA Civ 514.

42 Under CJA 1991 s32(6).

43 This is in contrast to the position where article 5 of the Convention requires the Board to have directive powers of release, where the courts have held that such directions cannot be binding as they interfere with the Board's independence as a court – *R (on the application of Girling)* [2005] EWHC 546 (Admin).

44 See ministerial statement of Paul Goggins, 18 March 2004, and Appendix 5.

45 Ibid.

46 CJA 1991 ss44(2) and 35(1).

sentence commensurate with the seriousness of the offence, release at the halfway point can be on the same criteria as for DCR cases. As noted in the section on recalls (see Chapter 12), article 5 of the Convention is engaged where there is a recall during the extension period, as that element of the sentence is not imposed punitively, but in order to protect the public and secure rehabilitation. This means the test the Board must pose when considering recalls is different.[47] However, for practical reasons the Board does not appear to distinguish between the test applicable to those recalled prior to the statutory commencement of the extension period, and those recalled afterwards.

CJA 2003 extended sentence prisoners

6.36 The guidance in PSO 6000 suggests that when the initial release of CJA 2003 extended sentence prisoners is considered by the Board, the procedures adopted should be the same as those applicable to CJA 1991 DCR cases outlined above.[48] The assumption that release at the halfway point of the custodial term of a CJA 2003 extended sentence case should be treated the same as release at the halfway point of a CJA 1991 DCR case relies on the fact that in both cases the prisoner is applying for release during the currency of term of imprisonment commensurate with the seriousness of the offence.

6.37 Accepting this analysis there is no risk of arbitrary detention should the prisoner be detained beyond this point (at least until the beginning of the extension period). The Board is not responsible for considering the legality of detention for the purposes of article 5, and the test for release can therefore be set by the executive in statutory directions, and the Board can consider the prisoner's eligibility for release on the papers without the need for an oral hearing.

6.38 This view of the custodial term of the CJA 2003 extended sentence is, to some extent, supported by the House of Lords decision in *R (on the application of Giles) v Parole Board*.[49] The sentence being analysed in that case was the 'longer than commensurate' sentence imposed under section 80(2)(b) of the PCC(S)A 2000.[50] This can be imposed where the court is of the view that a longer than commensurate sentence is needed to protect the public from further offences of serious

47 The situation is complicated by the fact that the extension period in CJA 1991 extended sentence cases commences at the three-quarter point of the custodial term: CJA 1991 s44(5)(a).

48 PSO 6000 para 8.4.5.

49 [2003] UKHL 42.

50 Which is still available for offences committed before 4 April 2005.

harm. Unlike with a CJA 1991 extended sentence,[51] the court is not required by statute to divide the sentence up into 'punitive' and 'preventative' elements, and further the statutory framework does not distinguish normal fixed term sentences and longer than commensurate sentences in determining release dates. Accordingly, when the prisoner in Giles argued that he was entitled to an article 5(4) review of his detention when eligible for parole at the halfway point of the sentence, the House of Lords held that there were no fresh issues of legality that could arise during the sentence that required such a review.

6.39 However, the position of the release of CJA 2003 extended sentence prisoners at the halfway point of the custodial term is arguably different and may lead to challenges asserting that the Board should consider such applications for release at oral hearings and apply a test that further detention can be justified only on a finding of continued dangerousness.

6.40 The reason for this can be seen by comparing the sentence both with the previous version of the extended sentence, and with the CJA 1991 DCR sentence. The CJA 1991 extended sentence could be imposed by the court for sexual or violent offences where the court was of the opinion that the licence period applicable to the normal commensurate term 'would not be adequate for the purpose of preventing the commission by him of further offences and securing his rehabilitation'.[52] Accordingly, it has been held by the courts that detention during the extension period can only be justified in relation to a risk of the commission of further offences of the kind for which the sentence was imposed, namely sexual or violent offences.[53] What was not needed, by comparison with indeterminate sentences, was a finding by the court that the offender posed a risk of 'serious harm'.

6.41 This has changed with the new CJA 2003 extended sentence, which can only be imposed where the court considers that the offender poses 'a significant risk to members of the public of serious harm', or in other words, is dangerous.[54]

6.42 As noted above, those serving an SDS of 12 months or more under the CJA 2003 are automatically released on licence at the half-

51 The House of Lords decision in *Giles* was distinguished when the Court of Appeal came to consider the situation of recalled CJA 1991 extended sentence prisoners in *R (on the application of Sim)* [2004] 2 WLR 1170.

52 PCC(S)A 2000 s85(1) – see *R v Nelson* [2002] 1 Cr App R (S) 565.

53 See *R (Sim) v Parole Board* [2003] EWHC Admin 152 para 42.

54 CJA 2003 ss227(1)(b) and 228(1)(b) – 'serious harm' is defined as 'death or serious personal injury, whether physical or psychological' (CJA 2003 s224(3)).

way point.[55] By contrast, extended sentence prisoners are eligible for release halfway through the custodial term only where the Parole Board directs release.[56] The Board can only make a direction where 'it is satisfied that it is no longer necessary for the protection of the public that the prisoner should be confined'.[57] There is therefore an argument that as, but for the finding of the sentencing court of dangerousness, the offender would have been released automatically at the halfway point of the custodial term, the ongoing justification for detention beyond this point can only be continued dangerousness.

6.43 If continued dangerousness is the test for detention then, for the same reasons applicable to hearings in indeterminate cases at the end of the punitive term, there is an argument that article 5(4) is engaged. The same argument does not apply to CJA 1991 extended sentence cases because such prisoners are not disadvantaged in relation to CJA 1991 DCR cases. The discretionary and automatic release dates for both are the same.

6.44 This is therefore a situation in which the Parole Board may be required by article 5(4) of the Convention to review the legality of the offender's detention under article 5(1). The fact that the statute uses the same language as that applicable to release in indeterminate and CJA 1991 extended sentence cases[58] indicates that article 5 is engaged.[59]

6.45 This analysis may lead to an anomaly that an SDS prisoner can be recalled on the basis of a risk of lesser offending than an CJA 2003 extended sentence prisoner who is released halfway through the custodial term, even though until the end of the custodial term he/she is serving the sentence commensurate with the seriousness of the offence. This is, however, an anomaly that also exists with discretionary lifers as against determinate sentence prisoners, as the tariff is set at the notional halfway point of what the offender would have received but for the finding of dangerousness.[60]

Parole Board decisions

6.46 The Board will issue decisions to the prison in all cases except DCR cases where the sentence is 15 years or longer. In those cases the

55 CJA 2003 s244.
56 CJA 2003 s247(2).
57 CJA 2003 s247(3).
58 See C(S)A 1997 s28 and CJA 1991 s44A.
59 See *R (Giles) v The Parole Board and another* [2003] UKHL 42 para 21.
60 *R v Secretary of State for the Home Department, ex p Furber* [1998] 1 All ER 23.

Parole Board decision is treated as a recommendation[61] by officials in the RRS who make the final decision on behalf of the Home Secretary.[62] The Board may defer a decision if it considers further information is necessary.[63] The Board will give reasons for its decision, and if the decision is to refuse parole, and where the sentence is long enough, the prisoner will be informed of any entitlement to further annual reviews.[64]

6.47 If the outcome is positive, the governor should ensure that the release arrangements (such as a hostel place arranged by the Probation Service) are in place[65] and once the release date has been agreed the governor must issue the licence on behalf of the Home Secretary.[66] The governor or authorised officer must sign the licence to confirm that its conditions have been explained to the prisoner. If the prisoner refuses to sign the licence, this will be reported to the Parole Board or RRS, as a refusal to comply with the conditions of release could lead to suspension of release on licence.[67]

Further reviews

6.48 If parole is refused, the prisoner is entitled to further annual reviews, as long as at the beginning of the review process there are at least 13 months until the date of automatic release on licence at the two-thirds point of the sentence/custodial term (for DCR and CJA 1991 extended sentence cases) or the automatic release date at the end of the custodial term (for CJA 2003 extended sentence cases).[68]

6.49 Beyond these annual reviews, PSO 6000 para 5.10.1 contains the policy on when early or special reviews may be agreed outside the normal timetable:

> The Early Release and Recall Section (on behalf of the Secretary of State) has the power to authorise special or early reviews in exceptional circumstances. The Secretary of State has delegated to

61 Under CJA 1991 s35(1).

62 Parole Board (Transfer of Functions) Order 1998 SI No 3128.

63 PSO 6000 para 5.18.2.

64 PSO 6000 para 5.19.1.

65 PSO 6000 para 5.19.3.

66 PSO 6000 para 5.25.

67 PSO 6000 para 5.25.2 – compare with the position on automatic release dates where a refusal to sign the licence cannot prevent release, for example in relation to the SDS sentence: see PSO 6000 para 4.10.5.

68 PSO 6000 para 5.9.3.

the Parole Board the authority to determine whether to reconsider an earlier decision in the light of representations. If the Board declines to reconsider a case, the prisoner or his representative may apply to the Early Release and Recall Section to re-refer the case back to the Board. Exceptionally, the Early Release and Recall Section may ask for an early review. The Board and/or the Early Release and Recall Section will advise the Governor if a special or early review is ordered by letter, when appropriate. *In such cases any subsequent reviews must commence 26 weeks after the special/early review panel date.*

6.50 The courts, when examining the policy on special or early reviews have held that it is not just a change of circumstances, such as completion of an offending behaviour course, that will justify a special review as such a change will not always be 'exceptional'. However, the court stated that the Board should have a flexible approach to what does constitute 'exceptional circumstances' and not merely limit them to instances where the reasons for the decision were flawed, or where there had been procedural errors, or decisions made due to a material basis of fact.[69] A common situation where the Board will agree to a further review is where material that should have been placed before the Board, such as a report on an offending behaviour course completed before its decision was made, is for some reason not included in the dossier.

Non-parole release

6.51 If not released on the recommendation of the Board at the halfway point of the sentence or at any subsequent reviews:

- existing CJA 1967 prisoners are released unconditionally at the two-thirds point;
- DCR and CJA 1991 extended sentence prisoners with a custodial term of four or more years are released at the two-thirds point of the sentence;[70]
- DCR prisoners are released on licence to the three-quarter point;[71]
- CJA 1991 extended sentence prisoners are released on licence to the end of the extension period;
- CJA 2003 extended sentence prisoners are released at the end of the custodial term on licence to sentence expiry.

69 *R (on the application of McCalla)* [2001] EWHC Admin 396.

70 CJA 1991 s33(2).

71 CJA 1991 s37(1), unless for sexual offences committed before 30 September 1998, the court ordered that the licence extend to sentence expiry under PCC(S)A 2000 s86.

Prisoners liable to removal

6.52 Prisoners who are liable to removal and are not released under the ERS scheme (see para 5.33) and who are serving sentences which fall to be administered under the CJA 1991 (imposed for offences committed before 4 April 2005) are subject to the normal early release schemes which depend on sentence length.

6.53 However, in DCR cases no referral is made to the Board and the Home Secretary is responsible for the release decision.[72] Those liable to removal cannot opt out of the process and a dossier is produced in the same way as for other prisoners.[73] The decision is made by officials at RRS on behalf of the Home Secretary on the basis of directions which are the same as those applied to the enhanced assessment under the ERS (see Appendix 6). The fact that deportees do not have their case referred to the Board has been held by the Court of Appeal not to be unlawfully discriminatory under the Human Rights Act 1998.[74]

6.54 SDS prisoners who are liable to removal will be released at the halfway point as with other prisoners.

72 CJA 1991 s46(1).

73 See Chapter 9 of PSO 6000 for the procedure.

74 *R (on the application of Headley and Hindawi) v Home Secretary* [2004] EWCA 1309.

CHAPTER 7

Indeterminate sentences: an overview

The various types of life and indeterminate sentence

7.1 There are a number of different life and indeterminate sentences available to the courts. While all of these sentences are administered by the Prison Service and the Parole Board in the same manner, the legal basis for the imposition of the sentence can have relevance when assessing risk issues for the purposes of parole, and so it is important to be aware of which life sentence has been imposed. The various life sentences available to the courts are listed below.

Murder

7.2 Following a conviction for murder it is a mandatory statutory requirement to impose a life sentence. The three sentences which can be imposed are:

- The life sentence which is imposed automatically on persons convicted of murder who are aged 21 or over when the offence is committed.[1] This is commonly referred to as the 'mandatory life sentence' and people serving the sentence are often described as 'mandatory lifers'.
- Custody for life, which is imposed automatically on people convicted of murder who are aged 18 or over but under 21 when the offence was committed.[2] For practical purposes, there is no real legal distinction to be made between this class of lifers and adult mandatory lifers.
- Detention at Her Majesty's Pleasure (HMP) is imposed on people convicted of murder who were under the age of 18 when the offence was committed.[3] This sentence has a complex history, originally being introduced at the start of the 20th century to replace the death penalty for minors with indefinite detention. When the death penalty was abolished for adults, the sentence effectively became subsumed into the adult mandatory life sentence, but a series of cases over the past 15 years have allowed the courts to reaffirm the distinctive nature of HMP detention. The relevance of these differences are discussed as they arise in context, but the fundamental distinction is that this sentence contains an intrinsic

1 Murder (Abolition of Death Penalty) Act 1965 s1.

2 Powers of Criminal Courts (Sentencing) Act (PCC(S)A) 2000 s93.

3 PCC(S)A 2000 s90, which replaced the Children and Young Persons Act 1933 s53(1).

welfare element as well as the normal punitive and protective elements in sentences imposed on adults.

Life sentences for other serious offences

Discretionary life sentences

7.3 The discretionary life sentence can be imposed where life is the maximum sentence – eg, for a range of offences such as attempted murder, manslaughter, arson with intent to endanger life or where there is recklessness, rape, buggery where the victim is under 16, armed robbery or other serious offences of violence. It is currently imposed under Criminal Justice Act (CJA) 2003 s225 for offences committed after 4 April 2005 (this requires the imposition of a life sentence where the offence attracts a maximum of life, and the court considers that the seriousness of the offence is such to justify the imposition of a life sentence). Before the enactment of the CJA 2003, the statutory authority for the sentence was found in section 80 of the PCC(S)A 2000.

7.4 The justification for the imposition of a discretionary life sentence is where the sentencing court believes that the offender is dangerous. It is therefore meant to be reserved for offenders whose mental state makes it difficult to predict future risk or where the offences or so serious that there may be ongoing risk. *R v Hodgson*[4] established the following criteria for the imposition of a discretionary life sentence:

- where the offence or offences in themselves are grave enough to require a very long sentence;
- when it appears from the nature of the offences or from the defendant's history that he/she is a person of unstable character likely to commit such offences in the future;
- where, if further offences are committed, the consequences to others may be especially injurious, as in the case of sexual offences or cases of violence.

7.5 However, subsequent case-law has suggested that the sentence is available in cases where the severity of the offence justifies it, even if there is no direct evidence of mental instability. This development seems to have been particularly concentrated on sexual offending.

4 [1968] 15 CAR 13.

Automatic lifers

7.6 The automatic life sentence ceased to be available to the sentencing courts as from 4 April 2005, when it was replaced by the sentence of imprisonment for public protection (see below). However, the sentence was so prevalent for while that there are large numbers of automatic lifers serving the sentence in custody and on licence.

7.7 The sentence was originally introduced by the Crime (Sentences) Act 1997 s2 (subsequently replaced by the PCC(S)A 2000 s109). It required the courts to impose a life sentence on anyone convicted for the second time of the following offences specified by the statute:

(1) attempted murder, incitement or conspiracy or soliciting to commit murder;
(2) manslaughter;
(3) wounding or committing GBH with intent;
(4) rape or attempted rape;
(5) sexual intercourse with a girl under 13;
(6) possession of a firearm with intent to injure;
(7) use of a firearm with intent to resist arrest;
(8) carrying a firearm with criminal intent;
(9) armed robbery.

7.8 Although the second conviction must have been after the Act came into force, the first conviction can have occurred at any time.

7.9 The automatic life sentence, after an uncertain start, to a large extent eventually came to mirror the discretionary life sentence. The rationale for the sentence is founded on the premise that persons convicted of a second serious offence are presumed to be dangerous, unless exceptional circumstances displace that presumption. In the early days of the sentence, the Court of Appeal created a very narrow test of exceptional circumstances. However, following the application of the European Convention on Human Rights to the sentence,[5] the Court of Appeal accepted that this construction breached article 5(1) of the Convention in that it rendered the sentence arbitrary. As a consequence, the Court of Appeal stated that if an offender could establish that they did not pose a continuing danger to the public, the exceptional circumstances criteria would be met. The result is that persons subject to this sentence will have been found to present a potential for continuing danger to the public at the outset, albeit to a lesser extent in many cases than persons receiving discretionary life sentences.

5 *R v Offen* [2001] 1 WLR 253.

Sentence of imprisonment for public protection

7.10 This has replaced the automatic life sentence and is imposed where the offender commits a 'serious offence' attracting a maximum sentence of ten years or more after 4 April 2005[6] and the court is of the opinion that 'there is a significant risk to members of the public of serious harm'[7] – but where the court does not consider the offence so serious as to justify a life sentence. The sentence may also be imposed on those under 18 when the offence was committed.[8]

7.11 The custodial part of the sentence is served in precisely the same manner as any other life sentence. However, it is distinguished from the life sentences listed above as it is the only kind of indeterminate sentence where the licence can be terminated rather than continuing for life.[9]

The length of the sentence

7.12 The period of time that a lifer must spend in custody before the Parole Board can consider suitability for release is known as the 'minimum term'. This is the punitive part of the sentence that is imposed for the purposes of retribution and deterrence. Historically, this part of the sentence was referred to as the 'tariff', but was changed on the advice of the Sentencing Advisory Panel as it was felt that 'minimum term' would convey more clearly that release at the end of this period is not automatic but dependent on risk being reduced sufficiently. The terms 'tariff' and 'minimum term' are now used interchangeably, although minimum term is the correct expression.

7.13 Although the detailed history and the precise mechanics for setting the minimum term are outside the scope of this book, a basic understanding of the principles applied by the courts when imposing a life or indeterminate sentence can be important to the parole process in terms of the assessment of how seriously the sentencing courts viewed the offence.[10]

6 CJA 2003 s224(2) and Criminal Justice Act 2003 (Commencement No 8 and Transitional and Saving Provisions) Order 2005 SI No 950.

7 CJA 2003 s225(2).

8 CJA 2003 s226.

9 CJA 2003 Sch 18.

10 For a detailed discussion of the history and practice of life sentences see Creighton, King and Arnott, *Prisoners and the law* 3rd edn, Tottel Publishing, 2005.

Minimum term for murder

7.14 Since 18 December 2003, the CJA 2003 s269 has required the court that imposes a mandatory life sentence to set the minimum term. Very strict statutory guidelines are contained in CJA 2003 Sch 21. In the event that the offender is aged over 21 when the offence was committed, the court has the power to impose a whole life term.[11] There are three statutory starting points for the length of the term, and aggravating and mitigating features are then added or subtracted from those starting points.

7.15 The sentencing court is also required to specify whether allowance is being given for time spent on remand and, if so, how time has been allowed.[12] The term that is imposed is subject to the normal provisions for an appeal against sentence to the Court of Appeal, either by the prisoner or on an Attorney-General's reference.[13]

Whole life terms

7.16 A whole life order is to be imposed in cases where the offender is over 21 at the time the offence was committed and the offence involves:

(a) the murder of two or more persons, where each murder involves any of the following –
  (i) a substantial degree of premeditation or planning,
  (ii) the abduction of the victim, or
  (iii) sexual or sadistic conduct,
(b) the murder of a child if involving the abduction of the child or sexual or sadistic motivation,
(c) a murder done for the purpose of advancing a political, religious or ideological cause, or
(d) a murder by an offender previously convicted of murder.[14]

30-year starting point

7.17 A starting point of 30 years is deemed appropriate for persons aged 18 years or over who are convicted of the following offences:

(a) the murder of a police officer or prison officer in the course of his duty,
(b) a murder involving the use of a firearm or explosive,
(c) a murder done for gain (such as a murder done in the course or

11 CJA 2003 s269(4).

12 CJA 2003 s269(3).

13 CJA 2003 ss270–271 which also amends Criminal Appeal Act 1968 s9(1).

14 CJA 2003 Sch 21 para 4.

furtherance of robbery or burglary, done for payment or done in the expectation of gain as a result of the death),

(d) a murder intended to obstruct or interfere with the course of justice,

(e) a murder involving sexual or sadistic conduct,

(f) the murder of two or more persons,

(g) murder that is racially or religiously aggravated or aggravated by sexual orientation, or

(h) a murder falling within [CJA 2003 Sch 21] paragraph 4(2) committed by an offender who was aged under 21 when he committed the offence.[15]

15-year starting point

7.18 The starting point for any case that does not fall within these two categories and where the offender was aged 18 years or over at the time of the offence is 15 years.[16]

Aggravating features

7.19 The factors which will justify a higher sentence being imposed are:

(a) a significant degree of planning or premeditation,

(b) the fact that the victim was particularly vulnerable because of age or disability,

(c) mental or physical suffering inflicted on the victim before death,

(d) the abuse of a position of trust,

(e) the use of duress or threats against another person to facilitate the commission of the offence,

(f) the fact that the victim was providing a public service or performing a public duty, and

(g) concealment, destruction or dismemberment of the body.[17]

Mitigating factors

7.20 The relevant factors which mitigate the length of the sentence are:

(a) an intention to cause serious bodily harm rather than to kill,

(b) lack of premeditation,

(c) the fact that the offender suffered from any mental disorder or mental disability which (although not falling within section 2(1) of the Homicide Act 1957 (c 11)), lowered his degree of culpability,

(d) the fact that the offender was provoked (for example, by prolonged stress) in a way not amounting to a defence of provocation,

15 CJA 2003 Sch 21 para 5(2).

16 CJA 2003 Sch 21 para 6.

17 CJA 2003 Sch 21 para 10.

(e) the fact that the offender acted to any extent in self-defence,
(f) a belief by the offender that the murder was an act of mercy, and
(g) the age of the offender.[18]

Transitional cases

7.21 There are very large numbers of prisoners serving life sentences for murder that were imposed prior to 18 December 2003. These comprise of one group who had minimum terms set by the Secretary of State when he still retained this power, and a smaller group who never had a minimum term set by the Secretary of State as their convictions occurred after it was decided it was in breach of article 6 of the European Convention on Human Rights for him to fix these sentences.[19]

7.22 Both of these groups of lifers will now have a judicially set minimum term. The difference between the two groups is that those who never had a minimum term fixed will have their cases considered by a High Court judge automatically, whereas those who did have a tariff or minimum term set by the Secretary of State must apply to the court if they wish it be reset by a High Court judge[20] (providing the previously set tariff has not already expired). The court is prohibited from setting a minimum term greater than the previously notified tariff or the term that would have been set by the Secretary of State at the time – but must have regard to the term previously set, the judicial recommendations and the guidance contained in CJA 2003 Sch 21 for current sentences.[21]

7.23 The procedure for setting the minimum terms is a written one, although the final decision is given in open court.[22] All decisions are published on the Court Service's website.[23] Once the High Court has given a decision, there remains a right of appeal by either the prisoner or the Attorney-General to the Court of Appeal.[24]

18 CJA 2003 Sch 21 para 11.
19 This occurred in December 2002 when the House of Lords ruled in *R (Anderson) v Home Secretary* [2003] AC 837.
20 CJA 2003 Sch 22 paras 6 and 3(1)–(2).
21 CJA 2003 Sch 22 para 4.
22 See also *R (Hammond) v Home Secretary* [2004] EWHC 2753 where the Divisional Court held that the judge setting the term should have the discretion to convene an oral hearing if necessary. At the time of writing, this decision was awaiting the outcome of an appeal to the House of Lords.
23 See www.hmcourts-service.gov.uk.
24 CJA 2003 Sch 22 paras 14 and 15 amend the Criminal Appeals Act 1968 to include this type of case in the normal procedures for an appeal against sentence.

All other life sentences

7.24 For all other lifers and indeterminate sentenced prisoners, the minimum term is fixed in open court at the conclusion of the trial. The power to set these sentences was transferred from the executive to the judiciary many years ago (1992 for discretionary lifers and 1998 for HMP detainees) and so there are no further transitional cases.[25]

HMP detainees

7.25 The minimum term for this group is set according to the principles applied in CJA 2003 Sch 21 para 7 which specifies that the starting point will be 12 years. The normal aggravating and mitigating factors specified in the Act should then be applied to the sentence.

Discretionary lifers, automatic lifers and IPP detainees

7.26 All of these prisoners have their minimum terms set by the trial judge in the same manner as any other. A succession of cases over the years has established that the sentencing judge should address the following matters when imposing the sentence:

- specify the determinate sentence that would have been imposed if a sentence of life imprisonment had not been imposed
- proceed to set the minimum term at a point between one-half and two-thirds of the determinate sentence;
- specify the amount of remand time that will be allowed against the minimum term.

7.27 There have been a large number of cases over the years that have looked at the relationship between the minimum term and the notional determinate sentence. The decision that it should be somewhere between one-half and two-thirds is to reflect the point at which a determinate sentenced prisoner will be considered for parole or, eventually, released automatically. By setting the minimum term in this way, the lifer will not be disadvantaged in the punitive part of the sentence in relation to prisoners serving determinate sentences. While the norm has been for the sentence to be one half of the determinate sentence, the Court of Appeal has refused to be too prescriptive allowing leeway up to the two-thirds point in more serious cases.[26]

25 The last group of transitional HMP detainees had their position clarified in July 2005 in *R (Smith and Dudson) v Home Secretary* [2005] UKHL 51 and 52.

26 The two cases which clarify these principles are: *R v Home Secretary ex p Furber* [1998] 1 All ER 23 and *R v Marklew* [1999] 1 CAR (S) 6.

CHAPTER 8

Serving the life sentence

How indeterminate sentences are served

8.1 All lifers will normally be expected to follow a similar path from conviction to release. Although there will obviously be scope for individual cases to vary from the core structure, the Lifer Manual (PSO 4700), a document which contains the centralised policy on life sentences, sets out a general overview of the normal life sentence. The Lifer Manual is available from the Prison Service's records centre at Branston. A copy should also be available to all lifers in prison libraries.[1] The core document deals with adults serving relatively long minimum terms whose entire sentences will be served in the adult estate. Many of the principles will apply to other classes of lifer, and the points of variation are set out below.

Home Office structure

8.2 The method by which the Home Office organises decision making for lifers has changed constantly over the past 20 years. The current system has been in place since around January 2004 following the introduction of the National Offender Management Service (NOMS).

8.3 Historically, lifers have always posed a particular organisational problem for the Home Office due to the tension between the desire of the Home Office to maintain control over the life sentence and the practicalities of the sentence, as it is the prison in which the individual is located that actually has the task of making the relevant assessments and writing reports. Until the latest reorganisation, a specialist unit at the Prison Service – Lifer Unit – was responsible for making decisions on lifers' categorisation and allocation and for dealing with parole reviews and recalls to prison custody. The department was initially split into two arms, with the *review unit* taking responsibility for decisions on progress and release and the *lifer management unit* addressing transfer and allocation issues. These two arms were amalgamated in 2000 so that one team dealt with all aspects of the lifer's progress. Prisons would simply submit reports and recommendations to this unit, as opposed to making final decisions on these matters. However, in February 2004 operational responsibility was removed from the unit when it became part of the Home Office as NOMS.

1 This document is now slightly out of date and was in the process of being updated in October 2005.

8.4 Under the current system, the Lifer Review and Recall Section (LRRS) has the following responsibilities:[2]

- to monitor the whole parole review process for all lifers;
- to consider directions for release made by 'paper' panels and to decide whether to refer those case to an oral hearing;
- to consider individual recommendations in those cases where the Parole Board has recommended the transfer of a lifer from closed to open conditions;
- to consider and, where appropriate, to refer cases to the Parole Board for advice on a lifer's continued suitability for open conditions;
- to monitor the progress of life licencees in the community, including recall to custody and the cancellation of supervision;
- to oversee and develop policy in respect of lifers in the above areas;
- to liaise with the Prison Service on operational lifer policy development.

8.5 Until June 2004, LRRS would also be asked to give final approval on matters relating to high profile prisoners, such as decisions on temporary release, but this is now a matter for area managers.

8.6 As LRRS is a department of NOMS, it falls under the direct jurisdiction of the Home Office. It is no longer a department of the Prison Service. It remained located at Prison Service headquarters, although a move to new premises was envisaged for early 2006. It is divided into a number of teams which deal with lifers on an alphabetic division (see Appendix 10).

8.7 All operational decisions – save for decisions pertaining to Category A prisoners – are made by the prison in which the lifer is held. Therefore, all inquiries about matters such as categorisation, transfers, access to courses, prison discipline and temporary release should be made to the lifer manager of that prison. In difficult cases, or in situations where the matter may have direct relevance to a parole review, LRRS may sometimes be able to intervene to try to broker a resolution to the problem. This most commonly occurs when a prison approves a progressive transfer but cannot find another prison to accept the individual. Although LRRS does not have any operational powers, it can sometimes assist in seeking to persuade a new prison to accept the lifer.

8.8 Finally, with Category A prisoners, there is an another level of administration to negotiate. Categorisation decisions for this group are made by the Director of High Security Prisons under devolved authority from the Home Secretary. The Directorate of High Security

2 PSO 4700 para 3.

Prisons[3] has casework teams which deal with Category A reviews and the allocation and movement of Category A prisoners.

Initial allocation

8.9 On conviction, adult male lifers will be sent to a prison with a stage 1 main lifer centre. There are several of these around the country and all are in either Category B training prisons or high security prisons (formerly known as 'dispersals' after the policy of dispersing high risk prisoners around the system). For female lifers, there are a number of designated stage 1 lifer prisons.[4] This initial decision is made by the lifer manager of the prison in which the lifer is held at the time of conviction. A form LSP 1 should be completed and forwarded to the Population Management Unit of the Prison Service (a unit which oversees transfers) as well as the relevant case work team at LRRS. This transfer request should include a list of suitable prisons to which the lifer could be transferred. The Lifer Manual contains a list of all prisons which can hold lifers and the types of courses and regimes they can offer.

8.10 All Category A prisoners will be allocated to a high security prison, of which there are currently five. Non-Category A prisoners can also be allocated to a high security prison if it felt that the offence or the lifer's history justifies these conditions. For Category A prisoners, the LSP 1B form should be used and marked 'high security allocation'. This is processed by the Directorate of High Security Prisons at Prison Service headquarters. In all cases, allocation decisions should be made within 28 days of the transfer request being received.

8.11 Juveniles will be allocated to an appropriate Young Offenders Institution (YOI), or a Local Authority Secure Children's Home if under 16 years of age.

8.12 Guidance on the factors which should inform allocation decisions, both initially and at subsequent transfers, can be found in PSO 4700 at para 21. These include:

- security issues relating to escape risk;
- control issues, including behaviour and progress in custody;
- risk assessment based on work completed in respect of offending behaviour;

3 Based at Prison Service Headquarters, Cleland House, Page Street, London SW1P 4LN.

4 For a fuller discussion of the establishments which can hold life sentenced prisoners see Creighton, King and Arnott, *Prisoners and the law* 3rd edn, Tottel Publishing, 2005.

- regime issues to ensure that the suggested prison can meet the prisoner's treatment, healthcare and resettlement needs;
- life sentence issues which will take account overall progress through the sentence, public interest in the case and the proximity to or outcome of parole hearings.

Progress reviews

Annual sentence planning

8.13 All lifers are supposed to have regular reviews of their progress. The first of these reviews are annual sentence planning reviews which must be held at intervals of no more than 12 months. The reviews are conducted by the prison holding the lifer at the relevant time and the reports for this review should normally be completed by the personal officer and seconded probation officer in advance of the meeting to discuss progress. These reports are completed on forms known as LSP 3B forms.

8.14 It is standard practice for the prison to disclose these forms to the prisoner in advance of the board meeting and to invite the prisoner to be present at the meeting itself. At the first board, it is required that there should be attendance by a psychologist, probation officer, personal officer and wing manager with the board being chaired by the lifer manager. At subsequent boards, the lifer manager will decide on whose attendance is necessary. The home probation officer will also normally be invited to attend, although such attendance is patchy. There is no provision for the attendance of solicitors and this is very rarely allowed. Legal representatives can make written submissions where necessary.

8.15 Following the completion of these boards, the outcome and recommendations are usually made available to the prisoner. The reports should be forwarded to LRRS and copies retained on the individual's life sentence plan (LSP).

Interim progress reviews

8.16 In addition to the annual reviews, all lifers will normally have a more detailed report on progress up until the first parole review. These reviews used to be termed 'F 75 reviews', having been named after the forms used to complete the review. They are now conducted primarily through forms known as 'LSP 3 progress reports'. The LSP 3 documents the setting and achievement of sentence planning targets. It incorporates Sentence planning and Review Board reports, progress reports for allocation during custody and for Parole Board reviews. It provides a permanent record of the lifer's participation in offending behaviour programmes, treatments, courses, activities and targets, both those directly related to the offence and others, such as educational or vocational qualifications that the lifer may achieve while in custody.

8.17 As a safeguard, LSP 3E reports must be prepared at certain fixed points of the sentence. These are:

- for parole reviews;
- if the lifer has a short tariff and has not been allocated to a Second Stage establishment within two years of arrival at the First Stage prison;
- when five years have passed since the last set of LSP 3E reports.

8.18 In between these fixed points, reports will only be called for when it is considered that the lifer may be suitable for a progressive transfer or reallocation within the closed prison estate, based on the recommendations of the LSP 3B Sentence Planning and Review Board report and the lifer manager.

8.19 The backstop dates are to ensure that reports are written on those prisoners who may be unable to progress due to being Category A, or who are unwilling or unable to participate in the normal sentence planning and review process. The purpose of the five-year backstop LSP 3E reports is to enable a review of the case of a prisoner who has made no significant progress on the basis of a set of detailed reports from all staff involved in the prisoner's management. A 'fresh start' transfer is one of the options that can then be considered.

8.20 LSP 3E reports will be disclosed to the prisoner and a period of seven days should be allowed for any comments to be made. Lifers may take legal advice on this and representations may be made by a solicitor on their behalf.

First parole review

Timing

8.21 The first formal review of a lifer's case by the Parole Board takes place approximately three years before the expiry of the minimum term. In cases where the minimum term is less than six years, the start date will be adjusted (see the section on short tariffs below). The purpose of this review is to enable consideration to be given as to whether the lifer has made sufficient progress to be moved to open conditions. The review time is set at three years before the earliest release test, in order to allow for the lifer to spend some time in open conditions before the minimum term expires. This is to reflect the requirement that before most lifers can be released, they will need to spend time in open conditions to establish a release plan and to demonstrate that they can be trusted to comply with supervision on life licence in the community.[5] The Lifer Manual explains the rationale of the policy as follows:

> A period in open conditions is essential for most life sentenced prisoners ('lifers'). It allows the testing of areas of concern in conditions which are nearer to those in the community than can be found in closed prisons. Lifers have the opportunity to take home leave from open prisons and, more generally, open conditions require them to take more responsibility for their actions.[6]

8.22 The date of this review can be brought forward by six months in cases where the prisoner has been in a Category C prison – or a second stage female prison – for at least one year before it is reached (ie for 12 months before the three-and-a-half years prior to the expiry of the minimum term).[7] Generally speaking, it will be extremely rare to find a case where a referral to the Board will take place earlier than this, and the one attempt to challenge the normal 'three-year policy' – in a case where a lifer argued that she had completed all necessary work in closed conditions and would benefit from a longer period of time in open conditions – was rejected by the High Court.[8]

The statutory grounds for referral

8.23 There is no requirement in statute for cases to be referred at the pre-tariff stage, nor for a move to open conditions to be dependent on a recommendation from the Parole Board. This practice has arisen

5 Ministerial statement of 7 November 1994. This policy was affirmed by the Court of Appeal in *R v Secretary of State for the Home Department, ex p Stafford* [1998] 1 WLR 503 and this part of the judgment was not criticised by either the House of Lords or the European Court of Human Rights.

6 Lifer Manual, Appendix 7 p4.

7 See *R v Secretary of State for the Home Secretary, ex p Roberts* [1998] 8 July, unreported and the ministerial statement of 9 July 1998.

8 *R (on the application of Payne (Kelly)) v Secretary of State for the Home Department* [2004] EWHC 581 (Admin).

solely as a matter of policy. However, the statutory authority for cases actually to be referred to the Board and considered under this policy can be found in Criminal Justice Act 2003 s239(2), which requires the Board to advise the Secretary of State on matters relating to the early release of prisoners where the Secretary of State has requested advice.

8.24 As the review is to examine progress prior to release, it does not fall within the ambit of article 5(4) of the European Convention on Human Rights, and this is why an oral hearing is not required. There is extensive case-law, both domestically and before the European Court of Human Rights, that makes it clear that decisions on the movement of prisoners to open conditions do not engage article 5 rights, as the concept of liberty is absolute in this context. The transfer of a prisoner to an open prison remains a decision taken on the conditions of imprisonment as opposed to one that engages liberty.[9] The Board does retain the discretionary power to convene an oral hearing if it feels it necessary as a matter of fairness on a case-by-case basis.[10]

The review process

8.25 The review, as with oral hearings, is fixed to take place on a six-month timetable. The first stage is the disclosure of the parole dossier. The dossier will be identical in form to the dossier prepared for an oral review on the expiry of the minimum term (see para 10.15 below) with a skeleton dossier being prepared by LRRS and the reports added to this by the prison. There will normally be reports from the lifer manager, personal officer, the wing manager, the prison and field probation officer, the prison medical officer and usually a psychologist or psychiatrist.

8.26 Following disclosure of the dossier, the prisoner will be given one month in which to make representations in writing. Prisoners are encouraged to seek legal advice and representatives will commonly make representations for their clients. Again, the format of the written representations is unlikely to vary a great deal from those prepared for the paper sift in the reviews which lead to an oral hearing.[11] The difference between the oral review and this pre-tariff review is that the written representations constitute the end of the active role

9 The most recent domestic decision on this issue which analyses the key case-law is *R (on the application of Day) v Secretary of State for the Home Department* [2004] EWHC Admin 1742.

10 *R v Parole Board ex p Davies* [1996] 27 November, unreported.

11 See para 10.54 below.

the prisoner can have in the review. The representations are considered by a three-member panel of the Board and their written decision is sent to LRRS. LRRS will then issue the outcome of the review to the prisoners.

The Secretary of State's directions

8.27 The Secretary of State has issued directions to the Parole Board setting out the matters they should take into account when deciding whether to authorise a transfer to open conditions. It has been held that the practice of the Home Secretary issuing directions to the Parole Board breaches the concept of judicial independence and so impinges on article 5(4).[12] Nonetheless, as the court also held that the directions related to considerations which any sensible Parole Board would take into account in any event, it is necessary to bear these in mind when drafting representations to the Board. Also, as the review at this stage does not engage article 5, there is no reason why the Secretary of State should not issue directions.

8.28 The overall instruction to the Board[13] is to 'balance the risks against the benefits to be gained by such a move'. The following specific factors inform that assessment:

(a) whether the lifer has made *sufficient* progress towards tackling offending behaviour to minimise the risk and gravity of re-offending and whether the benefits suggest that a transfer to open conditions is worthwhile at that stage; and
(b) whether the lifer is trustworthy enough not to abscond or to commit further offences (either inside or outside the prison).[14]

8.29 The detailed guidance is as follows:

(a) the extent to which the lifer has made sufficient progress during sentence in addressing and reducing risk to a level consistent with protecting the public from harm, in circumstances where the lifer in open conditions would be in the community, unsupervised, under licensed temporary release;
(b) the extent to which the lifer is likely to comply with the conditions of any such form of temporary release;

12 *R (on the application of Girling) v Parole Board and Home Secretary* [2005] EWHC Admin 546.

13 The Directions to the Parole Board on the Transfer of Mandatory Life Sentence Prisoners to Open Conditions; Lifer Manual, appendix 7 – the directions may also be found on the Board's website.

14 Ibid.

(c) the extent to which the lifer is considered trustworthy enough not to abscond;

(d) the extent to which the lifer is likely to derive benefit from being able to address areas of concern and to be tested in a more realistic environment, such as to suggest that a transfer to open conditions is worthwhile at that stage.

8.30 These directions are supplemented by Training Guidance on the Transfer of Life Sentence Prisoners to Open Conditions. The Board is instructed to consider any outstanding areas of concern in the lifer's offending behaviour and the benefits to the lifer of a transfer to open conditions. The Board is told that the emphasis should be on the 'risk' aspect of a move to open conditions, and the 'need to have made significant progress in changing attitudes and tackling offending behaviour'.

8.31 The Board is also specifically instructed that advice is only sought on the suitability of a move to an open prison – or for lifers at the end of their minimum term, release – and it is not required to comment on the timing of the next review or moves to other categories of prison.[15]

Special considerations

Short tariff lifers

8.32 When the automatic life sentence was first introduced, the Prison Service was suddenly confronted with large numbers of life sentenced prisoners with short tariffs, in some cases as short as 12–18 months. As the life sentence had previously been reserved for very serious offending, the normal structure of the life sentence did not translate properly to people who would become eligible for release before they even had their first full internal review. In order to address the difficulties this created, special directions were put in place for those with tariffs of under five years. These are:

- The Parole Board confirmed that there was no absolute requirement for short tariff lifers to go to open conditions, with an assessment being made on the merits of each case.
- On conviction, priority should be given to allocating this group to main lifer centres.

15 *R (on the application of Spence) v Secretary of State for the Home Department* [2003] EWCA Civ 732.

- Where the tariff is under five years, initial progress reports should be prepared after six months at the first stage prison.
- Pre-tariff parole reviews will generally only be feasible in cases where the tariff is three years or more. However, if the six-month review considers that a move to open conditions might be appropriate, steps will be taken by LRRS to try to facilitate a pre-tariff expiry parole review.[16]

8.33 The numbers of lifers with very short tariffs actually remained quite low, as the post-*Offen* test meant that where a very short tariff might be imposed, there is more likely to be exceptional circumstances making the life sentence inappropriate. However, in cases where short tariffs are imposed, these directions should be followed.

Deportees

8.34 Prisoners who are to be deported at the end of their life sentence should, in theory, not face any difference in their progress through the sentence and their parole reviews. For many years the Secretary of State did not permit this group of lifers to take town visits from Category C conditions or to move to open conditions. Now, in theory, there is no reason why deportees should not go to open conditions. In practice, they will find this more difficult to achieve than lifers not facing deportation, as they will need to overcome any concerns that they might seek to abscond from open conditions to avoid deportation. LRRS will also consult with the immigration authorities so that any objections they might have can be considered. In cases where it is decided that the lifer is not suitable for open conditions, release and deportation will normally take place from a Category C prison.

16 It is understood from LRRS that cases in this category are extremely rare.

CHAPTER 9

The test for release

The test for release

9.1 There is a statutory test for the release of a prisoners serving indeterminate sentences, which must be applied by the Parole Board in every case. The test is that:

> the Board is satisfied that it is no longer necessary for the protection of the public that the prisoner should be confined.[1]

9.2 There is an historical background to this statutory test arising from case-law. It is often referred to as the 'life and limb' test, as the danger posed by the lifer must be of re-offending which would cause serious harm to the public.[2] For mandatory lifers, this replaces the much narrower test which authorised detention if they were at risk of committing 'any imprisonable offence', which applied until the European Court of Human Rights (ECtHR) decision in *Stafford v UK*.[3]

9.3 The 'life and limb' test was first expressed in relation to a challenge by a discretionary lifer. The manner in which it was described by the court was as follows:

> If risk to the public is the test, risk must mean risk of dangerousness. Nothing else will suffice. It must mean there is a risk of Mr Benson repeating the sort of offence for which the life sentence was originally imposed; in other words risk to life and limb.[4]

9.4 These comments might, a first sight, seem to imply that the type of offending has to be the same as for the conviction, even perhaps if it were a different type of dangerous offending. This debate was reignited following the *Stafford* decision. In *Stafford*, the applicant had been convicted of murder, released on life licence and then recalled to prison following a conviction for fraud. The ECtHR found that the decision to imprison Mr Stafford pursuant to his original life sentence on the grounds that he might commit further non-violent offences was in breach of article 5(1) of the European Convention on Human Rights (ECHR), as there was no causal link between the original conviction and the subsequent detention. This resulted in an argument that the Board could not detain a lifer who posed a risk of offending that differed from the index offence.

1 Crime (Sentences) Act 1997 s28(6)(b).

2 *R v Parole Board ex p Bradley* [1991] 1 WLR 134.

3 [2002] 35 EHRR 32.

4 From *R v Secretary of State for the Home Department, ex p Benson (No 2)* 16 November 1988, *Independent*, but quoted in full in *Bradley* [1991] 1 WLR 134 at 142C.

9.5 The flaw in this argument was that the basis for the original imposition of a life sentence is that the offender is considered to be dangerous.[5] Therefore, any further offending that poses a risk of serious harm to the public is causally connected to the conviction which resulted in the life sentence as it pertains to dangerousness. Under the statutory test that the Board is required to apply, detention is therefore justified.

9.6 Although all lifers will have been considered dangerous at the time of their conviction, there is a distinction to be drawn between those convicted of murder and other lifers. For those convicted of murder, the sentence is mandatory, whereas for all others, there must be some finding of dangerousness based on the individual's behaviour at the time of sentencing. When the case eventually comes before the Board, it should not therefore be assumed that those convicted of murder have any underlying pathology or behavioural traits that render them dangerous:

> It is quite wrong to make any assumptions about the dangerousness of an HMP detainee. When considering whether the prisoner poses a risk to life and limb that is more than minimal, the Board must apply the most careful scrutiny since a fundamental human right, the right to liberty, is at stake. I am prepared to accept the submission [of the Applicant] that the Board require cogent evidence before being satisfied that a prisoner poses more than a minimal risk of danger to life and limb.[6]

9.7 Finally, the Board's duty is to assess risk wherever the release will take place. This is of particular importance to lifers facing deportation at the end of their sentence as it will still be necessary for the Board to reach a decision that they do not pose a risk of harm on release, even when the actual release will be to a different country.[7]

The Secretary of State's directions

9.8 Prior to the Criminal Justice Act (CJA) 1991, the decision whether to release all life sentenced prisoners was a matter of executive discretion and this remained the case for mandatory lifers up until the CJA

5 For discretionary lifers because a finding of dangerousness has been made by the courts; and for mandatory lifers because the offence of murder is inherently so serious that the person convicted can be deemed to pose a risk to the public.

6 *R v Parole Board, ex p Curley* (1999) 22 October, HC, unreported.

7 *R v Parole Board ex p White* (1994) *Times* 30 December.

2003. The Home Secretary issued directions to the Parole Board on how to deal with cases he had referred to it. Directions were issued for both lifers and determinate sentenced prisoners for many years. These directions encompassed the factors to be taken into account when transferring lifers to open conditions, those factors relevant to release and guidance on the recall of lifers on life licence.[8]

9.9 The practice of issuing directions to the Board in cases where it is acting as a court pursuant to article 5(4) of the ECHR has been held to be unlawful. In *Girling v Parole Board*[9] it was held that it breached judicial independence and article 5(4) for the executive to issue directions to the Board when sitting as a court like body. However, despite the breach identified by the court, it went on to dismiss the substantive challenge to the Board's decision finding that the Board would take into account the matters contained in the directions as a matter of common sense in any event. Therefore, although the directions do not have any formal legal status, their contents do provide some helpful guidance on the matters which the Board will focus on when assessing the suitability of a lifer for release:

> 4. The test to be applied by the Parole Board in satisfying itself that it is no longer necessary for the protection of the public that the prisoner should be confined, is whether the lifer's level of risk to the life and limb of others is considered to be more than minimal.
>
> ...
>
> 6. In assessing the level of risk to life and limb presented by a lifer, the Parole Board shall consider the following information, *where relevant and where available*, before directing the lifer's release, recognising that the weight and relevance attached to particular information may vary according to the circumstances of each case:
> (a) The lifer's background, including the nature, circumstances and pattern of any previous offending;
> (b) the nature and circumstances of the index offence, including any information provided in relation to its impact on the victim or victim's family;
> (c) the trial judge's sentencing comments or report to the Secretary of State, and any probation, medical, or other relevant reports or material prepared for the court;
> (d) whether the lifer has made positive and successful efforts to address the attitudes and behavioural problems which led to the commission of the index offence;

8 The directions on transfers to open conditions are set out in Chapter 10 below (pre-minimum term expiry reviews).

9 [2005] EWHC 546 QBD.

(e) the nature of any offences against prison discipline committed by the lifer;
(f) the lifer's attitude and behaviour to other prisoners and staff,
(g) the category of security in which the lifer is held and any reasons or reports provided by the Prison Service for such categorisation, particularly in relation to those lifers held in Category A conditions of security;
(h) the lifer's awareness of the impact of the index offence, particularly in relation to the victim or victim's family, and the extent of any demonstrable insight into his /her attitudes and behavioural problems and whether he/she has taken steps to reduce risk through the achievement of life sentence plan targets;
(i) any medical, psychiatric or psychological considerations (particularly if there is a history of mental instability)
(j) the lifer's response when placed in positions of trust, including any absconds, escapes, past breaches of temporary release or life licence conditions and life licence revocations;
(k) any indication of predicted risk as determined by a validated actuarial risk predictor model, or any other structured assessments of the lifer's risk and treatment needs
(l) whether the lifer is likely to comply with the conditions attached to his or her life licence and the requirements of supervision, including any additional non-standard conditions;
(m) any risk to other persons, including the victim, their family and friends.

7. Before directing release on life licence, the Parole Board shall also consider:
(a) the lifer's relationship with probation staff (in particular the supervising probation officer), and other outside support such as family and friends;
(b) the content of the resettlement plan and the suitability of the release address;
(c) the attitude of the local community in cases where it may have a detrimental effect upon compliance;
(d) representations on behalf of the victim or victim's relatives in relation to licence conditions.[10]

9.10 Although the directions do not add anything to the release test, they do assist in filling in the practical application of that test to the facts of individual cases. As can be seen, the risk assessment must focus on the historical background which resulted in the commission of the offence for which the sentence was imposed, the manner in which

10 These directions can be found on the website of the Parole Board: www.paroleboard.gov.uk/release. Emphasis in original.

the lifer has progressed in custody and the extent to which the resettlement plans will provide sufficient protection for the public.

The limits of the Parole Board's powers

9.11 The only statutory power granted to the Board is to direct the release of life sentenced prisoners. If the Board is not directing release, its power does not extend beyond giving advice to the Secretary of State.[11] Although the Board is master of its own procedure, it must operate within this statutory framework.[12] The Secretary of State has agreed to accept the Board's recommendations for the release of determinate sentenced prisoners serving under 15 years even though this is not a statutory power[13] but for lifers, a very tight reign is kept on the Board's remit.

9.12 When lifers' cases are referred to the Board, if the Board does not direct release; the referral note only asks the Board to advise on suitability for open conditions. This referral note specifically instructs the Board not to advise or comment on other matters, such as movement between closed security categories (ie Categories A to C) or the timing of the next review. Before the terms of referral were set in this manner, it had not been uncommon for prisoners to ask the Board to comment on matters relating to their general progress and when their next review should be held.[14] It has been held by the domestic courts, and confirmed by the ECtHR, that the requirements of article 5(4) of the ECHR extend only to the need for a court to have the power to direct release. Any other decision, even if it ultimately may have an important bearing on release, does not engage article 5(4). The Board is not, therefore, empowered to:

11 CJA 2003 s239(2).

12 See, eg: Lord Woolf in *R (on the application of Roberts) v Parole Board* [2005] UKHL 45 at para 44.

13 *R (on the application of Clift) v Secretary of State for the Home Department* [2004] EWCA Civ 514.

14 One case which demonstrates the importance that used to be attributed to the Board's observations on these issues was *R (on the application of Williams) v Secretary of State for the Home Department* [2002] EWCA Civ 498. In this case a Category A lifer received a recommendation from the Board that he should be downgraded, resulting in a finding that the discrepancy between the Board's view of his case and the view of the Home Secretary justified special procedures being put in place for his Category A review, including the possibility of an oral hearing.

- direct a move to open conditions – it can only offer advice to the Secretary of State on this issue;[15]
- set the time between parole reviews – even though the courts have suggested this might be desirable, it is not a requirement of article 5(4);[16]
- comment on moves within the closed prison estate.[17]

Burden of proof

Pre-HRA position

9.13 The original wording of the 'life and limb' test highlighted the possibility that there was a burden of proof in lifer parole reviews. It was not clear if there was a burden and if so, whether it fell on the Home Secretary to prove the necessity for the prisoner to be detained or the prisoner needing to prove that he/she is safe for release. This question has not been answered definitively, but there is now a far clearer indication that the courts are unlikely to consider that the traditional concept of a burden of proof is truly relevant to the review process.

9.14 The favoured approach of the courts has been to suggest that the task of the Parole Board is to make a decision based on the material before it. In one case heard fairly soon after the oral parole system had been established, the early judicial indication was that there was no duty on the Secretary of State to 'prove' that the prisoner would pose a risk if released, but that the Board needed to be satisfied that the risk was low enough for release:

> the Board must be satisfied that it is not necessary that he should be kept in prison and not that there would be a substantial risk if he were released. In other words it must be shown that the risk is low enough to release him, not high enough to keep him in prison.[18]

9.15 Although the judgment did not provide a definitive response to the burden of proof question, the clear implication is that the onus is on the prisoner to establish that he/she is safe for release.

15 *Blackstock v UK* 27 April 2004 (App No 59512/00), affirming a long line of domestic authorities.

16 *R (on the application of Day) v Home Secretary* [2004] EWHC Admin 1742.

17 *R (on the application of Spence) v Secretary of State for the Home Department* [2003] EWCA Civ 732.

18 *R v Parole Board ex p Lodomez* [1994] 26 BMLR 162 at p 18.

Post-HRA position

9.16 The issue has been reopened several times since the Human Rights Act (HRA) 1998 was enacted. The original discretionary lifer panel scheme was based very closely on the Mental Health Review Tribunals, not least because it was often very hard to distinguish between those who received discretionary life sentences and those who received hospital orders. When it was established that the correct post-HRA test in mental health context was that the burden of proof rested with the Secretary of State to justify detention,[19] it was clear that the issue needed to be resolved in the parole context.

9.17 Lord Bingham commented on this subject[20] in *R v Lichniak and Pyrah*.[21] Parole reviews were touched upon as part of Lord Bingham's finding that the system of review ensured the mandatory life sentence did not breach article 3 and he cast considerable doubt on whether there was actually a place for a burden of proof when considering risk assessments in the parole context:

> I doubt whether there is in truth a burden on the prisoner to persuade the Parole Board that it is safe to recommend release, since this is an administrative process requiring the Board to consider all the available material and form a judgment. There is, inevitably, a balance to be struck between the interest of the individual and the interest of society, and I do not think it objectionable, in the case of someone who has once taken life with the intent necessary for murder, to prefer the latter in case of doubt.[22]

9.18 The judgment left as much open as it resolved, to the extent that it shied away from the burden of proof approach while at the same time hinting that it was not for the prisoner to prove anything. It also dates from a time when the release of mandatory lifers had not been held to fall within the ambit of article 5 and so the Board's duty remained administrative rather than judicial.

9.19 The one case that attempted to confront the problem head on was *R (on the application of Hirst) v Parole Board*.[23] The application was made by a lifer prior to his parole review taking place. A declaration

19 *R (H) v North London and East Region Mental Health Review Tribunal* [2001] 3 WLR 512.

20 Although his comments were obiter dictum as the main decision in the case was that the mandatory life sentence itself was not an arbitrary punishment and so was compatible with article 5(1) and article 3.

21 [2002] UKHL 47.

22 At [16].

23 [2002] EWHC 1592 Admin.

was sought in relation to the burden of proof, but the application was dismissed as being premature. Although the court declined to make a finding, it indicated that, if forced to reach a conclusion, the opinion expressed by Lord Bingham would be most likely to prevail. The position of Mental Health Act (MHA) detainees was distinguished on the grounds that lifers are only detained once a court has already established that they posed a risk to the public. MHA detainees are subject to executive detention and so there needs to be judicial supervision to determine whether the grounds for detention are made out. In the post judgment discussion, the court indicated that it did consider the issue to be a serious one which merited full consideration, but that it was simply impossible to reach a decision in a vacuum. In order for a judgment to make any sense, it would need to proceed with a settled factual outcome that would enable the practical application of the arguments to be tested. However, once again, the implication of the judgment was to cast doubt on the very idea that this approach was relevant at all.

Conclusions

9.20 Although it not possible to provide a definitive answer to this question, the very clear indication is that the courts are highly unlikely to hold that it is appropriate to approach the task of risk assessment at a parole review in this way. The comments of various courts strongly suggest that the Board's duty is to consider all the available material and form a judgment on risk. In order to properly exercise its judgment, the Board will not be requiring either party to 'prove' its case, but will reach a view as to whether the prisoner poses a risk or not.[24]

9.21 There is one exception to this approach and that is where there is a material factual dispute, for example, where a prisoner is accused of a criminal act which is denied. This situation will arise most commonly, but not exclusively, at recall hearings. In those cases, it is far harder to envisage the burden of proof not being applicable and it would seem to be grossly at odds with the general principle of fairness if the person making the allegation were not required to stand the burden of proving it.

9.22 The outcome of these judicial observations does allow the Board an extremely wide discretion. As risk assessment is not an exact science,

24 Although where an extended sentence prisoner is recalled, as the extension period is designed to be served in the community the Board must assume a default position in favour of liberty and so have to be positively satisfied of the need for detention – see Chapter 12 below.

providing decisions are properly reasoned the Board will generally have the leeway to accept any reasonable view on risk assessment that is put to it. In the event that a case ever does come before the courts which allows this issue to be resolved, the obvious danger is that it will resolve any ambiguity against the prisoner.

CHAPTER 10

Reviews of life sentences by the Parole Board

continued

Overview of the review procedure

10.1 The timetable for parole hearings for lifers who have served their minimum terms is fixed by the Parole Board Rules (PBR) 2004. The review process is based around a timetable which allows the review to be completed within six months. The overriding aim is to complete review speedily and without an oral hearing wherever possible. An overview of the procedure as it is intended to operate is shown in the table below.

Referral of cases to the Parole Board

10.2 Crime (Sentences) Act 1997 s28(7) allows life sentenced prisoners to require the Home Secretary to refer their cases to the Parole Board once the minimum term has been served and at least every two years thereafter. Although the statute is worded to place the onus on the prisoner to seek the referral, in practice the referral is made by the Lifer Review and Recall Section (LRRS) on behalf of the Home Secretary automatically. It is arguable that as the duty to review is a positive obligation on the part of the state, any system that in practice actually required the prisoner to make the application, would be in breach of article 5(4) of the European Convention on Human Rights (ECHR).

10.3 The initial referral of cases on the expiry of the minimum term is made automatically. Occasionally, it may be necessary to contact LRRS to make sure that the first referral takes place at the correct time, most often in cases where there are concurrent life and determinate sentences which can cause confusion in calculating the correct review dates. However, as the vast majority of lifers will have a pre-tariff parole review before the expiry of their minimum term (see Chapter 8 above), these problems have usually been addressed by the time that the right to an oral hearing arises. The position concerning the timing between future reviews and the referral process is dealt with in Chapter 11.

10.4 The obligation is to conduct a review before the end of the minimum term to ensure that release can take place, if appropriate, at the first opportunity. This duty has been held to extend to the Home Secretary's duty to refer cases sufficiently early to allow the Parole Board to complete the review process in time[1] and also to the Parole Board to ensure

1 *R v Secretary of State for the Home Department and the Parole Board, ex p Norney* [1995] 7 ALR 861.

Week 1
Parole Board lists case – notification sent to LRRS and prisoner.

↓

Week 5
LRRS sends out skeleton parole dossier. Prisoner to notify PB of legal representative.

↓

Week 8
Prison discloses the completed dossier to prisoner and sends copies to PB and LRRS.

↓

Week 12
Prisoner sends written representations to PB and copy to LRRS.

↓

Week 14
Single member of the PB considers case on papers.

Single member does not recommend release

↓

Week 15
Decision notified to prisoner and LRRS.

↓

Week 19
Prisoner to notify PB and LRRS if oral hearing required. If hearing not requested, single-member decision becomes final.

↓

Week 20
Prisoner and LRRS to make written witness requests.

↓

Single member refers case for oral hearing

↓

Week 15
Decision notified to prisoner and LRRS.

↓

Week 20
Prisoner and LRRS to make written witness requests.

↓

Single member makes a provisional release decision

↓

Week 17
Three-member panel considers provisional release decision.

↓

Week 18
Decision of three-member panel notified to prisoner and LRRS.

↓

Week 22
LRRS and prisoner to notify PB if oral hearing required. If both parties accept decision, it becomes final.

↓

continued

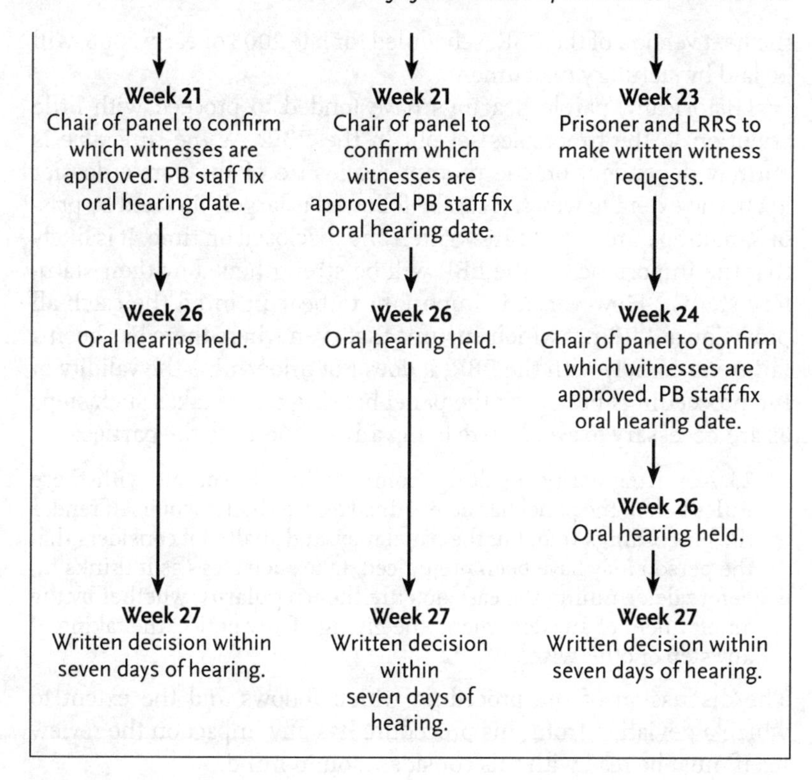

that they organise their procedures to allow for release to be possible the moment the minimum term ends.[2] As the entire review process is designed to be completed in six months, the process should commence at least six months before the expiry of the minimum term.[3]

A general note about the Parole Board Rules

10.5 The procedure following the referral of a case to the Board is governed by the PBR. These aim to provide a comprehensive guide to the timetable and procedural steps to be followed on a parole review where there is a right to an oral hearing. The PBR are not laid by statutory instrument but are simply drafted by the Secretary of State with no mechanism for parliamentary approval. It is proposed that

2 *R (on the application of Noorkoiv) v Secretary of State for the Home Department (No 2)* [2002] EWCA Civ 770.

3 Recall cases are referred pursuant to the Criminal Justice Act (CJA) 2003 s254(3) and are dealt with below.

the next version of the PBR, scheduled for late 2005 or early 2006, will be laid by statutory instrument.

10.6 Historically, parole hearings have tended to proceed with little attention to the timetables set out in the PBR. As the timetable is entirely dependent on the prompt disclosure of the parole dossier itself, the extent to which it can be followed is largely dictated by prisons making sure reports are written and disclosed on time. It is likely that the importance of the PBR will be strengthened by their statutory status.[4] However, it is important to bear in mind the catch-all provision at PBR r23 which ensures that even where there has been a failure to comply with the PBR, it does not undermine the validity of the proceedings providing the panel hearing a case takes such steps as are necessary to avoid there being any prejudice to the parties:

> **23.** Any irregularity resulting from a failure to comply with these Rules before the panel has determined a case shall not of itself render the proceedings void, but the panel may, and shall, if it considers that the person may have been prejudiced, take such steps as it thinks fit, before determining the case, to cure the irregularity, whether by the amendment of any document, the giving of any notice, the taking of any step or otherwise.

10.7 The discussion of the procedure which follows and the extent to which a deviation from this procedure has any impact on the review itself must be read with this consideration in mind.

10.8 It should also be borne in mind that the prisoner cannot be compelled to go ahead with a review. The review is to vindicate prisoners' right to have their detention reviewed by an independent tribunal. If the prisoner does not wish the review to take place at that particular time, it is possible to apply for a deferral. The procedure for applying for a deferral and the considerations taken into account when this request is made are examined in detail below.

Steps following referral

10.9 The PBR apply to all cases which have been referred to the Board by the Secretary of State, where the minimum term has expired or following recall.[5] Following referral, the PBR require that cases are

4 This should also ensure that the concerns about the potential for a breach of article 5(4) arising as a result of the executive dictating procedure rather than the legislature will not materialise: see *Girling v Parole Board and Home Secretary* [2005] EWHC 546.

5 PBR r2.

allocated to a member of the Board who has responsibility for conducting the paper review of the case.[6] In practice, cases will be allocated to a member once the parole dossier is received by the Board.

10.10 The Board is also required to list the oral hearing for the case and notify the parties – the prisoner and LRRS – within five working days.[7] Where the Board has details of legal representatives who have acted at previous reviews they will often send the notification to the lawyer. In practice, cases are rarely if ever given a precise hearing date at this stage and the notification forms sent out will usually indicate that the case is to be listed in a particular listing period. The Board's listing process divides the year into quarters, and cases are placed in one of the listing periods for the quarter in which the review should conclude. The precise date of the oral hearing is usually fixed much closer to the end of the review when it is apparent whether a hearing is actually necessary and when the Board have worked out the dates on which panels can attend particular prisons.

Legal representation

10.11 It is also envisaged that a prisoner will notify the Board of who is to act as the prisoner's legal representative within five weeks of the listing notification.[8] This requirement is perhaps the least important in the PBR. Except in cases where a representative has acted for a lifer at a previous review, and so their details are already on record, it is rarely followed. Certainly, the Board is usually content to allow for representatives to be appointed at any stage of the review process.

10.12 Although the choice of representation is left to the prisoner, certain persons are prohibited from this role. These are:

- anyone liable to be detained under the Mental Health Act 1983;
- anyone serving a prison sentence;
- any person currently on licence following release from prison;
- anyone with an unspent previous conviction.[9]

10.13 In cases where the prisoner is unrepresented, it is also possible for the Board to appoint a legal representative if the prisoner consents to this course of action. In practice, it is very difficult to envisage

6 PBR r3(1).
7 PBR r4.
8 PBR r5(3).
9 PBR r5(2).

any circumstances where this is likely to happen other than where a prisoner is unable to find a solicitor and the Board is able to assist.

10.14 There is one situation where it is possible that the Board may seek to appoint a representative without the prisoner's consent and where this might be held to be permissible. In the rare situations where the Board decides that material cannot be disclosed to either a prisoner or the prisoner's appointed representative, it is possible that the Board may decide that a special advocate should be appointed to protect the prisoner's interests, whether or not the prisoner consents. The extent to which the appointment of a special advocate is possible in any circumstances is discussed further at para 10.39 below.

Contents of the parole dossier

10.15 The parole dossier should be disclosed within eight weeks of the Board listing a case following referral.[10] LRRS will have prepared a 'skeleton' dossier that should be sent to the prison at the same time as the referral to the Board has taken place. The prison then has responsibility for adding current reports. The disclosure of the dossier is the key to the progress and timing of the entire review. All the substantive stages of the review can only take effect once the full dossier has been disclosed. It is therefore essential that close attention is paid to the preparation of reports in sufficient time to allow for disclosure to be made promptly.

10.16 The PBR require that the following information is contained in the parole dossier.

Information relating to the prisoner (PBR Sch 1 Part A)

10.17 (1) The prisoner's full name and date of birth.

(2) The prison in which the prisoner is detained, details of previous prisons where the prisoner has been detained and the dates and reasons for transfer.

(3) Details of the offence for which the life sentence was imposed and details of previous convictions.

(4) The trial judge's sentencing comments (if available).

(5) Details of any appeal to the Court of Appeal.

10 PBR r6(1).

(6) The parole history, if any, of the prisoner including any periods spent on licence during the currency of the life licence or extended sentence.

10.18 This information will all be contained in the skeleton dossier which is sent to the prison. Information relating to the trial, sentencing and any appeal will be taken from the prisoner's life sentence file. The details of the prisoner's progress in custody are prepared by LRRS and are usually based on the LSP 3E reports submitted by the prison at the three yearly progress reviews. These will usually contain summaries of the principal findings of the progress reports, details of identified risk factors and courses undertaken to address those risk factors and details of the prisoner's disciplinary history taken from both formal adjudications and informal disciplinary measures such as segregation and security reports.

10.19 The contents of this history will need to be very carefully checked to ensure that it is both factually accurate and that it contains the full details of all relevant assessments of risk. As lifers are entitled to copies of their sentence planning documents and life sentence plan (LSP) reports when they are prepared, it is important to advise clients to retain copies of these in case there is a need to resolve a factual dispute or to supplement material. For example, a summary of a favourable psychological assessment may not be sufficiently detailed and it may be necessary to submit the entire psychology report. Also, in cases where independent reports are needed, it may be helpful to have further information from historical reports to aid any assessment.

Reports relating to the prisoner (PBR Sch 1 Part B)

10.20 In addition to the general background information, the PBR require that the following specific reports are included in the dossier:

(1) Pre-trial and pre-sentence reports examined by the sentencing court on the circumstances of the offence.

(2) Reports on a prisoner while he was subject to a transfer direction under section 47 of the Mental Health Act 1983.

(3) Current reports on the prisoner's risk factors, reduction in risk and performance and behaviour in prison, including views on suitability for release on licence as well as compliance with any sentence plan.

(4) An up-to-date home circumstances report prepared for the Board by an officer of the supervising local probation board, including information on the following where relevant:

(a) details of the home address, family circumstances and family attitudes towards the prisoner;
(b) alternative options if the prisoner cannot return home;
(c) the opportunity for employment on release;
(d) the local community's attitude towards the prisoner (if known);
(e) the attitudes and concerns of the victims of the offence (if known);
(f) the prisoner's attitude to the index offence;
(g) the prisoner's response to previous periods of supervision;
(h) the prisoner's behaviour during any temporary leave during the current sentence;
(i) the prisoner's attitude to the prospect of release and the requirements and objectives of supervision;
(j) an assessment of the risk of reoffending;
(k) a programme of supervision;
(l) a view on suitability for release; and
(m) recommendations regarding any non-standard licence conditions.

10.21 Although the PBR do not specify precisely who should prepare up-to-date reports other than the home probation officer, the Board expects that as a minimum the dossier should contain, in addition to the home probation report, reports from the lifer manager, the seconded probation officer, the personal officer, the wing manager and the medical officer or a member of healthcare staff.

10.22 It is not a mandatory requirement for there to be a report from a psychologist or psychiatrist. In cases where there has been recent treatment or assessments by a specialist, then the Board would normally expect that person to prepare a report for inclusion in the dossier. Indeed, it is difficult to see how a valid assessment of risk can be made without such reports. In cases where there is a historical psychological report and no ongoing concerns or treatment needs were identified, it is unlikely to be necessary for there to be a current psychological assessment.

Disclosure of the parole dossier

Obtaining the dossier

10.23 The responsibility for disclosing the dossier rests with the prison at which the lifer is held at the time of the review. This used to be a responsibility of LRRS but is now devolved entirely to the prison, although where late reports are received LRRS will sometimes take responsibility for adding these to the dossier and disclosing them. As disclosure is a local responsibility, there is no uniform procedure for obtaining the dossier. The practice at most prisons is to provide one copy of the dossier to the prisoner free of charge and to retain a second copy to be sent to a legal representative on request. In order to ensure that there are no delays in obtaining the dossier, it is advisable to prepare a written authority signed by the prisoner authorising disclosure to the legal representative. The request for disclosure should be addressed to the lifer clerk or parole clerk at the prison.

10.24 Some prisons will make a charge to cover the costs of copying and postage and some will require that this is paid in advance of disclosure. It is therefore sensible to agree to pay reasonable copying and postage charges when requesting the dossier. These charges can be claimed as a disbursement under the CDS funding scheme.

10.25 Some prisons do not send out dossiers to solicitors but will instead provide the prisoner with two copies. They see it as the prisoner's responsibility to send the dossier to their legal representative and do not wish to become involved in this process in case there is any confusion over the correct representative. Where this occurs, it is acceptable practice to send the prisoner a stamped, addressed A4 envelope to enable the dossier to be forwarded.

Obtaining further information

10.26 In addition to the procedures for disclosure of the dossier, it is possible to obtain further details of the prisoner's records under the Data Protection Act (DPA) 1998. This enables prisoners to apply for copies of all their prison records, subject to the exemptions contained in the Act.[11] An application can be made by a legal representative on behalf of the prisoner by submitting a signed authority from the prisoner. A fee of £10 is payable and the request should be made to

11 See *R (on the application of Lord) v Secretary of State for the Home Department* [2003] EWHC Admin 2073.

the Prison Service's Information Management Section.[12] The DPA requires disclosure to be made within 40 days and requests are dealt with more speedily where specific information is sought as opposed to all prison records. The request might, for example, seek copies of medical records, security intelligence reports, wing history sheets or other information that might not ordinarily be included in the dossier or might not have been disclosed under the normal reporting procedures.

Challenging erroneous information

10.27 There will be occasions when the dossier contains information that is simply factually inaccurate. This has tended to be a problem which arises most commonly in parole reviews for determinate prisoners rather than for lifers, for example, by including pre-trial police reports rather than accurate information after conviction. Although this does not tend to be a major issue in lifers' reviews, there will be occasions when there is factual information in the dossier which is inaccurate and highly prejudicial.

10.28 When assessing whether information falls into this category, it is important to distinguish between information that may be unproven but relevant (such as disputed risk assessments or details of security concerns which never formed the subject of formal disciplinary proceedings), and information that is simply untrue. In cases where the information falls into the first category, the proper method of challenging it is through the submission of representations and additional evidence during the review itself.

10.29 On the rare occasions when there is material that is factually incorrect and cannot be rectified satisfactorily through representations, the correct procedure to follow will depend on whether the dossier has been supplied to the Board. The Board is under a statutory duty to consider all material placed before it[13] and so if the dossier has been sent to the Board, it has no power to remove material from it.[14] This is a function that can only be performed by the Home Secretary and so must be resolved with the prison or LRRS. If it has not been

12 Branston Registry Building 16, S & T Store, Burton Road, Branston, Burton Upon Trent, Staffs, DE14 3EG.

13 CJA 2003 s239(3).

14 See *R v Parole Board ex p Harris* [1998] COD 233 and *R v Parole Board ex p Higgins* (1998) 22 September, unreported. Both of these cases concerned determinate prisoners but the principles apply equally to dossiers prepared for life sentenced prisoners.

unresolved prior to the submission of the dossier to the Board, it will be necessary for the Board to agree to return the dossier for the inaccuracies to be corrected and then resubmitted. As this can be time consuming, it is always worth considering whether the problems can be corrected through representations or whether the material is so prejudicial that it must be removed.

Withholding information

10.30 The normal principle applied to disclosure is that all material to be considered by the Board should also be disclosed to the prisoner. This is a requirement that arises as a matter of domestic law fairness and as part of the requirements of article 5(4). As such, it is recognised in the PBR that the norm is full disclosure.

10.31 PBR r6(2) authorises the Secretary of State to withhold material contained in the dossier where:

> its disclosure would adversely affect national security, the prevention of disorder of crime or the health and welfare of the prisoner or others (such withholding being a necessary and proportionate measure in all the circumstances of the case) ...

10.32 Where it is proposed to withhold material under this rule, it must be served upon the Board separately from the dossier itself, together with the reasons for that decision.

10.33 On receipt of this material, the chair of the panel which is to consider the case is required to make arrangements for it to be served on the prisoner's representative providing the representative is a barrister or solicitor, a registered medical practitioner or someone whom the chair considers suitable to receive the material by virtue of their experience or qualifications.[15] This representative is forbidden to disclose the material either directly or indirectly to the prisoner without the consent of the chair.

10.34 If the Board proposes to serve material on a representative in accordance with these provisions, this can create a serious professional problem. Some representatives will not feel that it is ethical to proceed with a review in such circumstances and it may also create problems if the material is received without the client consenting to the representative receiving it under these constraints.[16] To try to minimise

15 PBR r6(3).

16 Solicitors Practice Rule 16-06 states that the solicitor must normally disclose all relevant information to the client.

these problems, the appropriate procedural step to be followed is for the Board to ask the representative whether he/she is prepared to receive material under PBR r6(3). This allows the representative to explain to the client how the rule operates and to obtain the client's consent to receive material which might not be seen by the client at all.

10.35 On a purely practical level, it will normally be in the prisoner's best interests for the representative to accept material under this rule. Very often, the Home Secretary will have taken an overly restrictive view of what cannot be disclosed and may be paying undue deference to the wishes of the person providing the material without giving proper consideration to the overall requirements of fairness and the extent to which non-disclosure can genuinely be justified. It is only if the representative has access to the material that this can be addressed in representations to the Board.

10.36 Following are examples of cases where material has been initially withheld under PBR r6(2) only for it to become apparent that this is not justified when it is passed to the representative:[17]

- Where the information was an allegation that had already been the subject of criminal trial (and acquittal).
- Where the information in a 'confidential' police report had already been largely disclosed to the prisoner in the lifer manager's report which summarised the police records.
- Allegations where there was no evidence of danger to the source but where the source had been given an assurance the allegations would not be disclosed. It was eventually decided that it was appropriate to provide a gist of the material to the prisoner.

10.37 As can be seen from these examples, there will be many instances where a representative can receive material under the restrictions contained in PBR r6(3) and can then effectively challenge the decision not to disclose the material to the client. Representations should be made to the chair of the panel dealing with the case and an oral directions hearing requested if necessary. The chair has express power to make directions relating to the disclosure or non-disclosure of this material under r8(2). In any case where directions are made in relation to disclosure (eg, to disclose the material to the prisoner or to withhold it), it is possible for either the prisoner or the Secretary of State to appeal the decision to the chair of the Parole Board within

17 There is no reported case-law on this issue; these are examples taken from practical experience.

seven days of the notification.[18] This decision is then final and the only further remedy is by way of judicial review.

10.38 The real ethical difficulties for a representative will arise if the final decision prevents disclosure of the material, or a gist of the allegations, to the prisoner. In such cases the representative will have to make a decision as to whether it is possible properly to represent the prisoner's interests at a 'secret' hearing where the prisoner is not present and, if so, whether the prisoner is prepared to authorise the representative to embark on this course of action. It is necessary to make a decision on a case-by-case basis as to whether it is possible for the prisoner's interests to be safeguarded in these circumstances and whether the procedure, taken as a whole, will comply with the requirements of article 5(4) of the ECHR. These issues are considered further in the following discussion of the role of special advocates.

Special advocates

10.39 There may be very rare circumstances where the Board decides that it is impossible to disclose safely material that has been withheld under PBR r6(2) to the representative. This has only arisen in a case concerning a life sentenced prisoner on one occasion in circumstances where it was found that the source of the material in question faced a genuine threat to life and limb and where there was a risk of inadvertent disclosure of the material to the prisoner if it was disclosed to the representative: *R (on the application of Roberts) v Parole Board.*[19]

10.40 The case of *Roberts* concerned a prisoner serving mandatory life sentences for the murder of three police officers. The Parole Board decided that it was not safe to disclose the material either to the prisoner or his representative and decided that in order to ameliorate the unfairness to the prisoner, the best course of action was to appoint a 'special advocate' to represent his interests at a closed hearing at which neither he nor his legal representatives would be present. The special advocate procedure was imported from the Special Immigration Appeals Commission (SIAC) where there is statutory provision for material to be withheld in this way where national security issues are at stake and for the material to be tested in closed hearings by special advocates who are allowed no contact with the individual or his/her legal team once they have received the material in question.

18 PBR r8(3).
19 [2005] UKHL 45.

10.41 It was argued by the prisoner that this decision was ultra vires, as the PBR did not make any provision for a special advocate procedure and that any procedure which allowed for a secret hearing to take place to determine liberty was in breach of article 5(4) of the ECHR. The House of Lords rejected this argument by a 3:2 majority. Underpinning the majority decision was the view that the special advocate procedure is not an infringement of a right but a potential enhancement of rights in a situation where there might otherwise be no other way of testing the material in question. Although the decision has sanctioned the Board's decision to appoint a special advocate, the strength of the dissent raises serious questions as to whether this would be followed by the European Court of Human Rights (ECtHR).

10.42 The logic of the majority view is difficult to reconcile with the general principle that parole hearings are an adversarial process at which the prisoner is entitled to the highest standards of procedural fairness which ordinarily includes the right to test the evidence of witnesses.[20] It was firmly rejected by Lord Bingham and Lord Steyn who both expressed the view that the use of a special advocate was such a departure from the normal standards of procedural fairness that it could only be permissible with express parliamentary approval. Lord Steyn analysed the issue as follows:

> Taken as a whole the procedure completely lacks the essential characteristics of a fair hearing. It is important not to pussyfoot about such a fundamental matter: the special advocate procedure undermines the very essence of elementary justice. It involves a phantom hearing only.[21]

10.43 Lord Bingham also commented that it was contrary to 'legal principle and good democratic practice' to allow such a procedure to be read into a statute.[22] He went on to state that if a special advocate procedure is adopted, it might not lead to a breach of article 5(4) as the process could result in the allegations being withdrawn and the prisoner freed. However, if the process entailed a final 'secret' hearing which did not result in release, his view was that it would inevitably breach article 5(4).[23]

10.44 Lord Woolf, in a confusing judgment, followed the majority opinion that a special advocate could lawfully be appointed, but appears

20 See eg *Hussain & Singh v UK* [1996] 22 EHRR 1.

21 Para 88.

22 Para 30.

23 Para 19.

to suggest that the role of the special advocate has to be limited to procedural testing of the evidence as a final determination based on a secret hearing would breach article 5(4):

> There are two extreme positions as far as the prisoner is concerned. On the one hand there is full disclosure and on the other hand there is no knowledge of the case against him being made available to the prisoner so that even with a SAA he cannot defend himself. In between there is a grey area and within that grey area is the border which is the parameter between what is acceptable and what is not acceptable ... The Board's existing statutory framework, including the Rules, do not entitle the Board to conduct its hearing in a manner that results in a significant injustice to a prisoner and in view of Article 5(4) I do not anticipate that primary legislation can now be introduced that expressly authorises such a result.[24]

10.45 It remains to be seen how the Board interprets this judgment and the extent to which it will allow a special advocate procedure to deal with issues beyond the procedural arguments on disclosure. The very strong warnings given by Lord Bingham and Lord Steyn suggest that any decision to allow the procedure to make final determinations on the suitability for release would be unlikely to survive the scrutiny of the ECtHR. While it was accepted that issues of witness safety were of importance, it was suggested that the balance between the competing interests had not been properly addressed and that less intrusive measures, such as witness protection schemes as are used in criminal proceedings, had not been properly explored.

10.46 The decision does raise wider concerns about the whole issue of non-disclosure, even where it is to a legal representative as is envisaged in the normal course of PBR r6(2). There may well be situations where a prisoner's own legal representative is unable to secure disclosure of the material to the prisoner and feels that it is not possible to properly contest the allegations without instructions. In such cases it is difficult to see how a 'secret' hearing where the representative is present but not the prisoner can be any more fair or complaint with article 5(4) than the special advocate procedure. The message of the Lords in *Roberts* appears to be that when faced with that situation, the representative should attempt to represent the prisoner's interests as far as possible and then seek to challenge the outcome if it is unfavourable.

24 Para 77.

Victim's charter reports

10.47 The one exception to the normal rule that all material should be disclosed are the reports prepared as a result of inquiries made of victims and in murder cases, their relatives. The purpose of these reports is not to take the victims' and families' views on whether the lifer should be released, but to ascertain whether they wish restrictions to be imposed on the life licence to prevent there being any contact between them and the prisoner. As these reports will contain details of the victims' location and concerns, they will not be disclosed to the prisoner. Unless the victim has recent and relevant knowledge of circumstances that relate to the current assessment of risk, these reports cannot have any bearing on release and are solely relevant to licence conditions. If there is a significant dispute over the conditions imposed on a life licence, it might prove necessary for a gist of the victim's concerns to be made available to the prisoner without disclosing any sensitive material. Alternatively, it might conceivably be necessary for disclosure of the report to be made to the legal representative under the PBH r6(2) procedure. The manner in which licence conditions are set and can be challenged, including the relevance of the victims' views is addressed in more detail below.

Independent reports

10.48 Once the dossier has been disclosed, consideration can be given to commissioning independent reports. Independent reports are most likely to be necessary where the client disagrees with an expert assessment made by a psychologist or psychiatrist. Occasionally, reports from independent social workers or probation officers might be helpful if there are concerns about probation reports. If a medical issue is relevant to the assessment of risk, the independent medical reports may also be helpful.

10.49 When considering whether an independent report is necessary, it is important to consider the reasons why the prisoner is unhappy with the report under challenge and precisely what an independent expert might be able to address. For example, if a prisoner is unhappy with a Sex Offender Treatment Programme (SOTP) report, then it will be necessary to identify whether the prisoner wants to challenge the suggestion that the SOTP is an appropriate treatment method in his particular case or whether the challenge is to the accuracy of the risk assessment itself on the conclusion of the SOTP. The client should always be advised that a favourable expert report is not a guarantee that the Board will be required to prefer that evidence over the Prison Service's experts. Risk assessment is not a precise science and will always carry a degree of subjective interpretation (see Chapter 4 above).

10.50 This does mean that it is very important to select an expert with appropriate expertise in the relevant area of risk assessment. It is usually helpful for the expert to have had some experience of prisons, as this will ensure familiarity with the methods and tools used in the contested assessments. Ideally, the expert should also have some experience of treating ex-offenders in the community as this will provide some basis for assessing the extent to which risk levels are manageable under supervision on licence. Prisoners will often suggest particular experts whom they perceive as writing reports which are favourable to prisoners. There can be a risk when instructing experts who may be perceived by the Board as writing stock reports on behalf of prisoners, as there can be tendency to give less weight to their assessments. Clients should always be advised of these risks so that an informed choice can be made as to the appropriate expert. It can often be extremely helpful to contact regional secure units to try to identify expert psychologists and psychiatrists who have experience in treating and managing high risk offenders. It is always essential to discuss the case with the expert before sending written instructions.

10.51 Expert reports can be paid for under the CDS funding scheme where it is considered necessary by the representative. Justification will need to be recorded on the file and it will usually be necessary to obtain an extension to cover the cost using the form CDS 5. The CDS extensions team operate on a general rule that expert fees should be in the region of £85 per hour, and so if the estimate is higher than that, an explanation will need to be given as to why the higher hourly rate is justified.

10.52 Most experts who prepare these reports will contact the prison to make their own arrangements for entry to the prison, although they may occasionally require the legal representative to make the arrangements with the prison to allow them to see the prisoner. The normal practice is for facilities for psychologists and psychiatrists to be provided in the health care centre and the prison medical records will usually be made available for the expert to inspect.

10.53 If the client is unhappy with the views of the independent expert, there is no requirement for this to be disclosed to the Parole Board or LRRS and it can simply not be used in the review process. LRRS has initiated discussions as to whether there should be an obligation to disclose all independent expert reports or whether it is possible to implement arrangements for joint experts as exists under the Civil Procedure Rules (CPR) 1998. It seems unlikely that this will ever be a realistic possibility given the differences between the aims and purposes of the CPR and the parole review process. There have been occasional cases, however, where all the parties have agreed that a particular expert report should be commissioned which is not in the original dossier and the prisoner and LRRS agree to one expert being instructed in the first instance. Prisoners should only be advised to agree to this where they have the power to veto experts. In any event, it is difficult to see how the Board could lawfully refuse to consider a further expert report if the prisoner did not agree with the joint expert and managed to obtain funding for another report.

The prisoner's written representations

Timing

10.54 Following disclosure of the parole dossier, the prisoner has four weeks in which to submit written representations.[25] The four-week deadline is set to enable the case to be considered on the papers at a paper 'sift' before proceeding to an oral hearing. In routine cases where there are no problems arising with disclosure, this is the first stage at which the involvement of a legal representative is generally needed.

Deciding whether or not to make a representation

10.55 It should be noted that there is no requirement for prisoners to make representations for the paper sift. In most circumstances, it is difficult to see what advantage can be gained for the prisoner by not making representations. However, there are two occasions when it may not be appropriate to make detailed representations at this stage.

10.56 The first situation is where it has been decided to commission an expert report and it is not possible to have that report ready within the four-week period (see above). This is a very common problem with psychological and psychiatric reports, as there are relatively few suitably qualified experts available and they tend to be heavily oversubscribed. The second situation is where the dossier is not complete and a report which the prisoner considers to be important is not avail-

25 PBR r7(1).

able. It may be that the Board will agree that the absence of the report means the case is not ready for a paper sift but in most circumstances, the Board may consider that the report is not so crucial as to justify a delay. An example might be an updated report of attendance on an offending behaviour programme or reports of a prisoner's performance on an unescorted absence from the prison. In both situations it is sensible to write to the Board to explain why detailed representations have not been made for the sift as this may persuade the Board to delay initial consideration; but in any event, there will then be a record of why decisions have been made should this need to be produced at a later stage in the review.

Deferral

10.57 Before preparing representations, prisoners will also want to consider whether it is appropriate for the review to proceed or whether they wish to apply for a deferral of the review. An example of when a prisoner may wish to defer might arise where a key piece of offending behaviour work – which is likely to be determinative of future progress – has been started but not finished. If the prisoner proceeds with the review and does not receive a favourable response, the next review is unlikely to take place for between 12 and 24 months. A deferral of three to six months may enable the loose ends to be tied up and provide the information needed for a positive decision and this short delay is obviously preferable to the lengthier alternative. The earlier in the review process that this application is made, the more likely it is to be granted. The procedure for applying for a deferral and the considerations applied by the Board on receipt of these requests are dealt with in detail below.

Format

10.58 There is no standard format for the submission of representations, and representatives are at liberty to adopt the style they find most comfortable. The most common formats are a letter, a document of numbered paragraphs or a statement from the client. Generally, the use of a statement from the client to cover both factual and legal matters can appear slightly artificial and it can lead to the client appearing overbearing or pompous. In cases where a personal statement from the client is going to advance the case, separating this from the more general submissions can work to the client's favour as it allows some room for the expression of their personality and personal views without this being subsumed into observations that may come across as pedantic or even bombastic. A statement is most likely to be needed if there are disputed facts and it is necessary to have the prisoner's version. As in all litigation, the representative will need to be sure that the prisoner can come up to proof should the matter proceed to an oral hearing.

Contents of representations

10.59 The preparation of these representations is one of the most crucial stages of the review, as it the first opportunity for the prisoner to address any concerns he/she may have about the contents of the dossier, to notify the Board of what is being sought from the review and to submit additional material which may be missing from the dossier. Although it is not possible to be prescriptive about the contents of representations as each case will require very careful individual consideration, as a general guide written representations should aim to cover the following matters:

- *Inform the Board at the outset of the direction/recommendation that the prisoner is seeking.* This will help focus attention on relevant matters. For example, if the prisoner is only seeking a move to open conditions and not release, it will mean that the review is unlikely to be delayed or hampered if the dossier does not contain full details of a proposed release plan.
- *Address any factual errors or concerns that the prisoner has about the contents of the historical details,* such as previous convictions or the details of progress in custody. If the errors are minor and are unlikely to be relevant to the outcome of the review, it may be worth noting them very briefly as a matter of record. If the errors or disputed records are material to the outcome of the review, more detailed representations may be required. This is also the opportunity to submit any material that will support the prisoner's account of historical events.
- *Comment on the current reports on behaviour, paying particular attention to the risk factors identified in the case and the extent to which these have been addressed, or alternatively, should not be treated as indicators of future risk.* This part will normally form the main substance of the representations and will need to be very carefully drafted with reference to the aims being sought by the prisoner and the recommendations of the reports. In cases where the prisoner is happy with the reports and there is nothing contentious in

them, it is usually advisable to make these comments fairly short. However, in cases where the reports do not agree with each other, or where the prisoner is unhappy with all of the reports, these may need to be extensive.

It is necessary to consider the nature of the contact the report writer has had with the prisoner and the basis of the report writer's expertise when drafting this part of the representations. A prison probation officer who has had extensive contact with a prisoner might, for example, be better placed to make an accurate risk assessment than a home probation officer who has had just one visit and is working mainly from historical records. An assessment of risk factors made by a psychologist is very likely to carry more weight than a risk assessment prepared by the medical officer or the prisoner's personal officer. Conversely, an assessment of custodial behaviour made by a wing manager who has day-to-day contact with the prisoner will probably be more accurate than an assessment made the psychologist.

- It is essential to *concentrate the Board on the real risk factors in a given case.* A prisoner may receive negative reports based on difficult prison behaviour, but this might not be relevant to the assessment of risk. Similarly, concerns about trustworthiness and compliance with licence conditions might not be sufficiently serious to impede release where there is no evidence that the prisoner poses any ongoing danger to the public.
- *If independent reports have been prepared at this stage, these should be enclosed and an explanation made as to why they are being relied upon.* In cases where these reports disagree with expert reports contained in the dossier, an explanation should be given as to why the Board should prefer the independent expert's assessment. This may be based on the greater experience or expertise of the author of the independent report or simply because the approach of the independent report is more realistic.
- *Any additional material which the prisoner wishes the Board to consider,* such as work references, offers of employment, letters from family members or certificates of attendance on courses. These should be enclosed, and the relevance of this material in terms of risk and rehabilitation issues should be drawn to the attention of the Board.
- *Final submissions on legal considerations,* such as how the test for release has been applied by report writers and the weight which the Board should give to evidence.

Distribution

10.60 All written representations, both at this stage and in the future, should be sent to the Parole Board and copied to the relevant casework team at LRRS.[26] As the Home Secretary is also a party to the review, it is important to make sure that LRRS is copied into all correspondence with the Board at all times.

The paper sift

Options and decisions

10.61 The first stage at which the merits of a case are addressed by the Parole Board is at the 'paper sift', where a single member of the Board will 'consider the prisoner's case without a hearing'.[27] The single member has four options available (see table at start of chapter), these being:

(1) *To refer the case for an oral hearing.* This step is taken if the single member is of the view that there are factors in the case that require examination by a full oral panel.[28]

(2) *To make a provisional decision in favour of release.* In this event, the case will be referred to a three-person panel of the Board to consider the case on the papers. The reason why this additional paper review was introduced was to ensure that release decisions are not made without the case being considered by Board members with a range of expertise. The three-member panel can then confirm the decision to release or refer the case for an oral hearing. If the release direction is confirmed, the Secretary of State has 28 days in which to oppose the decision and require that the case is referred for a full oral hearing.[29]

(3) *To make a decision that the prisoner is not suitable for release but that he/she is suitable for open conditions.* In these circumstances, the case will be considered by a three-member panel which can confirm the recommendation or refer the case for consideration at an oral hearing. The prisoner will be given the decision and has 28 days in which to require the case to be referred for an oral hearing.

26 See the details of the casework teams at LRRS in Appendix 10.
27 PBR r11(1).
28 PBR r11(2)(a).
29 PBR r13.

This procedure is not actually mandated by the PBR but is a hybrid of the release and no release procedures.[30] It has been designed in this way in recognition that a move to open conditions is a step which is very close to release and requires careful consideration by the Board, but that as it is not a release decision, the prisoner still has the right to require consideration at an oral hearing.

(4) The final option is *to reach a decision that the prisoner is unsuitable for release or open conditions*. The prisoner is given this provisional decision and has the option within 28 days of requiring the case for the case to be considered at an oral hearing.[31]

10.62 The PBR require that written reasons are given for all decisions made by the single member or a paper three-member panel and that the reasons must be provided to the prisoner and LRRS within seven days.[32] This written decision will only become the final decision if it is a refusal of both open conditions and release and it is accepted by the prisoner. As it can only become a final decision with the consent of the prisoner, it is highly unlikely that it will ever be the subject of a legal challenge. In consequence, there is no requirement for this to follow a particular format and it probably does not need to be as detailed as the reasons given for the final decision (see below). Nevertheless, the single member will want to provide as detailed an explanation as possible for the preliminary decision, both to focus the prisoner's mind on the issues which are perceived to be relevant to the review in case it is to proceed to an oral hearing and to explain the rationale for the decision to a three-member panel. The single member's sift decision will form part of the dossier if the case proceeds to an oral hearing.

Case progression

10.63 The Board has developed its own variant on the spirit of the Civil Procedure Rules, recommending that the single members at the sifting stage give consideration to CPR – case progression requirements. The PBR contain provisions for panel chairs to issue formal directions under r8. Directions are generally required to allow for effective oral hearings and will usually only be made when the dossiers are sent to the oral panels around six weeks before the oral hearing. At this stage of the review, unless there has been a need for directions

30 PBR rr12–13.

31 PBR r12.

32 PBR rr11(3) and 13(3).

to address problems with disclosure, there will not have been any formal directions made.

10.64 At the sift stage, the single members are advised to give consideration to the steps that might help progress the case and to try to ensure that the case can proceed and be concluded within the time scale set out in the PBR. Experience has shown that many hearings are ineffective because of deficiencies in the dossier or because witnesses cannot attend. Formal directions will often not be able to resolve this type of problem in time to save a hearing date given the late stage at which they usually take place and so the CPR provide an opportunity to pre-empt these difficulties. In cases where a referral is made for an oral hearing, single members are encouraged to note any gaps in the dossier such as missing reports and which witnesses will be required for the hearing.

10.65 CPR suggestions are not directions within the meaning of the PBR but are simply a case management tool. They must be restricted to steps needed to ensure the case is being prepared properly and must not cross into sentence management matters. CPR must not, for example, include requirements for prisoners to be allowed further home leaves or to attend offending behaviour courses before the oral hearing.

Considering sift decisions

10.66 The sift decision that is sent to the prisoner (or legal representative) will only require positive action if it does not recommend release. If it is a provisional direction for release, the prisoner will obviously not require an oral hearing. If it is a referral for an oral hearing then the prisoner has no election to make.

10.67 The cases where the decision does not direct release[33] will not always be adverse to the prisoner as they incorporate those cases where a recommendation has been made for open conditions. It should not be an automatic response to request an oral hearing in these circumstances and very careful consideration should be given as to what could be achieved at an oral hearing. In making this decision it is important to bear in mind two factors:

(1) The Parole Board is only permitted to direct release or to recommend a move to open conditions and to give reasons for the decision they reach. The Board is not requested to give advice on a prisoner's general progress in prison custody and will only

33 Prisoners will usually refer to unfavourable parole decisions as a 'knockback'.

address progress insofar as it is relevant to explaining the reasons for its decisions. The Board will not comment on what security categorisation a prisoner should be within closed conditions.

(2) Nearly all lifers are required to go to an open prison before first release, the rationale being that after many years in custody it is necessary to have a slow and structured period of reintegration into the community as this allows risk factors to be further explored and tested, for the prisoner's trustworthiness to be tested and for proper release plans to be put in place and assessed by the supervising probation service.[34]

10.68 As lifers in closed conditions in the vast majority of cases need to go to an open prison before the Board will direct release, a recommendation for open conditions made in a case where the prisoner is in a closed prison might be all that was being sought from the review. In this type of case, there would be little point in requiring an oral hearing to take place as the lifer would already have achieved everything possible from the review.

10.69 In the first scenario, the question of whether an oral hearing is likely to produce any benefit will be very fact specific. A lifer in a Category C prison who does not receive a recommendation for open conditions is highly likely to require an oral hearing. In contrast, a prisoner in Category B conditions who is engaged in offending behaviour work prior to moving to a Category C prison is unlikely to obtain any real benefit from an oral hearing. Prisoners in this situation may find some benefit from an oral hearing if they wish to challenge a risk assessment which is delaying their progress or if they are able to put together enough evidence to demonstrate that their case warrants a departure from the normal progression towards release.

10.70 To balance against the possible benefits of the oral hearing is the delay that is caused to the case. A single member's decision may be notified to the prison as long as three months before the scheduled oral hearing. If this is accepted, the review will conclude at this point. The prisoner will then normally have the time set for the next review subject to the statutory two-year maximum period between reviews.

34 This policy was considered to be lawful and rational by the Court of Appeal in the case of *R v Home Secretary ex p Stafford* [1998] 1 WLR 503. The case eventually went to the House of Lords and the domestic decisions which found that article 5(4) does not apply to the mandatory life sentence were overturned by the ECtHR in *Stafford v UK* [2002] 35 EHRR 32. The ECtHR decision was only concerned with the application of article 5 to the life sentence. It is still the case that movement between security categories in prison does not engage article 5 and so this part of the domestic *Stafford* decision remains good law.

In contrast, if the oral hearing goes ahead and a more favourable decision is not made, the prisoner's review cycle will be put back by up to three months, leading to a longer period of imprisonment.

10.71 The final factor to consider is the merits test that must be applied under the CDS public funding scheme. Advocacy Assistance, the public funding available for oral parole hearings, is subject to both means and merit testing. It is essential to be able to demonstrate that there is a real benefit to the client in proceeding to an oral hearing in order to authorise this funding. It is likely that this type of decision making will come under closer scrutiny when prison law files are audited by the Legal Services Commission. The cost to the LSC of oral hearings is far higher, both in terms of the work that will be needed and the hourly rate that is allowed. The CDS policy unit is working to train auditors on prison law issues so that this type of decision making can be properly scrutinised.

CHAPTER 11

Oral hearing procedure

continued

Pre-hearing preparation

11.1 In cases where an oral hearing is to take place, 19 weeks after the review has commenced (or seven weeks before the scheduled hearing date) the prisoner should be in receipt of the following documentation:

- the parole dossier;
- the written sift decision;
- any independent reports that have been commissioned.

11.2 Ideally, this should comprise all the documentary material that is going to be needed for the oral hearing. In practice, the extent to which all this material will be available is entirely dependent on whether the complete parole dossier was in fact disclosed on schedule some 11 weeks earlier. It is at this stage that directions can be sought from the chair of the panel which is to eventually hear the case. The practice of the Parole Board is to send the dossier out to the panel six weeks before the hearing is scheduled. This timing is set to coincide with the requirement in the Parole Board Rules (PBR) 2005 to make written witness requests and representations six weeks before of the hearing.[1]

Directions applications

11.3 If the dossier is still incomplete, it is at this point that formal directions can be sought from the chair of the panel pursuant to PBR r8 to try to ensure that all material is made available.[2] The reports that are most commonly missing from the dossier will be the home probation report, and in cases where there are disputed allegations relating to the prisoner's behaviour in custody or on temporary release, the reports relating to that behaviour. In cases where material is still missing from the dossier at this stage, an application should be made to the chair of the panel that will consider the case for appropriate directions to be made in order to resolve the problem. By this stage, the Board is likely to have appointed a case manager who is responsible for providing administrative support to the panel. Wherever possible, it is always sensible to try to make contact with that person to ensure that applications are received and actioned. As with all other applications and representations, copies of all correspondence with the Board should be sent to the relevant casework team at the Lifer Review and Recall Section (LRRS).

1 PBR r15.

2 Directions can also be sought when witness requests are made – see below.

11.4 When applying for directions, particularly when seeking a direction which will require the disclosure of additional material or the preparation of a fresh report, it is essential to explain the evidential purpose behind the request and the reasons why it will help facilitate the assessment of risk and suitability for release. In some cases this may be self-evident, such as where a probation report is missing. In other cases, it may be necessary to provide a more detailed explanation. A common example is where reports refer to undisclosed security material alleging misbehaviour, or where reference is made to an historical report that has not been previously disclosed to the prisoner.

11.5 In the event that there is substantial disagreement between the parties, or where complex legal or factual matters arise in the application, the chair may decide to convene an oral directions hearing. Oral directions hearings will usually be held where it is most convenient for the chair – either in the courthouse where the chair is sitting (if it is a judicial member) or at the Parole Board itself. At least 14 days' notification of the directions hearing date should be given,[3] but it will often be in the interests of all parties for the hearing to be convened more quickly. The representative of the prisoner and the Secretary of State (usually someone from LRRS) will be present, but the prisoner will not. There is no formal procedure to be followed for the hearing and the chair will usually ask the party making the application to make submissions and then the other party to respond. Where the application does raise legal arguments, it is always sensible to prepare a written summary of the argument and to have copies of any cases or other materials relied upon available for all the parties. Wherever possible, these should be served well ahead of the hearing to avoid delays on the day itself.

11.6 Written decisions containing any directions made by the chair – whether after considering written applications or after an oral hearing – shall be served on the parties 'as soon as practicable'.[4] Surprisingly, this has proven to be a major failing by the Parole Board over the years, with case managers often failing to send prisoners' representatives copies of the written decisions, although they do usually send them to LRRS. This is possibly symptomatic of the very slow progress towards the recognition of the Parole Board as a court and the consequent requirement for its administration to be of the quality one would expect from other courts rather than the administration being

3 PBR r8(5).

4 PBR r8(9).

viewed as being an off-shoot of the functions of the Prison Service. This is a further reason why it is sensible to identify the named case manager in each case so that there is a point of contact to chase decisions and notifications.

The hearing date

11.7 The actual hearing date will normally be fixed no later than six weeks before it takes place, although in some cases it may have been set much earlier. This timing coincides with the date on which the dossier is sent to the chair of the panel that will hear the case and when witness requests should be made. If the hearing is to be at a prison where there are a large number of cases to be heard, the panel may be at the prison for two to three days, and the hearing will be scheduled for any of those days. If a 'floating' date of this type is given and there is a particular reason why one of the days is more suitable than another (eg, for witnesses to attend or the availability of an advocate), the case manager should be informed immediately so that efforts can be made to try to accommodate that date.

11.8 In cases where the bulk of the documents is ready, requests for the attendance of witnesses should be made within six weeks of the hearing date.[5] By this stage, the parole dossier will have been sent to the panel appointed to hear the case and a final hearing date should have been arranged and notified to the parties, although the PBR do not require the exact hearing date to be fixed until three weeks before the hearing is to take place.[6] It is also a requirement that the parties are consulted before fixing a hearing date, but in practice this obligation is rarely if ever followed, except in cases where a second hearing is being fixed following an adjournment or deferral. It is worth bearing this in mind if a hearing is fixed without any consultation and the hearing date is likely to cause prejudice to the prisoner.

Witness requests

11.9 The PBR require that all witness requests should include the name, address and occupation of the witness and the substance of the evidence that the witness will give at the hearing. In the vast majority of cases, the witness will be one of the report writers in the dossier or an independent expert who has written a report for the hearing.

5 PBR r15(1).
6 PBR r17(2).

If the independent expert's report has not previously been served on the Board and LRRS, then it should be sent at this stage to coincide with the witness requests. As the witnesses will nearly always have written some form of report, it is not necessary to repeat the contents of their evidence. Instead, it is advisable to set out what the purpose of the oral evidence will be and the reasons why oral evidence is needed to enable the panel to reach a decision on the case. There will be cases where there are relevant witnesses who have not prepared any form of report, such a family members with whom the prisoner intends to live on release. In those cases, slightly more detail about the nature of the evidence to be given will be needed. It should be remembered that witness requests can be made by both the prisoner and LRRS.

11.10 The Parole Board's internal guidance on witness requests contains the assumption that witness requests will normally be granted so as to ensure the prisoner does not have the perception that his/her access to justice is being impeded. This is not, however, an open invitation for every witness to be approved and panels are reminded that the consideration does have to be given to the substance of the evidence and the overall length of the hearing. As a very rough rule of thumb, the general advice is:

- independent experts and family members should normally be permitted to attend;
- witnesses who have prepared evidence that is unfavourable to the prisoner should always be allowed to attend;
- witnesses who can make a further contribution to risk assessment should always be allowed to attend;
- if the prisoner is in an open prison, the home probation officer should usually be required to attend;
- witnesses who have written favourable reports and whose evidence is not likely to be in dispute should only be allowed if they can materially add to the evidence in the dossier.

11.11 Once the chair of the panel has considered the requests, notification should be given to the parties of the permitted witnesses. If the request is refused, reasons should be given for that decision.[7] When considering these requests, the chair is also permitted to make a decision as to whether the panel require any other witnesses to attend. If the parties making the witness requests have not sought the attendance of a witness whom the panel chair considers should give evidence, it is open to the chair to make a direction for the witness to attend. If the

7 PBR r15(3).

panel chair does decide a further witness should be called, written notification must be sent to the parties containing the name, address and occupation of the witness and the substance of the evidence it is proposed to adduce.[8]

11.12 In the draft new version of the PBR, when making a decision on which witnesses should attend, the chair is also required to give consideration as to whether it is desirable and practical for the witness to give evidence other than by appearing in person.[9] This proposed new addition to the PBR is intended to allow for witnesses to give evidence by video link, the aim being to save the costs and inconvenience caused by witnesses travelling to the prison, and also to allow for vulnerable witnesses to give their evidence without coming into contact with the prisoner. The Probation Service have been lobbying for permission to give their evidence by telephone while video link facilities are being made available in prisons, but it seems highly unlikely that this will ever be the norm due to the difficulties it would cause in terms verifying the identity of the witness and in allowing for effective cross-examination. The occasions when it has taken place are when the parties all consent.

Securing the attendance of witnesses

11.13 It is the responsibility of the person who has sought permission for a witness to attend to ensure that witness is present at the hearing. This means that when a request for a witness to attend is made on behalf of a prisoner and is granted, it will fall to the prisoners' legal representative to notify each witness of the hearing date and time and that their attendance is required. This remains the responsibility of the prisoner even if the witness is a hostile witness (such as a prison psychologist or probation officer) but their attendance has been requested to cross-examine them on the contents of the report.

11.14 It is always advisable to send a fax directly to the witness at the witness's work address providing notification of the hearing details and asking for confirmation that they will attend the hearing. In the case of persons employed in the prison where the hearing will take place, it can also be useful to notify the lifer manager of the witnesses whose attendance has been approved by the Parole Board.

11.15 Often the most difficult witnesses to persuade to attend the hearing is the home probation officer. Although probation directives have

8 PBR r15(2).
9 Proposed new PBR r15(5).

now emphasised the importance of attendance at parole hearings,[10] there remains a reluctance on their behalf to travel to prisons, especially when this is being arranged by the prisoner's representative. In cases where the home probation report is favourable, or in cases where the lifer is to be released to a different area and so will not actually be supervised by the home officer who has written the report, one way around this problem is to ask for the seconded probation officer based at the prison to attend as a witness. The seconded officer can then liaise with the home officer and give a view on behalf of the probation service as a whole, including details of particular licence conditions and the supervision arrangements. In cases where the prisoner is being released to a hostel close to the prison, especially in situations where the hostel have a close relationship with the prison probation department, the attendance of the hostel manager or key worker can be adequate. This approach is only likely to be viable where there is no significant dispute about the contents of a probation report and where both the prison and home probation officer are in agreement as to the best course of action.

11.16 Where the chair of the panel has requested the attendance of a witness, the Board's advice to panels is that it is preferable for witnesses to attend voluntarily. The standard form of wording that is recommended in letters to witnesses is as follows:

> The Board directs that [name of witness] shall attend the hearing to give evidence. The witness should note that the proceedings will be as informal as possible, but that the Board will nevertheless sit as a court. Non-attendance is only permitted in compelling circumstances and the Board does have the power to enforce attendance by way of a witness summons. Full reasons must be given by anyone unable to attend.

11.17 There has been considerable confusion as to the correct procedure to be followed to secure the attendance of witnesses where the request for the attendance has been made by the Board, or where the witness is clearly one who is to give evidence for the Home Secretary. This was resolved by the Court of Appeal, which indicated that the Board should direct the Secretary of State (through LRRS) to notify the witness and to obtain a witness summons from the court if necessary.[11]

11.18 The Board has no power to issue a witness summons itself, although this is a power which may be granted to the Board in the future. This means that any party wishing to summons a witness

10 PC 45B/2004.

11 See *R (on the application of Brooks) v Parole Board* [2004] EWCA Civ 80.

to the hearing must make use of the power of the County Court and High Court to issue a witness summons pursuant to Civil Procedure Rule 34.4. In order to make such an application it is necessary to provide the court with evidence confirming that the Parole Board has directed the attendance of the witness at the hearing and evidence as to why a summons is considered to be necessary. In cases where the witness is one whom the Board itself has directed should attend or where the witness is required to give evidence to support the Secretary of State's case, even if their attendance has been requested by the prisoner, LRRS will be directed to apply for the summons. This situation is most likely to arise with non-professional witnesses, such as members of the public or other prisoners who have provided evidence which the Secretary of State proposes to reply upon against the prisoner. In cases where the witness is a professional, such as a prison or probation officer, there is no reason why the prisoner's representative should not apply for the witness summons if their attendance has been requested by the prisoner.

11.19 The use of witness summonses is extremely rare in the parole context.[12] The Parole Board's internal guidance suggests that panel chairs should have in mind the following considerations when deciding whether a reluctant witness should be required to attend:

- A witness should only be summonsed where their oral evidence is crucial to the outcome of the case.
- Where a witness is reluctant, a panel chair should always consider the alternative of written evidence.
- It is never appropriate to compel a minor to attend.
- The likely outcome should be considered. Although a witness can be compelled to attend, the witness cannot be compelled to give evidence. It may be pointless directing the Secretary of State to compel attendance if the witness will ultimately refuse to give evidence.

11.20 Although these guidelines only apply to situations where the Board are being asked to direct the Secretary of State to obtain a witness summons, they are also useful points for prisoners' representatives to bear in mind when making a decision on whether to summons a reluctant witness.

12 It was precisely because this is so unusual that none of the parties in the *Brooks* case (as above) were really sure about what to do.

Observers

11.21 Parties to the hearing may apply for observers to be present at the hearing.[13] The application is usually made at the same time as applications for the attendance of witnesses. The chair of the panel should seek to obtain the consent of the prison governor before authorising the attendance of observers.

11.22 Applications for observers to attend usually fall into three categories:

(1) Prisoners may wish to apply for a close friend or family member, or even a personal officer, to attend to provide support. Prisoners making such an application should be reminded that the hearing is likely to go over the details of the index offence and general offending history. Some prisoners may actually find it inhibiting to talk about these matters in front of family members, especially of the offences are sexual or particularly violent.

(2) The prison or LRRS may ask for new staff, such as trainee lifer managers to attend, to give them a greater insight into the parole process and to learn how to present cases on behalf of the Home Secretary.

(3) The Parole Board might ask for new or trainee members to attend for the same reasons. Occasionally, a request may be made for academic researchers to attend.

11.23 When considering such requests, the chair should have regard to the numbers of persons likely to be at the hearing and the need for the prisoner to feel at ease. Although there is no provision in the PBR for prisoners to veto requests for observers made by the Board or LRRS, panel chairs are usually very mindful of the need for prisoners to feel comfortable at the hearing and will take very seriously any objection raised by a prisoner to the attendance of an observer. Issues relating to the Data Protection Act 1998 may well arise if an observer were to attend against the prisoner's wishes.

Final preparation for the hearing

11.24 If a hearing date has not already been fixed, the PBR require that at least three weeks' notice should be given, although a shorter time can

13 PBR r16.

be given with the consent of the parties.[14] The parties are supposed to be consulted before the hearing is fixed, but this rarely happens as most parole hearings are fixed with reference to the dates at which panels are scheduled to visit particular prisons. It is only in the rare cases where a hearing is particularly complex and is being fixed to take place on its own that the parties are routinely consulted.

11.25 Although there is rarely any consultation, case managers are extremely helpful in trying to minimise any difficulties that might arise. In cases where the panel is sitting at the prison over several days, requests for a case to be fixed on a particular date or time are treated sympathetically. The general provision in the PBR to allow the chair to vary the timetable so long as it does not cause prejudice to the parties does mean that unless genuine prejudice is going to rise from a listing which is late or where there has been no consultation, it is unlikely that it will be possible to have the hearing date altered.

11.26 This general power to vary the timetable set out in the PBR does ensure that there is a great deal of flexibility which permits late requests for witnesses, the late submission of documents or late requests for directions. Panel chairs will almost always be willing to deal with additional issues as they arise and it is extremely rare for applications to be refused simply because they are made outside of the time limits. The chair is far more likely to be concerned with ensuring that the hearing will be effective and that all evidence and material relevant to a fair and accurate risk assessment is available.

11.27 At this stage, the areas where additional directions are most likely to be needed are:

- additional witness requests where there have been late reports, including late expert reports;
- special measures for vulnerable or reluctant witnesses, including ensuring that video conferencing facilities are available if required and making sure that any special measures for vulnerable witnesses are in place;
- making directions for interpreters to be present if necessary for either the prisoner or any witnesses;[15]
- assessing whether there is any need to change the location of the hearing for security or practical reasons.

11.28 Prisoners' representatives should ensure that they have checked whether any additional directions should be sought and that all the

14 PBR r17.

15 This is normally the responsibility of the prison.

witnesses whose attendance they have requested are aware of the hearing date and can attend.

11.29 The Board is in the process of seeking to introduce a system which requires the parties to file certificates of readiness 14 days before the hearing. The certificate is available on the Parole Board's website.[16] There is no requirement in the PBR to file this certificate, although it is obviously in the interests of all parties to the review if this practice is followed.

11.30 If the representative is concerned that the case cannot proceed as crucial material is unavailable or there is a difficulty with witness attendance, it is possible to apply for a deferral (see below).

The Secretary of State's view

11.31 Shortly before the hearing, usually within the final week, the Secretary of State's view will be sent to the Board and the prisoner. This is prepared by LRRS and will explain how the Home Secretary views the case, whether release or a move to open conditions is being opposed and the reasons for that view. The quality of these views will vary enormously depending on who has prepared it. Sometimes they run to more than a page and contain detailed comments on the evidence. In other cases they will only be a perfunctory paragraph that does not engage with the facts of the case at all. If no view is prepared by the Secretary of State, this does not prevent the hearing going ahead and hearings will not be deferred simply to allow one to be issued.

Applications for a deferral

11.32 Once a parole hearing has started, there may be reasons arising at the hearing that require it to be adjourned and resumed at a later date. If it becomes apparent before the hearing has commenced that there are difficulties that are likely to prevent the panel from reaching a fair decision, an application should be made for the hearing to be deferred. There is no specific provision for this in the PBR and no reported case-law, so the guidance on how to apply for deferrals and how the Board treats such requests is taken from practical experience and the guidance issued by the Board to panel members.

16 See www.paroleboard.gov.uk.

Applications before the review has begun

11.33 If a case has been referred to the Board but the review has not yet begun (ie, the case has not been listed under PBR r5) an application for a deferral should be made to the oral hearings team at the Board and it will normally be processed without any reference to a judicial member of the Board. The application should explain why the request has been made and the length of time for which the prisoner wishes the case to be deferred. The presumption operated by the Parole Board in these cases is that the request to defer should be accepted.

Applications after the review has commenced

11.34 If the review has started but it is in the early stages and has not been allocated to a panel, applications to defer should be made in writing to the oral hearings team and will be referred to the duty judge for consideration. The duty judge should consider:

- whether additional written or oral information is needed for the review and, if so, whether it will be available within a short and specific time; and
- will this information have a material bearing on the outcome?

11.35 If the duty judge decides it is not appropriate to agree to a deferral, written reasons should be given for the decision. If the deferral is approved, a letter should be sent to all parties confirming the period of deferral, specifying what information is missing, who should provide it and the time period in which it should be made available.

Applications after the case has been allocated to a panel

11.36 In this instance, the request should be made to the oral hearings team and it must be referred to the chair of the panel. The chair will have in mind the same considerations as the duty judge. Generally, it does prove harder to obtain a deferral the further into the review the case has reached. Although the reasons to be applied by the Board do not change, it has been suggested that as the costs to the Board increase enormously once the case has been referred to a panel, there is a greater reluctance to defer cases once they have reached this stage.

11.37 It is implicit in the guidance issued by the Board to panel members that deferrals should be allowed where relevant material is unavailable which will become available in a reasonably short period of time. The manner in which this is applied to particular circumstances is more apparent from the guidance on when an application should be refused and these considerations can help guide representatives in making applications:

- If a deferral is sought to allow a course to be finished, consideration must be given to whether the reports will be available within three months and if the course was successful, whether a period of monitoring is likely to be needed after completion. If not, it should be refused.
- If the course is unlikely to be determinative – for example, in cases where there are still multiple risk factors and the course will only address one – it should be refused.
- Where the prisoner has only recently arrived in open conditions and wishes to have a programme of home leaves, this will be refused as the process of taking the home leaves and having reports written is likely to take six months or more.

11.38 The Board also suggests that deferrals pending the outcome of criminal charges should usually be refused. This is a highly contentious view and one which is arguably very difficult to sustain. Although the Board operates to a lower standard of proof than the criminal courts,[17] it is very difficult to see how a fair inquiry can take place before the criminal trial and how an accurate assessment of risk can be made until it is known whether a criminal offence has been committed. This is far more likely to be an issue on recall hearings and is explored further in that context (see Chapter 13 below).

11.39 In cases where a material witness will not be available, the panel chair will need to consider the reasons why they cannot attend and to make an assessment of whether it is reasonable or not.

11.40 If a deferral application is refused, it is still possible to renew this application at the start of the oral hearing itself. As a matter of good practice, the panel should be notified in advance that the application is being renewed and it should be made at the commencement of the hearing and before any evidence has been taken. If evidence has been taken, technically the case can no longer be deferred but must be adjourned. This is a far more difficult procedural step, as an adjournment will normally require that the same panel reconvenes to re-hear the case when is resumes. It is necessary to have the same panel, as otherwise the panel making the final decision will not have heard all of the relevant evidence.

17 See the discussion of evidence at oral hearings, below.

Location of proceedings

11.41 The PBR provide for the oral hearing to be held at the prison where the prisoner is detained, although the chair can direct the hearing is held elsewhere, providing the Home Secretary consents.[18] There is an obvious efficacy in holding the hearing where the prisoner is detained as the majority of the witnesses are likely to be from the prison and there will be no need to consider security issues arising from moving the prisoner to a different location.

11.42 As the number of oral hearings has increased over the years, the Parole Board has explored the situations when it is more sensible to have hearings outside of the prison where the prisoner is detained or to have alternative methods of giving evidence such as through video links. Consideration is being given to having parole hearings at regional trial centres. The next version of the PBR may make explicit provision for this, although the Secretary of State will retain the power to veto any direction that the hearing should be held elsewhere, an obvious requirement given the security issues involved.

11.43 The PBR also require that the hearings are held in private.[19] The reasons for this are partly tied to the security concerns of making hearings held inside prisons (especially high security prisons) open to the public and partly to ensure that the privacy of victims is properly protected. A challenge to this was found to be inadmissible by the European Court of Human Rights in 2000.[20] Arguably, there may be cases where the presumption that the hearings should be conducted in private could be displaced, but it is difficult to envisage circumstances where this might arise.

11.44 The precise location of the hearing will vary greatly from prison to prison. Some prisons set aside a large room for the hearing itself, with side rooms for witnesses and private consultation with the client. Other prisons have the most basic of facilities, holding hearings in the middle of draughty gyms with poor consultation facilities. It is possible that conditions could be so poor that they could undermine the ability to hold a fair hearing.[21] However, given that an application

18 PBR r18(1).

19 PBR r18(2).

20 *Hirst v UK* [2001] CLR 919 – the case was successful in challenging the interval set between parole reviews, but the part of the application challenging the holding of parole hearings in private was dismissed at the admissibility stage.

21 Conditions at one hearing in Wormwood Scrubs approached that level, being held in a hut in the middle of the prison yard with solicitor and client consultation having to take place in the prison yard while other prisoners played football.

to adjourn or defer a hearing would result in a delay in the prisoner having his/her case considered, the conditions would have to be bad enough to prevent the representative from adequately presenting the case before an application on these grounds would be of benefit to the client.

The persons present at the hearing

11.45 The physical arrangements for the hearing have all the persons sitting at a table or on seats while waiting to give evidence in the hearing room. Witnesses do not give evidence on oath and the members of the panel should be addressed as 'sir' or madam'. Other than the prisoner and his/her legal representative, the following persons will be present at the hearing.

The panel

11.46 The panel will consist of three members of the Parole Board. The chair of the panel is required to have held a legal qualification as a barrister or solicitor for at least five years.[23] When oral hearings were first established by the Criminal Justice Act 1991, panel chairs were required to hold judicial office and there was a requirement for a High Court judge to hear certain types of case. As the number of cases heard has expanded exponentially and now includes large numbers of cases involving determinate sentences, the pressure to increase the numbers of members of the Parole Board has led to a relaxation of the requirements. Complex or high profile cases will still be allocated to panels chaired by a judge.

11.47 The other two members of the panel are drawn from the lay members of the Parole Board. In the early days where all panels were for discretionary lifers, it was a requirement that one panel member should be a psychiatrist. It is still very common for one member to hold a psychiatric or psychological qualification, and in any case where psychiatric or psychological issues are relevant to the assessment of risk this should always be the norm.

23 PBR r3(6).

The panel administrator

11.48 In the majority of cases, a panel administrator will be present. The role of the administrator is to assist the panel with the routine administration on the day (checking whether parties are ready, showing them to the room etc) and to make a written note of the hearing. For a while, oral hearings were tape recorded so that transcripts of evidence could be prepared, this practice being instituted in response to the requirement on panel chairs to keep a note of key points of evidence and points of law as well as giving written reasons for decisions[24] until the mid-1990s in case a challenge was made to the decision and a transcript of the evidence was required. This practice was halted as the number of hearings increased and requests for the tapes or transcripts began to rise. The panel administrator's note is therefore part of the record of the hearing which can be referred to in the event of a dispute at a later date.

11.49 If no panel administrator is available, this will not result in the hearing being postponed. This will simply increase the administrative burden on the panel itself and the need for other parties present to keep an accurate note of the proceedings.

The Secretary of State's representative

11.50 The Secretary of State will normally be represented at the hearing by the lifer manager of the prison where the hearing takes place. In particularly complex cases, a representative from LRRS may attend as the representative or a barrister may be instructed. This will also happen in all recall cases, as the prison in which the lifer is held may not know anything about his/her case and may not even have a lifer department.

11.51 One problem that sometimes arises is where the lifer manager does not agree with the Secretary of State's view on the case. It is not uncommon for a lifer manager to be in favour of a progressive transfer or release, only for the Secretary of State to oppose this view. In those circumstances, the lifer manager may be needed to give evidence and so cannot present the case. In any event, good practice dictates that the lifer manager should not present a case where he/she disagrees with the Secretary of State and LRRS should arrange for someone else of governor grade at the prison or a member of LRRS to represent this case at the hearing.[25]

24 *R v Parole Board ex p Gittens* (1993) *Times* 3 February.

25 Guidance from LRRS on representation for the Secretary of State is contained in *Lifer News*, Spring 2004.

The witnesses

11.52 For the vast majority of hearings, all the witnesses will be present for the entire hearing. The reason for this is that the evidence given at the hearing might be relevant to the assessment of risk and so it is helpful for the witnesses to hear that evidence.

11.53 The exception to this general rule is when there are contested factual allegations, possibly matters which have already been the subject of a criminal trial or discontinued criminal charges and which the Board wishes to re-investigate. In that instance, it may be appropriate for the evidence to be heard in a manner which more closely resembles the criminal trial process with witnesses only entering the hearing to give their own evidence. This is most likely to arise when dealing with recall hearings and is a matter which should be raised at the directions stage if possible.

Observers

11.54 Observers will normally be present for the whole of the hearing.

Hearing procedure

An overview

11.55 Guidance as to how the hearing should be conducted is contained in PBR r19. This provides some guidance on the nature of the hearing at r19(2):

> The panel shall avoid formality in the proceedings and so far as possible shall make its own enquiries in order to satisfy itself of the level of risk of the prisoner; it shall conduct the hearing in such manner as it considers most suitable to the clarification of the issues before it and generally to the just handling of the proceedings it.

11.56 A number of important principles which underpin the style of the hearing and inform judicial decisions on challenges to parole review can be taken from r19:

- the hearing should be as informal as possible;
- the panel has an inquisitorial role;
- the panel has flexibility as to how to conduct that inquiry.

11.57 There is room for some debate as to whether the proceedings should be adversarial or inquisitorial. Case-law from the European Court of

Human Rights suggests that an adversarial hearing is a necessary guarantee of article 5(4) of the Convention in the parole context:

> The Court is of the view that, in a situation such as that of the applicant, where a substantial term of imprisonment may be at stake and where characteristics pertaining to his personality and level of maturity are of importance in deciding on his dangerousness, Article 5(4) requires an oral hearing in the context of an adversarial procedure involving legal representation an the possibility of calling and questioning witnesses.[26]

11.58 It is possible that the reference to 'adversarial' in this context is not a term of art, but a recognition of the practice and procedure of the oral hearings process as it already existed in this country at the time of the judgment.[27] 'Adversarial' might arguably be a way of describing a process where there are two parties, both of whom are represented and can call and cross-examine witnesses. This would not undermine the distinction between the more stringent adversarial process that exists in the civil and criminal courts and the essentially inquisitorial nature of the parole hearing which is seeking to make an assessment of risk rather than a precise finding of fact.

11.59 In cases where the Board is required to make a factual determination, the panel conducting the hearing are far more likely to dispose of that part of the case in a manner which is closer to traditional criminal proceedings. As was outlined above, the procedure will often be varied to ensure that witnesses are only present for their own evidence and the order of the evidence will be changed. Where, as in most cases, the evidence is more concerned with reaching a decision as to what the correct assessment of risk is for an individual, although the evidence before the Board will be tested through cross-examination, the inquisitorial model is arguably more appropriate.

Order of evidence

11.60 The PBR require the panel chair to explain at the outset how the panel intends to proceed and then to invite each party to present their view on the suitability for release.[28] Invariably, the Secretary of State's representative will first read out the written view and the prisoner's legal representative is then invited to comment on that view.

26 *Hussain and Singh v United Kingdom* [1996] 22 EHRR 1 paras 59–60.

27 This case was where the European Court of Human Rights held that there should be an extension of the oral hearings process from discretionary lifers to HMP detainees.

28 PBR r19(1).

11.61 In cases where a deferral is being sought, the application should be made at this stage before any evidence is heard. If it is a case where there have been late reports or late written submissions, it is also sensible to check at the outset that everyone at the hearing is working from the same documents.

11.62 In the vast majority of cases, the first person to give evidence will be the prisoner. The prisoner's representative will commence by asking questions. Once this examination-in-chief has concluded, the panel will then ask questions of the prisoner, although it is not uncommon for panel chairs to interject during the examination-in-chief. The Secretary of State's representative then has the opportunity to put questions and finally, the prisoner's representative has a further opportunity to put questions to the client.

11.63 Once the prisoner's evidence is completed, the same procedure is followed with each of the witnesses called by the prisoner. If any witnesses have been called by the Secretary of State or the panel, it is usual for the examination-in-chief to be conducted by the Secretary of State with the prisoner's representative having the opportunity to cross-examine. However, it must be remembered that although this is the standard procedure, the aim of the proceedings is to be flexible and so this can be varied as and when necessary.[29] In cases where a departure from this standard model is proposed, then it is always advisable to raise this with the panel at the commencement of the hearing.

Advocacy style

11.64 The evidence given by the prisoner is often crucial and so it is important for legal representatives to give a great deal of thought as to the questions they will put to their clients. The considerations to have in mind when preparing those questions are:

- *Always discuss with the client the questions to be put to him/her in advance of the hearing.* It is essential that the client does not feel surprised or pressured when giving evidence.
- *Try to cover as much ground as possible that is relevant to the determination of the issues during the examination-in-chief.* A successful examination-in-chief will leave the panel with very little to ask the prisoner. A prisoner is likely to feel much more comfortable answering questions from his/her own lawyer, especially if it is understood why the question is being asked, than one put by a stranger.

29 See PBR r19(2) above.

- *Try to keep the evidence as focused and succinct as possible.* The key to this is the relevance test. In many cases, the panel will want the prisoner to provide an explanation of his/her offending history and an account of progression since that time. However, if it is clear from the evidence that the area of dispute is the suitability of a release plan, it may not be necessary to go over this history at all. Panels will often give an indication at the start of the hearing if there are areas they do not need to hear evidence on.
- *Always advise the prisoner that the panel, particularly the chair, may interject at any time.*

11.65 While there is no prescriptive advice to be given on a particular style of advocacy to adopt, the inquisitorial and informal nature of parole hearings does mean that a forensic, criminal court advocacy style is often inappropriate. For example, rather than trying to build up the background to a relevant point through a series of questions, it will usually be of more assistance to the panel to put points directly to the witnesses. Although the approach of panel chairs will vary, there is not the same blanket prohibition on leading witnesses, not least because in most cases the purpose of the hearing is not to examine contested factual matters. Obviously, in cases such as recall hearings where there is a contested factual matter, a more conventional advocacy style is likely to be appropriate.

Evidence

11.66 There are no formal rules of evidence for parole hearings. PBR r19(5) states:

> The panel may adduce or receive in evidence any document or information notwithstanding that such document or information would be inadmissible in a court of law, but no person shall be compelled to give any evidence or produce any document which he could not be compelled to give or produce on the trial of an action.

11.67 It should be noted from the outset that the criminal rules of evidence do not apply to parole hearings and that the criminal limb of article 6 of the European Convention on Human Rights has also been held not to apply.[30] Although there has been some room to explore whether the requirements of article 5(4) in this context are materially different

30 There have been numerous cases on this issue, possibly the most authoritative recent discussion can be found in *R (on the application of Smith) v Parole Board* [2005] UKHL 1.

from article 6, most recently in *R (on the application of Roberts) v Parole Board*,[31] the view of the domestic courts has always tended towards allowing the Parole Board significant discretion to regulate how, and in what form, it receives evidence. In the *Roberts* case, the decision of the Lords was that the Board's primary statutory duty is to protect the public and that this does allow flexibility in determining procedure and receiving evidence. The safeguard for prisoners is that the Board must not adopt procedures which would effectively extinguish the right to a fair hearing. Although the Lords were divided on whether a particular procedure – in that case the adoption of a special advocate[32] – would cross the dividing line, the overall analysis emphasises the flexibility that the Board has in relation to evidential matters.

11.68 The PBR permit panels of the Parole Board to receive evidence which would not be admissible in a court of law.[33] A great deal of the evidence at parole hearings is in the form of hearsay evidence, whether written or oral. Where hearsay evidence is not contested or contentious, this is uncontroversial. One of the key evidential issues that has arisen over the years is whether contested hearsay evidence, especially in relation to disputed factual matters, is admissible.

11.69 Two decisions of the Court of Appeal firmly concluded that hearsay evidence is permissible at parole hearings, even in cases where the hearsay evidence is contested and contradicted by oral evidence. The issue identified for the panel by the Court of Appeal was not whether this evidence is admissible, but the degree of weight that is given to it. In *R (on the application of Sim) v Parole Board*[34] Keene LJ analysed the issue in the following manner:

> That passage seems to me to be generally applicable to proceedings before the Parole Board when it is assessing risks, especially bearing in mind that recall decisions are not criminal proceedings within the meaning of Article 6: *R (West) v Parole Board* [2002] EWCA Civ 1641; [2003] 1 WLR 705. Merely because some factual matter is in dispute does not render hearsay evidence about it in principle inadmissible or prevent the Parole Board taking such evidence into account. It should normally be sufficient for the Board to bear in mind that that evidence is hearsay and to reflect that factor in the weight which is attached to it. However, like the judge below, I can envisage the possibility of circumstances where the evidence in question is so fundamental

31 [2005] UKHL 45.

32 See above in the section on disclosure of evidence for a discussion on the implications of the *Roberts* case for the special advocate procedure.

33 For example, none of the evidence is given on oath.

34 [2003] EWCA Civ 1845.

to the decision that fairness requires that the offender be given the opportunity to test it by cross-examination before it is taken into account at all. As so often, what is or is not fair will depend on the circumstances of the individual case.[35]

11.70 This was followed and applied to particular facts in *R (on the application of Brooks) v Parole Board*.[36] The facts of the case are worth considering, as they illustrate how a process which can appear fundamentally flawed by comparison with the criminal trial process has been deemed acceptable in parole reviews. The case concerned a discretionary lifer who had been recalled to prison following allegations made by his partner that he had raped her. The allegations had been made to the Probation Service and repeated to the police, but the complainant had declined to pursue criminal charges and indicated to the prisoner's solicitors that she wished to withdraw the charges. She declined to attend the parole hearing[37] but evidence was given about her allegations by the interviewing probation officer and the written statements were available. The panel went on to find the rape had occurred on the balance of probabilities. The Court of Appeal held that the review had been conducted fairly, Kennedy LJ commenting:

> I, like Keene LJ in *Sim* can envisage the possibility of circumstances where the evidence in question is so fundamental to the decision that fairness requires that the offender be given the opportunity to test it by cross-examination before it is taken into account at all. As Elias J indicated in the present case, that could require production of the complainant if someone in the position of [the complainant] was willing to testify, but as Keene LJ went on to point out, the requirements of fairness depend on the circumstances of the individual case, and in my judgment there was nothing unfair about the decision of this panel to proceed as it did. As I have made clear, neither the Parole Board nor the Secretary of State did anything to inhibit the claimant's opportunity to test by cross-examination the allegations of [the complainant] before those allegations were taken into account, but in the particular circumstances of this case that opportunity was not worth much, and the claimant's solicitor was entitled to decide not to pursue it more than she did.[38]

11.71 As the Board operates to the civil standard of proof rather than to the criminal standard when dealing with factual findings, there is

35 Para 57.

36 [2004] EWCA Civ 80.

37 Part of the case was concerned with whether appropriate steps had been taken to secure her attendance – this is discussed in the section on securing the attendance of witnesses above.

38 Para 37.

no prohibition on the evidence which has been considered during criminal proceedings being reheard at a parole hearing with the lower standard of proof applied. The courts have cautiously approved the approach applied in cases decided under the Children Act 1989, whereby a criminal acquittal is not considered determinative and does not preclude the tribunal from making its own inquiry applying the civil standard of proof. The leading Children Act authority on this subject is *H (minors) (sexual abuse: standard of proof), Re*[39] in which Lord Nicholls explained the duty as follows:

> When assessing the probabilities the court will have in mind as a factor, to what ever extent is appropriate in the particular case, that the more serious the allegation the less likely it is that the event occurred and, hence, the stronger should be the evidence before the court concludes that the allegation is established on the balance of probability.[40]

11.72 The Children Act analogy has always been considered apposite in the parole context, as the predominant statutory requirement to protect the best interests of the child is mirrored by the Board's primary duty to protect the public. Despite this, there has been some judicial reservation as to whether this can be transposed to the parole process in its entirety.[41] Although the admissibility of evidence will be fact-specific, the most succinct summary of the guidelines the Board will apply can be found in *R v Parole Board ex p Watson*:[42]

> In exercising its practical judgment the Board is bound to approach its task under the two sections in the same way, balancing the hardship and injustice of continuing to imprison a man who is unlikely to cause serious injury to the public against the need to protect the public against a man who is not unlikely to cause to such injury. In other than a clear case this is bound to be a difficult and very anxious judgment. But in the final balance the Board is bound to give preponderant weight to the need to protect innocent members of the public against any significant risk of serious injury.[43]

39 [1996] AC 563 at 586.

40 At 586.

41 See, for example, Elias J in *R (on the application of Sim) v Parole Board* [2003] EWHC 152 Admin at paras 76–78 in the Administrative Court, although this was not an issue raised on the appeal. In contrast, in the *Brooks* case in the Court of Appeal, the Board did adopt the *H* approach and this was not criticised by the court.

42 [1996] 1 WLR 906.

43 At 916H – the judgment was given by Lord Bingham when he was Master of the Rolls and so has even greater force.

New confidential evidence

11.73 The submission of confidential material usually happens before the hearing itself (see the discussion on disclosure above). If, however, during the course of the hearing the Secretary of State's representative seeks to introduce evidence that is not to be disclosed to the prisoner under PBR r6, the panel should ask everyone to leave the room except for the two representatives and the panel administrator. The panel will have to determine why the application is being made and why it is being made at such a late stage. The prisoner's representative must be allowed the chance to read the material and to make representations on disclosure, subject of course to the prisoner approving this course of action. Once representations have been received, the panel will need to make a decision on disclosure pursuant to r8(2)(d) and the two representatives should be called back into the room for the decision to be conveyed. As r8(3) permits an appeal to be made to the chair of the Parole Board within seven days, if either party indicates that they wish to appeal, the hearing will need to be adjourned (or deferred if no evidence has yet been taken) to allow that appeal to take place.

Disruptive behaviour

11.74 The Board does not have any powers to hold persons in contempt. The PBR do permit the panel to exclude any persons present at the hearing who are behaving in a disruptive manner. Once excluded, the chair of the panel can place conditions before permitting a return.[44]

Children and young persons

11.75 Occasionally children and young persons may be present at oral hearings, either as witnesses or as prisoners. In whatever capacity the child appears, particular care needs to be taken to ensure that his/her evidence can be adduced as effectively and fairly as possible.

11.76 Insofar as child witnesses are concerned, the panel will need to be satisfied that the witness is competent to give evidence, namely that they have the ability to understand questions and to give answers which can be understood. Ordinarily this will be a matter for the chair of the panel to consider as a preliminary issue when making directions for the attendance of witnesses. The burden of proof lies

44 PBR r19(4).

with the party seeking to call the child to give evidence and is on balance of probabilities. Where a child or young person does attend to give evidence, panels are reminded to consider directions for 'special measures' subject to available facilities at the prison concerned.

11.77 When hearing evidence from a child witness or prisoner, the panel should have regard to the key principles of the Practice Direction issued by The Lord Chief Justice in relation to trials of children and young persons in the Crown Court. The over-riding principle being that the hearing itself should not expose the child or young person to avoidable intimidation, humiliation or distress and that all possible steps should be taken to assist the young person in understanding and participation in the proceedings. So far as possible, the ordinary hearing process should be adapted to meet those ends. Modifications to the hearing process may include:

- enabling the young person to see the hearing room prior to giving evidence in order that he/she can familiarise himself/herself with it;
- permitting the young person, if he/she wishes, to sit with members of his/her family in a place which permits easy informal communication with the young person's legal representative and others;
- the panel should explain the proceedings to the young person in terms he/she can understand;
- the hearing should be conducted according to a timetable which takes full account of a young person's inability to concentrate for long periods. Frequent and regular breaks will often be appropriate;
- a more informal approach to the proceedings may be required, including addressing the young person by his/her first name.

Adjournments

11.78 Panels have the power to adjourn hearings after the evidence has commenced if it is considered that further information might be needed to enable a final determination to be reached. The most common situations where this is likely to occur are cases where the release plan has not been properly prepared or the evidence suggests that amendments to the release plan might be necessary.

11.79 When a panel adjourns, the case should normally be re-listed before the same panel on a later date. This is different from a deferral where the case can be considered by an entirely new panel. The distinction is drawn as if evidence has already been received, then the same panel members will need to reconvene in order to be able to reach a decision on risk. New panel members would not usually be able to reach this assessment if they have not heard all of the evidence.

11.80 The point of the hearing at which a panel adjourns is important. If the panel reaches a decision on risk and then adjourns for reports on the release plan, it is not permitted to reopen the risk issue. In one case where this happened, at the resumed hearing LRRS and the probation service persuaded the panel that their initial risk assessment was incorrect and the provisional release direction was rescinded.[45] The High Court quashed this decision of the Parole Board, accepting the argument that the Board was functus officio on the issue of risk assessment and that it could not reopen this issue unless there was new factual material available. Fresh submissions and argument were insufficient. Following this decision, most panels will refrain from making a determination on risk at the time of the adjournment, not least because the nature of the release plan may be intimately tied to the management of risk in the community.

Concluding the hearing

11.81 At the conclusion of the evidence, the chair of the panel will invite the Secretary of State's representative to make any closing comments or submissions. The prisoner's representative will then also be given this opportunity. It is always the case that the prisoner should be given the last word.

11.82 The Secretary of State's representative will, in the vast majority of cases, simply repeat the view that was provided in writing at the start of the hearing. The representative is highly unlikely to have the authority to depart from that view and it is only in cases where the initial view was neutral that there might be scope for a more focused view to be provided on consideration of the evidence.

11.83 The closing comments made on behalf of the prisoner provide an opportunity to draw out any important themes from the evidence and to make legal submissions on the interpretation of that evidence or the appropriate test to be applied. It is important that submissions are made on all relevant points, but this does have to be tempered with the need not to alienate the panel by reminding them of legal principles with which they will be familiar. It is a question of judgment

45 *R v Parole Board ex p Robinson* (1999) *Independent* 8 November.

in each case, although some panels will provide an indication of their views on a case and the areas which are still causing them concern. In hearings where a great deal of evidence has been taken from the home probation officer about the precise licence conditions, this can be an indication that the panel are minded to release.

The decision

11.84 The test that the Board are required to apply on release is the statutory test in the Crime (Sentences) Act 1997 s28(6)(b) that:

> the Board is satisfied that it is no longer necessary for the protection of the public that the prisoner should be confined.

11.85 The precise nature and ambit of this test is discussed at length in Chapter 9 above. This section is concerned with the procedural aspects of the final decision made by the Board, whether this is release or otherwise.

11.86 The PBR require decisions to be recorded in writing with reasons and sent to the parties within seven days of the hearing.[46] In cases where the panel cannot agree, a majority decision is binding.[47] The Board will often send decisions to prison in the internal prison post, which can be slow and often leads to the decision not arriving at the prison until after the seven-day period has elapsed. The decision will usually be sent to the lifer manager or lifer clerk to be passed onto the prisoner. This can introduce further delay if the prison does not deal with this promptly. It is always sensible for representatives to contact the Board on the seventh day to have a copy faxed if it has not arrived and to arrange for the client to telephone that afternoon to find out the result.

11.87 The case-law that developed in relation to paper parole reviews where article 5(4) was not engaged emphasised the duty of the Board to give clear and cogent reasons for its decisions. This common law test is now one of the requirements of the PBR and remains a general principle of good administrative practice. Inadequate reasons can be a basis for a legal challenge and so decisions should be checked to ensure that the reasons:

- focus on the question of risk;
- identify the matters in favour of and against release;
- explain how the panel have weighed the varying evidence and reached a conclusion.

46 PBR r20.

47 PBR r10(1).

11.88 The internal guidance provided by the Board to panel members on the drafting of reasons is as follows:

> Reasons should be clear, accurate and concise. Simple, short sentences are best. However, the courts have criticised the terseness of some reasons which leaves them open to misconstruction and misunderstanding. Reasons should, therefore:
>
> - concisely cover the issues and leave the prisoner in no doubt how the panel arrived at its decision;
> - avoid jargon. For example, what does 'address offending behaviour' really mean? It means different things in different cases. Panels must say exactly what factors contributed to the 'offending behaviour';
> - avoid absolutes where possible. For example, 'no evidence that the prisoner has addressed ...' does not necessarily mean the problem has not been worked on and invites the prisoner to point to some evidence however slight, which shows the contrary. 'There is insufficient evidence ...' is preferable. Similarly, it is better not to say, eg, 'the prisoner has had 5 adjudications'. This invites an argument over the correct number. It is preferable to use the 'several' or 'a number of'.
>
> The panel should ask whether the reasons:
>
> - Identify the nature and circumstances of the index offence (including, where provided, information about its impact on the victim and/or the victim's family?
> - Deal with the lifer's background, including the nature, circumstances and pattern of previous offending?
> - Cover efforts made by the prisoner to reduce risk by addressing attitudes and/or behavioural problems that led to the index offence, including the achievement of sentence plan targets?
> - Address the lifer's awareness of the impact of the index offences, particularly in relation to the victim or the victim's family?
> - Address the nature of any offences against prison discipline?
> - Address the lifer's attitude to other prisoners and staff?
> - Cover the lifer's security category and, where available in reports, the reasons for it
> - Deal with response to trust, including, absconds, escapes, breaches of ROTL or life licence?
> - Deal with any medical, psychiatric or psychological considerations relevant to risk?
> - Cover any available indicators of predicted risk as determined by a validated actuarial risk score or any other structured assessments of risk or treatment needs?

In addition, do they:

- Address both the test for release and the directions for open conditions (see below)?
- Where absconding is an issue deal with the likelihood of that occurring?
- Identify risk factors and areas of concern that remain to be addressed?
- Avoid making any recommendation or comment on matters outside the terms of the referral (eg, treatment needs, specific courses, transfers within closed conditions or assessment under the Mental Health Act)?
- Balance positive factors against negative
- Take account of any oral evidence that adds to or persuades you to reject evidence in the documents?
- Deal with any procedural submissions made by either party (eg, on 'burden of proof', test for release, adjournment, admissibility of evidence)?

In addition, if considering open conditions do the reasons address:

- The extent to which the lifer has made sufficient progress in reducing risk?
- The extent to which the lifer is likely to comply with the condition of temporary release?
- The extent to which the lifer is considered trustworthy enough not to abscond?
- Any potential benefits to the prisoner of such a transfer (eg, institutionalisation, available courses, development of release plan, testing on work already completed) and balance these against the risk?
- If recommending open conditions, state why risk is still too high for release?

If directing release on licence, do the reasons also address:

- Relationships with probation staff and other outside support such as family and friends?
- The content of the resettlement plan and suitability of release address?
- Where it might have a detrimental effect on compliance, the attitude of the local community?

Licence conditions:

- Are the conditions recommended necessary, reasonable and proportionate?
- Are exclusion zones, in addition to the above, sufficiently specific?
- Have you addressed any representations on behalf of the victim or the victim's relatives in relation to licence conditions?

Processing decisions made by the Board

11.89 The Board has the power to direct release[48] but, as noted in Chapter 9 above, all other powers are advisory only. Where release has been directed, the duty to process the direction, to draw up the life licence and physically to organise the release rests with LRRS.

11.90 LRRS aim to process release directions within five working days, but once again, the precise time limit will depend on the circumstances of the release arrangements in each case. Where release is directed to a home address, all that needs to be done is for LRRS to liaise with the probation service and physically draw up the licence. If release is to a hostel, it will only be able to take place when the hostel has a bed for the prisoner. The time scale should hopefully be known at the hearing itself but sometimes this is impossible to predict and in the worst cases, prisoners can wait for four to six weeks for a bed to be available.

11.91 If the Board has recommended a move to open conditions, LRRS aim to make a final decision on this recommendation within six weeks. The decision is usually made by a senior caseworker at LRRS on behalf of the Secretary of State. The final decision will be sent to the prisoner with a memorandum explaining whether it has been accepted or not and if it has not, the reasons for rejecting the recommendation. The memorandum will also set out the time when the next parole review will take place.

11.92 Where the Board has not directed release or recommended a move to open conditions, LRRS simply notify the prisoner of when the next review will take place.

Timing of reviews

11.93 LRRS retains the responsibility for setting the timing between reviews.[49] The statutory requirement is for a review to take place at least every two years. As the rationale behind the requirement for article 5(4) reviews is that the person subject to the sentence is susceptible to change, the decision as to how long the gap should be between reviews is case sensitive.[50] The legal rationale for this restriction is discussed in Chapter 9 above and challenges to decisions made

48 C(S)A 1997, s 28(5).

49 *R (on the application of Day) v Secretary of State for the Home Department* [2004] EWHC Admin 1742.

50 The leading domestic law decision in *R (on the application of MacNeil) v HMP Lifer Panel* (2001) EWCA Civ 448.

by LRRS about the timing of reviews and moves to open conditions are discussed in Chapter 14 below.

Lifers facing deportation

11.94 In cases where the lifer is to be deported, the Board can direct release from the life sentence but does not have jurisdiction to interfere with any decision made by the immigration authorities to detain. In the majority of cases, lifers being deported will be released from closed prison conditions (see Chapter 8 above). In those cases, it will be normal for the immigration authorities to seek to continue the detention pending the physical deportation. In the rarer cases where the lifer has already been to open conditions and is released from there, it may be far more difficult for detention on immigration grounds to be justified.

11.95 The physical process for arranging deportation can be lengthy, even where the deportation is not contested. Arrangements are dealt with by the Criminal Casework Team of the Immigration and Nationality Directorate (IND). They will require proof of citizenship, such as a passport or birth certificate, to enable the receiving state to agree to accept the return of the prisoner. The physical arrangements will involve making a booking with an airline, which will nearly always require the prisoner to be escorted, and then finding a date on which escorts are available. Even in cases where it has been possible to arrange for the documentation issues confirming nationality to be resolved promptly, it can still take several weeks for the physical flight arrangements to be resolved.

CHAPTER 12

Licences

continued

Introduction

The purpose of licence supervision

12.1 While licence conditions form part of the sentence of the criminal court, the purpose of their enforcement is not to punish.[1] Licences, even for determinate sentence prisoners, are therefore primarily preventative. Those released on licence are supervised by the Probation Service,[2] who also will be responsible for initiating enforcement action where the conditions of the licence are broken. Both those serving determinate and indeterminate sentences are released on a licence that contains a set of standard conditions. As it is probation officers who have the responsibility for the supervision of licences, they also play a large part in determining which conditions, beyond the standard conditions, should be imposed in any particular case.

Limits on what licences can contain

12.2 Licence supervision can impose significant restrictions on the offender's life in the community. As will be seen below, licence conditions can, among other things, exclude the offender from specified geographical areas, determine who he/she can live with and place restrictions on the kinds of employment that can be undertaken. The courts have therefore recognised that the imposition of licence conditions is capable of engaging the offender's right to private and family life under article 8 of the ECHR.[3]

12.3 It will not be every licence condition that will engage article 8 (for example, the requirement to report to the supervising officer), but many will. Obvious examples are those conditions that restrict the offender's ability to maintain ties with close family members, or those which prevent him/her from continuing in their chosen profession or from living in his/her own home.

1 *R (on the application of Smith) v Parole Board* [2005] UKHL 1 para 40 where Lord Bingham stated that 'a challenge to revocation of a licence may lead to detention imposed to protect the public but it cannot lead to punishment' in deciding that the Parole Board was not determining a 'criminal charge' within the meaning of article 6 of the European Convention on Human Rights (ECHR) when considering recall.

2 Criminal Justice and Court Services Act (CJCSA) 2000 s1.

3 See *R (on the application of Craven) v Home Secretary and Parole Board* [2001] EWHC Admin 850.

12.4 Where licence conditions do constitute interferences with article 8 rights, the question then arises as to whether the interference is for one of the purposes set out in article 8(2) and whether it is proportionate. Guidance to the Probation Service states that

> to be lawful the [licence] condition has to be both necessary and proportionate. Necessary means that no other means of managing a particular risk is available or appropriate; and proportionate means that the restriction on the offender's liberty is the minimum required to manage the risk.[4]

Clearly the greater the risk the offender is assessed as posing to the public, the more restrictive will be the licence conditions that are permitted.

12.5 Although courts, when examining the lawfulness of licence conditions, will be required to come to their own view as to whether they disproportionately interfere with Convention rights,[5] they will also give considerable weight in making such assessments to the view of the Probation Service:

> The licence conditions and assessment of risks to the public, on which they are based, are matters of fine judgment for those in the prison and the probation service experienced in such matters not for the courts. The courts must be steadfastly astute not to interfere save in the most exceptional case.[6]

12.6 As licence conditions are preventative, they must bear a relationship to the kind of risk to the public that the sentence in question was imposed to address. Therefore conditions imposed on the basis of material errors of fact taken into account in assessing the risk (such as the number of convictions the sentence relates to) may render conditions unlawful.[7]

12.7 Licence conditions should only be reasonably imposed. For example, additional licence conditions may include a requirement to address offending behaviour, by attending community based programmes (see below). However, an offender who does not admit his/her guilt cannot be required to complete a course that is only open to

4 PC 16/2005 para 28.

5 *R (on the application of Daly)* [2001] 2 AC 532.

6 *R (on the application of Carman) v Secretary of State for the Home Department* [2004] EWHC (Admin) 2400 para 33.

7 *R (on the application of Carman) v Secretary of State for the Home Department* [2004] EWHC (Admin) 2400.

those who accept guilt.[8] In practice, the wording of such conditions is normally vague enough to be interpreted as requiring offenders to comply with assessments for courses.

12.8 In accordance with normal public law principles, policies on the supervision of licence conditions should not be applied inflexibly. In relation to the standard condition that those on licence should not travel abroad, the Probation Service policy states that in relation to determinate sentence prisoners permission for such travel should only be granted in exceptional compassionate circumstances, and not for holiday, business or recreation.[9] The Probation Service, following the grant of permission in one case, has conceded that there may be exceptional cases where permission should be granted for one of the excluded reasons, although obviously such cases will be rare.[10]

Liaison with other organisations to inform licence conditions

12.9 Multi Agency Public Protection Arrangements (MAPPA), if applicable to the offender, will inform any licence conditions recommended by the Probation Service, especially for high risk prisoners.[11]

12.10 The Joint National Protocol on the Supervision, Revocation and Recall for Prisoners released on licence[12] between the Probation, Prison and Police Services states that in respect of MAPPA level 2 and 3 cases and those identified as Prolific and Priority Offenders (PPOs) the Probation Service will make a formal request to the police for any information or intelligence that may impact upon what may be appropriate licence conditions.[13] This process should take place no later than 28 days prior to release.[14]

8 *R (Wilkes) v Home Secretary* [2001] EWHC Admin 210; although in *R (on the application of AT) v Parole Board* [2004] EWHC 515 (Admin), where a prisoner had pleaded guilty to a sexual offence but had been inconsistent during his sentence as to whether he admitted guilt, the judge doubted whether it was unreasonable to require the offender to attend a community sex offender treatment programme.

9 PC 16/2005 para 99.

10 *R (Mehmet) v London Probation Board and another* CO/1214/2005.

11 See, for example, PSO 4745 para 2.4.3.

12 Annexed to PC 3/2005.

13 Para 5.2.

14 Para 5.1.

Consultation with victims

12.11 Since the first Victim's Charter was introduced in 1996, the Probation Service has been required, where this is requested by the victim, both to inform victims as to when prisoners convicted of the more serious offences are released on licence, and also to consult on whether the victim wishes to make representations as to appropriate licence conditions.

12.12 This duty is now a statutory one[15] on the local probation board for where the prisoner is to be released, where an offender receives a sentence of 12 months or more for a sexual or violent offence. The duty is to take all reasonable steps to ensure that if the victim wants to make representations about licence conditions, these are forwarded to whoever is responsible for the setting of them. The victim is also entitled to information about what supervision arrangements are in place and such other information as the probation board considers appropriate to provide.[16]

12.13 This duty will be reinforced by a Code of Practice[17] describing the minimum services that criminal justice agencies should provide to victims of crime, which was due to replace the Victim's Charter in late 2005. The draft code[18] imposes duties to direct victims of crime, or where the crime resulted in death, the victim's 'family spokesperson'.[19] Under the draft code the Parole Board must consider any representations made by victims through the Probation Service regarding licence conditions, and 'reflect these considerations in the parole decisions', and if a condition has not been included the Board should provide an explanation.[20]

12.14 It is clear is that victims cannot insist on disproportionate or unreasonable licence conditions being imposed on released prisoners. What the courts have recognised is that, when deciding whether a licence condition which interferes with an offender's rights under article 8(1) of the Convention can be justified under one of the grounds in article 8(2), this can necessitate balancing the offender's rights with those of the victim. So a condition excluding an offender from entering a prescribed area imposed to minimise the risk of contact with the victim can be justified as protecting 'the rights and freedoms of

15 Domestic Violence, Crime and Victims Act (DVCVA) 2004 s35.

16 DVCVA 2004 s35(7).

17 Issued under DVCVA 2004 s32.

18 Victim's Code of Practice Consultation, March 2005.

19 Ibid paras 4.2–4.6.

20 Ibid para 14.2.

others'.[21] However, such conditions have to be proportionate, or the minimum necessary interference to meet the stated aim. Accordingly, any exclusion zone, and any terms which allow the offender access to it, must be carefully tailored to address the real risk of contact with victims balanced against the impact on the offender's private and family life.[22]

12.15 The courts have also suggested that there is a distinction to be drawn between the statutory period during which an offender is liable to recall, and the obligation to adhere to the requirements of supervision. In *Rodgers, Re*[23] the offender had wrongly been informed that his licence would expire before the statutory date. While this did not affect the liability to recall on the basis of risk to the public, it did render a decision to recall purely for failing to comply with supervision requirements unlawful.

Enforcement of licences

12.16 For sentences of less than four years for offences committed before 1 January 1999,[24] breaches of licence conditions are punished by the courts. In all other cases the only sanction is recall to prison (see below at para 12.35).

Licences and determinate sentences

12.17 All prisoners serving determinate sentences will be released on licence except:

- those serving sentences of less than 12 months whenever imposed (except offenders who are under 22 at the date of release who are on three months' minimum supervision[25]);
- CJA 1967 'existing prisoners' released at the two-thirds point; and
- recalled prisoners released at sentence expiry.

21 *R (Craven) v Home Secretary and Parole Board* [2001] EWHC Admin 850, where the court considered that 'a democratic society should be sensitive to the emotional harm caused to victims of crime'.

22 Following the *Craven* case, guidance was issued to the Probation Service on exclusion zones – see PC 28/2003.

23 [2003] All ER (D) 156 (Mar).

24 When the Crime and Disorder Act (CDA) 1998 repealed Criminal Justice Act (CJA) 1991 s38.

25 CJA 1991 s65.

Summary of length of licences

12.18
- *CJA 1967 cases (those sentenced before 1 October 1992)* – If released early, the licence expires at the two-thirds point.
- *CJA 1991 ACR and DCR cases (those sentenced on or after 1 October 1992 for offences committed before 4 April 2005 to terms of at least 12 months)* – The licence expires at three-quarter point, subject to recall.[26]
- In relation to *sexual offences committed prior to 30 September 1998* the court can order that the licence lasts for the whole of the sentence.[27]
- *CJA 2003 Standard Determinate Sentences (12 months and over for offences committed on or after 4 April 2005)* – Licences will always run until sentence expiry.[28]
- *Extended sentences under both CJAs 1991 and 2003 impose an extra period of supervision on licence to be served in the community* – Offenders are on licence until the end of the extension period.

CJA 1991 determinate sentence prisoners

12.19 The initial release dates, and licence expiry dates, for CJA 1991 prisoners were preserved when the relevant parts of the CJA 2003 were brought into force.[29] For prisoners released on licence under CJA 1991 provisions there is a duty to comply with the conditions specified in the licence, and the Home Secretary is empowered to make rules for the regulating of licence supervision.[30]

CJA 2003 determinate sentence prisoners

12.20 Under the CJA 2003 fixed term prisoners, including extended sentence prisoners, are released on licence[31] and the licences last for the whole of the sentence.[32] The conditions that can be attached to these sentences are authorised by section 250, which empowers the

26 CJA 1991 s37(1).
27 Powers of Criminal Courts (Sentencing) Act (PCC(S)A) 2000 s86.
28 s249(1).
29 Criminal Justice Act (Commencement No 8 and Transitional and Saving Provisions) Order 2005 SI No 950 Sch 2 para 19.
30 CJA 1991 s37(4).
31 CJA 2003 ss244 and 247, respectively.
32 CJA 2003 s249.

Secretary of State to prescribe standard and additional licence conditions by statutory instrument (see below). When exercising the power to prescribe licence conditions the Home Secretary must have regard to:

- the protection of the public;
- prevention of re-offending; and
- securing the successful re-integration of the prisoner into the community.[33]

12.21 Prisoners released under the 2003 Act provisions, as with those released under the CJA 1991, are required to comply with such conditions as are specified in the licence.[34]

Content of licences

12.22 In summary, where the Parole Board has responsibility for deciding whether a prisoner is released early, it is also consulted about appropriate licence conditions. In cases where prisoners are automatically released, the responsibility lies with the governor of the holding prisons to set the licence conditions on behalf of the Home Secretary.[35]

12.23 Although for CJA 2003 cases the licence conditions that can be imposed are specified by the Act and statutory instrument (see below), guidance to the Probation and Prison Services confirms that the same standard and additional licence conditions can be imposed on CJA 1991 cases. (see PSO 6000 Chapter 14 and PC 16/2005.)

Standard conditions

12.24 Licences will require the offender to immediately report to the supervising officer. In addition, all licences will contain standard conditions. For CJA 2003 cases the standard licence conditions are statutorily prescribed under section 250 of the Act.[36] For other determinate sentences the standard licence conditions are similar and set out in PSO 6000.[37] The standard conditions are that the prisoner must:

- keep in touch with the responsible officer as instructed by him/her;
- receive visits from the responsible officer as instructed by him/her;

33 CJA 2003 s250(8).

34 CJA 2003 s252.

35 See guidance in PSO 6000 Chapter 14.

36 Criminal Justice (Sentencing) (Licence Conditions) Order 2005 SI No 648.

- permanently reside at an address approved by the responsible officer and obtain the prior permission of the responsible officer for any stay of one or more nights at a different address;
- undertake work (including voluntary work) only with the approval of the responsible officer and obtain his/her prior approval in relation to any change in the nature of that work;
- not travel outside the UK, the Channel Islands or the Isle of Man without the prior permission of the responsible officer, except where he/she is deported or removed from the UK in accordance with the Immigration Act 1971 or the Asylum and Immigration Act 1999;
- be of good behaviour, and not behave in a way which undermines the purposes of the releases on licence, which are to protect the public, prevent re-offending and promote successful re-integration into the community;
- not commit any offence.[38]

Additional licence conditions

12.25 The Probation Service can also recommend additional licence conditions from a prescribed list.[39] The additional licence conditions are:

- *Drug testing orders* – These will be limited to those identified as 'Prolific and other Priority Offenders' (PPOs) who are convicted of specified offences committed on or after 4 April 2005.[40]
- *Contact requirement* – To attend appointments with a named psychiatrist/psychologist/medical practitioner.
- *Prohibited activity requirement* – For example, not to work with persons under a specified age, or not to access the internet without approval.
- *Residency requirement* – A stronger version of the standard requirement.
- *Prohibited residency* – For example, not to stay in the same household as a child under a specified age without approval.

37 PSO 6000 paras 14.5–14.6.

38 Criminal Justice (Sentencing) (Licence Conditions) Order 2005 SI No 648 article 2(2).

39 s250(4)(b) and SI 2005 No 648 article 3, and guidance in PC 16/2005 and PSO 6000 Chapter 14.

40 See PC 16/2005 para 33.

- *Prohibited contact requirement* – For example, not to contact a named victim without approval.
- *Programme requirement* – For example, to comply with requirements specified by Probation to address offending behaviour.
- *Curfew requirement* – Electronic monitoring is available for those notified to the Public Protection and Courts Unit as a critical case.[41] It can only be imposed by RRS as governors do not have authority to impose the condition.
- *Exclusion requirement* – Not to enter a specified area.
- *Supervision requirement* – For example, reporting regularly to a police station, or notifying probation officer of any developing relationship.
- *Non-association requirement* – For example, not to associate with specified offenders.

Setting licence conditions

CJA 1991 ACR and CJA 2003 SDS cases

12.26 For CJA 1991 ACR cases (ie, sentences of 12 months or more but less than four years imposed in respect of offences committed before 4 April 2005) and CJA 2003 SDS cases (sentences of more 12 months or more in respect of offences committed on or after that date) the licence is issued by the individual prison by the governor on behalf of the Home Secretary, who must also approve any additional licence conditions recommended by the Probation Service.[42] There is no Parole Board involvement, as release for these classes of prisoner is automatic.

12.27 If the Probation Service requests any licence conditions not included within the standard or additional conditions set out above, the governor must consult with RRS which will have the responsibility for deciding whether any such exceptional licence conditions can be added to the licence.[43] Guidance to the Probation Service states that in ACR cases probation should only recommend the standard/additional licence conditions applicable in 2003 Act cases.[44]

12.28 Licence conditions can be varied by application to the governor of the releasing prison.[45]

41 Under PC 19/2004b or MAPPA level 3 cases.

42 PSO 6000 Chapter 14 para 14.4.

43 PSO 6000 para 14.4.1.

44 PC 16/2005 para 25.

45 PSO 6000 para 14.8.1.

CJA 1991 DCR cases

12.29 For prisoners serving sentences imposed on or after 1 October 1992 of four or more years for offences committed before 4 April 2003, licence conditions beyond the standard conditions can only be imposed after consultation with the Parole Board.[46] The request for additional conditions should be made by the Probation Service in the report prepared for the parole dossier, and should only be from the set of additional conditions set out above.[47] The Board will set out any recommended conditions in its decision recommending release, and if release is not recommended the decision will confirm whether any additional licence conditions should be imposed at the NPD (when the prisoner is automatically released at the two-thirds point).

12.30 If the prisoner has not applied for parole and it is considered that additional conditions should be imposed, a report can be forwarded to the Parole Board for consideration as to whether such conditions should be imposed.[48] For DCR prisoners serving sentences of less than 15 years, the Board's decision on additional conditions is binding. For those serving 15 or more years, the Board's decision, as with release decisions, is considered by the Home Secretary, who makes the final decision.

12.31 Requests to vary licence conditions in DCR cases should be sent to the RRS which will ensure that they are forwarded to the Parole Board for consideration.[49]

Extended sentences

12.32 CJA 2003 extended sentence cases are dealt with in a similar way to DCR cases where the sentence is of 15 years or more in that additional licence conditions must be approved by the Parole Board but the final decision on which conditions will be added rests with the Home Secretary.[50]

12.33 With CJA 1991 extended sentences the length of the custodial term is decisive. If it is less than four years the offender is treated as an ACR prisoner for the purpose of the setting of licence conditions, and if it is four or more years the prisoner is treated as a DCR prisoner and additional conditions will be the responsibility of the Board.[51]

46 CJA 1991 s37(5) and (6) and PSO 6000 para 14.3.1.
47 PC 16/2005 para 24.
48 See PSO 6000 Chapter 6.
49 PSO 6000 para 14.3.1.
50 PSO 6000 para 14.7.2.
51 CJA 1991 s44(2).

Judicial recommendations

12.34 For sentences where release will be under the CJA 2003, the sentencing court can now recommend further conditions 'which in its view should be included in any licence granted to the offender'.[52] Those responsible for issuing licences must have regard to such recommendations, although it is accepted that circumstances may change during the currency of a sentence to such a degree that the recommendation may be no longer relevant, or in fact be counter-productive. In such cases the Probation Service will consult with the RRS to seek authority to omit the judicial recommendation. If the RRS feels it appropriate to omit the condition, it will inform the sentencing judge of this.[53]

Effect of recall on licences

12.35 The effect of recall on licences is only relevant to CJA 1991 cases as the SDS licence always lasts until sentence expiry, and indeterminate sentence licences (with the exception of the licence in relation to the indeterminate sentence for public protection) last for life.

12.36 For sentences administered under the CJA 1991 (including sentences of less than 12 months imposed after 4 April 2005), the position is complicated. Until the coming into force of the relevant parts of the Crime and Disorder Act 1998 on 30 September of that year, licence conditions always expired for this class of sentences at the three-quarter point.[54] However, for offences committed on or after that date, CJA 1991 prisoners, when recalled to custody, if not released on the recommendation of the Parole Board were released at the three-quarter point on licence to the end of the sentence. (CJA 1991 ss33(3) and 37(1A).)

12.37 What happens where offenders serving sentences imposed for offences committed before 4 April 2005 are recalled under the new CJA 2003 provisions is slightly more confused. When the relevant parts of the CJA 2003 were brought into force, the transitional and saving provisions preserved the *initial* release and licence expiry dates for this class of prisoner (see para 12.19 above). However, where such

52 CJA 2003 s238(1).

53 PSO 6000 para 14.9.2.

54 Unless the court ordered, in the case of sexual offences, that the licence should extend for the whole of the sentence – see now PCC(S)A 2000 s86.

offenders are *recalled* it appears that the statutory framework permits detention to sentence expiry, as the statutory right to be automatically re-released at the three-quarter point of the sentence has been removed.[55] Under the provisions of the CJA 2003, which apply to all offenders whenever the date of offence, all recalls are referred to the Parole Board, which has the power to decide when the offender is released.

12.38 However, the new directions to the Parole Board on recall state that prisoners sentenced under the CJA 1991 provisions 'cannot be disadvantaged by the recall provisions of the Criminal Justice Act 2003'.[56] Further guidance in PSO 6000 states that when such prisoners are recalled, the Parole Board 'must ensure that in all such cases, the prisoner is re-released no later than their LED, on licence, until SED'.[57]

12.39 It appears strange that the possibility of detention beyond LED for this class of prisoner is apparently sanctioned by the statutory framework, and then effectively prohibited by directions to the Parole Board. The courts have yet to consider the legality of detaining recalled CJA 1991 prisoners beyond their LED.[58]

12.40 While there is evident unfairness in changing the amount of time an offender may be subject to licence conditions after sentencing (and it was argued to be a breach of the requirement for certainty in sentencing required by article 6 of the Convention in *Buddington* – see fn 58), whether such a change offends against the prohibition on the retrospective increase of sentences contained in article 7 of the ECHR is unclear.[59]

55 As para 19 does not preserve the recall provision in CJA 1991 s39 which triggers the re-release at the three-quarter point in section 33(3): see *R (on the application of Buddington) v Secretary of State for the Home Department* [2005] EWHC 2198 (QB) para 50.

56 See Appendix 7.

57 PSO 6000 para 7.12.1.

58 In *R (on the application of Buddington) v Secretary of State for the Home Department* [2005] EWHC 2198 (QB) para 49 the Divisional Court held it did not have to rule on the issue partly because the Secretary of State contended that the statutory directions would prevent any perceived unfairness in the new regime.

59 *R (on the application of Uttley) v Secretary of State for the Home Department* [2004] UKHL 38 only considered the position when the legislative change occurred between commission of the offence and sentencing.

Indeterminate sentences

Statutory basis of licence supervision

12.41 All indeterminate sentence prisoners, when their release is directed by the Parole Board, are released on licence.[60] Licences remain in force until the offender's death[61] with the exception of the sentence imposed for public protection under the CJA 2003 (see below). Indeterminate sentence prisoners are placed under a duty to comply with the conditions contained in the licence and the Home Secretary is empowered to make rules relating to supervision.[62]

Responsibility for setting licence conditions

12.42 Although licences for indeterminate sentence prisoners are prepared by LRRS on behalf of the Home Secretary, conditions can only be imposed in accordance with the recommendations of the Parole Board.[63] In practice, lifers are released on licences containing the standard conditions and any additional conditions the Parole Board specifies in its decision directing release.

Contents of life licences – standard conditions

12.43 Although, as noted above, licences must be imposed in accordance with recommendations of the Board, there are seven standard licence conditions that LRRS has indicated should be included in indeterminate licences. These now largely mirror the determinate sentence standard conditions:[64]

(1) He/she shall place himself/herself under the supervision of whichever supervising officer is nominated for this purpose from time to time.
(2) He/she shall on release report tot the supervising office so nominated, and shall keep in touch with that officer in accordance with that officer's instructions.
(3) He/she shall, if his/her supervising officer so requires, receive visits from that officer where the licence holder is living.
(4) He/she will reside only where approved by his/her supervising officer.

60 Crime (Sentences) Act (C(S)A) 1997 s28(5).
61 C(S)A 1997 s31(1).
62 C(S)A 1997 s31(2).
63 C(S)A 1997 s31(3).
64 See LRRS *Lifer News*, Summer 2005.

(5) He/she shall undertake work, including voluntary work, only where approved by his/her supervising officer and shall inform that officer of any change in or loss of such employment.
(6) He/she shall not travel outside the United Kingdom (including the Isle of Man and Channel Islands) without the prior permission of his/her supervising officer.
(7) He/she shall be well behaved and not do anything which could undermine the purposes of supervision on licence which are to protect the public, by ensuring that their safety would not be placed at risk, and to secure his/her successful reintegration into the community.

Additional conditions

12.44 These are also imposed in accordance with recommendations of the Board. Although, unlike with determinate sentences, there is no prescribed list of additional conditions, such conditions will have to be lawful and otherwise not disproportionately interfere with the offender's Convention rights. In practice, the Board will generally only impose additional conditions in line with those approved for recommendation by the Probation Service for determinate sentence prisoners (see para 12.25 above).

Variation and cancellation of indeterminate sentence licences

12.45 Those serving the indeterminate sentence of imprisonment for public protection imposed under the CJA 2003 can, after ten years of supervision in the community, apply to the Parole Board, which can order that the licence ceases to have effect where it is satisfied that it is no longer necessary for the protection of the public.[65]

12.46 In all other cases, the licence lasts until the offender's death. However, consideration may be given to cancelling the supervision element (although this does not affect the offender's liability to recall) of the life licence after a minimum of four years, or ten years for sex offenders. Such cases will be dealt with by application to LRRS, and the supervision requirement can be re-imposed if further incidents suggesting this may be necessary come to the attention of the Probation Service.[66] LRRS will need to consult with the Board before varying or cancelling any licence condition.[67]

65 C(S)A 1997 s31A(4).
66 See PSO 4700 para 14.6.
67 C(S)A 1997 s31(3).

CHAPTER 13

Recall to prison

continued

Introduction

13.1 It has always been recognised that the consequences of being returned to prison from a state of liberty will have a greater impact on the offender than a refusal of initial release. Even when release on licence, including for those serving life sentences, was seen purely as a matter of clemency at the discretion of the executive, a distinction was been made between processes to determine initial release, and those applicable to licence revocation.[1] Both under the European Convention on Human Rights (ECHR) and common law it has been recognised that loss of liberty, even where conditional, requires the highest standards of fairness.

13.2 Not all licence breaches will justify a recall to custody, even for those serving determinate sentences. However, there is a distinction between indeterminate and extended sentences on the one hand, where the grounds for recall must have a 'causal link' with the purpose of the sentence to be lawful,[2] and the position with determinate sentence prisoners. The grounds upon which offenders on licence can be recalled to custody will therefore vary according to the sentence that has been imposed.

- For determinate sentence prisoners (not including extended sentence prisoners during the extension period) the Home Secretary has issued directions to the Parole Board as to recall which state that the Board should consider whether there is an unacceptable risk of further offending, or whether licence breaches indicate that the objectives of probation supervision have been undermined.
- For CJA 1991 extended sentence prisoners, as the sentence is imposed to protect the public from further sexual or violent re-offending, it is only where the offender's behaviour during the extension period demonstrates a substantial risk of further such offending that recall can be justified.[3]
- For CJA 2003 extended sentence prisoners during the extension period, and all indeterminate sentence prisoners, as the sentence is imposed to protect the public from offences of serious harm, it

1 When the Parole Board was created by the Criminal Justice Act (CJA) 1967, unlike with other decisions, reasons for recall were required to be given to prisoners, and the Home Secretary was bound to accept recommendations for their release: CJA 1967 s62.

2 *Stafford v UK* (2002) 35 EHRR 32, *R (on the application of Sim) v Parole Board* [2003] EWCA Civ 1845.

3 *R (on the application of Sim) v Parole Board* [2003] EWHC 152 (Admin) paras 42–45.

is only where the offender's behaviour demonstrates a substantial risk of such harm that recall can be justified.[4]

- Notwithstanding specific behaviour indicative of risk to the public, those on licence may be recalled if their behaviour suggests that supervision has fundamentally broken down (making the risk unmanageable in the community).[5]

Legal assistance

13.3 Prisoners can be assisted in relation to making written representations to the Board under the CDS advice and assistance scheme. If the initial written representations are rejected then representation can be provided at the oral hearing under the Advocacy Assistance scheme as with indeterminate sentence cases.

Determinate sentence recalls

Recall procedure

13.4 The procedure adopted in the recall of determinate sentence prisoners has been radically changed because of the decision of the House of Lords in *R v Parole Board ex p Smith and West*.[6] Prior to this decision, while the Parole Board accepted that it had a statutory discretion to hold oral hearings in determinate sentence recall cases, it only did so rarely. *Smith and West* reversed this position and the procedure now is that all determinate sentence prisoners when recalled are given the opportunity of an oral hearing for their representations to be considered if the Board does not direct release after an initial consideration on the papers.

13.5 The right of extended sentence prisoners to an oral hearing if recalled during the extension period existed prior to the decision in *Smith and West*. It arises, as with indeterminate sentence prisoners' entitlement to oral hearings to determine the legality of their detention on expiry of the minimum term, on the applicability of article 5(4) of the ECHR to the sentence.[7]

4 *R v Parole Board ex p Watson* [1996] 1 WLR 906.
5 *R (Sim) v Parole Board* [2003] EWHC 152 (Admin) para 44.
6 [2005] UKHL 1. For fuller discussion see Chapter 1 above.
7 *R (Sim) v Parole Board* [2003] EWCA Civ 1845.

The legal framework of recall

13.6 Since 4 April 2005 all determinate sentenced prisoners, irrespective of the date the relevant offences were committed, are recalled under section 254 of the CJA 2003.[8] It is the Home Secretary who has the power to revoke the licence and recall the offender to prison.[9] This marks a change from the previous power to recall under the CJA 1991[10] where, except in urgent cases,[11] the Home Secretary was under a duty to consult the Parole Board before recalling an offender.[12] Now the initial recall decision is entrusted wholly to the executive.

Prisoners released before, but recalled after, 4 April 2005

13.7 The commencement order that brought the CJA 2003 recall provisions for determinate sentence prisoners into force[13] appeared on the one hand to remove the old power to recall under the CJA 1991,[14] but then failed to make those who had been released prior to its coming into force liable to recall at all.[15]

13.8 Following a legal challenge by a prisoner released on licence before 4 April 2005 to his recall after that date[16] a further statutory instrument was brought into force to clarify that section 254 was intended to apply to CJA 1991 cases whenever they were released.[17] When the issue was considered by the court it held that, although the draftsman did not 'deserve any prizes' for its wording, the intention of parliament must have been to allow for the recall of prisoners released prior

8 Criminal Justice Act 2003 (Commencement No 8 and Transitional and Saving Provisions) Order 2005 SI No 950 Sch 2 para 23.

9 CJA 2003 s254(1).

10 See CJA 1991 s39(1).

11 CJA 1991 s39(2).

12 And even in urgent cases it was the practice to consult the Board on an extra-statutory basis as soon as possible after the recall.

13 Commencement Order No 8 2005 SI No 950 – see above.

14 SI 2005 No 950 Sch 1 para 44(k).

15 See SI 2005 No 950 Sch 2 para 23 – which applied the CJA 2003 recall power under section 254 only to a CJA 1991 prisoner 'who falls to be released *after* 4th April 2005' (emphasis added).

16 *R (on the application of Buddington) v Secretary of State for the Home Department* [2005] EWHC 2198 (QB) – a challenge also to the further effect of the commencement order of making those originally released under the CJA 1991 when recalled liable to detention until sentence expiry – see Chapter 12 above.

17 Criminal Justice Act 2003 (Commencement No 8 and Transitional and Saving Provisions) Order 2005 (Supplementary Provisions) Order 2005 SI No 2122 – in force from 29 July 2005.

to 4 April 2005. Therefore the original commencement order should be construed as permitting the recall of this class of prisoner.[18]

The recommendation for recall

13.9 In practice it is nearly always the supervising probation officer who will initiate procedures leading to recall. The RRS will consider all requests for recall within 24 hours of receipt although very urgent cases (where the offender is subject to Multi Agency Public Protection Arrangements (MAPPA) level 3 arrangements, or is considered to present a high and imminent risk of harm to the public, or where re-offending is believed to be imminent) RRS will consider the case within two hours.[19]

13.10 The Probation Service National Standards 2005[20] state that 'breach action' may be initiated where there has been 'one unacceptable failure' to comply with licence conditions where appropriate, and if such action is not initiated a formal written warning should be given. The Standards state that 'no more than two written warnings shall be given within the total sentence period before commencing breach action'. If the offender is recalled that Standards require the supervising officer to provide a new risk assessment to RRS within 14 days.[21]

13.11 The Probation Service will prepare a report on a standard form[22] for forwarding to the RRS, which should specify:

- the level of risk under MAPPA;
- the licence conditions that have been breached, details of the breach and its circumstances and 'any deterioration in behaviour/ compliance which has led to an assessment that the risk of harm or re-offending has increased to an unacceptable level, comment upon the offender's behaviour and general response to supervision during the licence period and detail any previous breaches and action taken in response';
- a risk assessment;
- a risk management plan.[23]

18 SI 2005 No 2122 para 33, although the court has granted permission to appeal.
19 PSO 6000 para 7.7.1.
20 See PC 15/2005.
21 National Standards GS9.
22 See Appendix A of PC 16/2005.
23 PC 16/2005 para 46(ii).

13.12 The Probation Service must also provide to RRS other core documents for the recall dossier such as previous convictions and any pre-sentence report. The recall request should be endorsed by the Assistant Chief Officer (ACO).

Where the licencee faces further criminal charges

13.13 In relation to situations where the offender has been charged with further offences, the Probation Service guidance suggests that supervising officers should 'disregard the charge, the plea and whether the offender has been remanded into custody' and instead, when deciding whether to recommend recall for breach of the condition to be of good behaviour, focus upon:

(i) the behaviour of the offender surrounding the incident that resulted in the charge being made;

(ii) whether the new offence is similar to the one for which the offender is on licence and was originally sentenced;

(iii) whether the new offence indicates any rise in the level and immediacy of the risk the offender presents to others.[24]

13.14 This guidance encourages a wholly unrealistic approach to the consideration of recall, but is also mirrored in the Parole Board approach, which is to assume that if criminal proceedings in respect of fresh allegations have not concluded, it is nevertheless usually possible to consider whether recall is appropriate in light of evidence of the offender's behaviour, short of that relating to the new charges themselves.[25]

13.15 While it has been held that the mere fact of a further charge and pending prosecution cannot on its own justify recall on the basis of a risk of re-offending[26] there will often be occasions when it is necessary for the Board to consider the evidence upon which the new charges are based in order to properly come to an assessment of risk.[27] Where the new charge does have a bearing on the risk assessment, it is difficult to see how the Board can fairly deal with it in advance of the criminal trial without prejudicing the prosecution. Although agreeing to a deferral of the Parole Board hearing pending the outcome of

24 PC 16/2005 para 61.

25 See also para 11.38 above.

26 *R (on the application of Broadbent) v Parole Board* [2005] EWHC 1207 (Admin) para 26.

27 Ibid para 29, *R (on the application of Brooks) v Parole Board* [2004] EWCA Civ 80.

the prosecution will inevitably lead to delay, this course may be advisable where a decision of the Board upholding the recall will potentially result in long periods of further detention.

13.16 However if the Board does uphold recall in advance of the hearing of any further charges by the criminal court, and the prisoner is subsequently found not guilty, then the Home Secretary does have a discretion to re-refer the original recall decision back to the Board where he considers that there is a realistic prospect that a different view may be taken by the Board.[28]

13.17 The Prison and Probation Services, the Police and the Home Office have agreed a joint protocol relating to the supervision and recall of offenders which came into effect from 1 February 2005.[29] This states that prosecutions should not be discontinued purely because an offender has been recalled to custody and in fact the commission of an offence while on licence 'is a significant public influence factor in charging and prosecuting an offender'.[30]

Consideration of the recall request by the RRS

13.18 The decision as to whether to recall the offender lies with the RRS. Where there is a divergence of view as to whether recall should be proceeded with, the Probation Service view can only be overridden by an RRS official of at least Higher Executive Officer (HEO) grade.

13.19 The fact that the executive decision to recall will be referred to the Board means that it will only be in exceptional cases that the courts will review the initial recall decision. This is because the referral to the Board is the appropriate remedy for the recall decision, and because the Board 'is in a better position than the court to assess where the balance should lie between, on the one hand, the risk to the public, and, on the other, the interests of the prisoner'.[31]

13.20 If RRS officials make the decision to recall on behalf of the Home Secretary the revocation order will be sent to:

28 *R (on the application of Francis) v Secretary of State for the Home Department* [2004] EWHC 2143 (Admin) para 49.

29 See PC 3/2005.

30 National Protocol para 8.3.

31 *R (on the application of Hare) v Secretary of State for the Home Department* [2003] EWHC 3336 (Admin); see also *R (on the application of Biggs) v Secretary of State for the Home Department* [2002] EWHC 1012 (Admin) which also confirmed that RRS is entitled to rely on the probation report in making the decision to recall and generally is not required to make further inquiries as to the facts behind the recommendation.

- the supervising probation officer;
- New Scotland Yard for entry onto the police national computer;
- the nominated police force communication centre;
- the releasing/holding prison.[32]

13.21 Once the revocation has been issued, if the offender is not already in custody (for example, having been recalled following arrest for a new offence) he/she is deemed to be 'unlawfully at large' until returned to prison.[33] The offender can then be arrested without warrant.[34] The National Protocol (see above) states that the police 'shall take speedy steps to arrest the offender'.[35] Time spent unlawfully at large is not then taken into account when calculating release dates and the eventual sentence expiry date.[36] The offender does not need to be aware of the revocation of licence to be unlawfully at large.[37] Following arrest, recalled offenders will be taken to the nearest remand prison.[38]

Referral of recall cases to the Parole Board

13.22 The prisoner should be informed of the reasons for the revocation of licence and of the right to make representations to the Parole Board.[39] PSO 6000 contains a model timetable for the initial consideration of recall cases.[40]

13.23 As the timetable shows, the procedure is that the Board initially consider the case on the papers and only if immediate release is not directed is the prisoner, in line with the *Smith and West* decision, offered an oral hearing.

13.24 A further change from the previous statutory framework relating to recall is that all cases are referred to the Board whether or not the prisoner makes representations.[41]

32 PSO 6000 para 7.7.4.
33 CJA 2003 s254(6).
34 Prison Act 1952 s49(1).
35 Para 10.1.
36 Prison Act 1952 s49(2) – see guidance in PSO 6650 Chapter 7.
37 *R (on the application of S) v Secretary of State for the Home Department* [2003] EWCA Civ 426, and this is the case even if the prisoner is wrongly released early from a sentence, see *R (on the application of Lunn) v Governor of HMP Moorland* [2005] EWHC 2558 (Admin).
38 PSO 6000 para 7.7.5.
39 CJA 2003 s254(2).
40 PSO 6000 para 7.81 – see box below.
41 CJA 2003 s254(3) – compare with CJA 1991 s39(4).

Timetable for consideration of determinate sentence recall

- Day 1 – return to custody of recalled prisoner. Notification to RRS by establishment of receipt of recalled prisoner. RRS issues representations against recall dossier to establishment. *The parole clerk must ensure the dossier is served on the prisoner immediately and that they understand that they have the right to make representations to the Parole Board.* RRS notify supervising probation officer of return to custody of prisoner, and give provisional panel date for review by Parole Board.
- Day 5 – Annex A [prisoner's intent to make representations] to be returned to RRS. All representations to be submitted to RRS by Day 14. *A Risk Management Plan must be submitted by the Probation Service simultaneously to RRS and the establishment, for disclosure to the prisoner.*
- Day 14 – Risk Management Plan and representations to be added to the recall dossier, and the complete dossier to be sent to the Parole Board, for distribution to panel members. Any additional representations made by the prisoner in response to the risk management plan must be submitted to RRS by no later than day 19.
- Day 20 – Parole Board panel sits. RRS notified of the outcome and result notified to Establishment. In all cases where the prisoner has submitted representations but is not given a release date, they will be advised that the decision to reject representations is provisional and they have the right to request an oral hearing. They have 14 days in which to seek an oral hearing. If they fail to respond within that time, the decision will be final.

Procedure and the Parole Board Rules

13.25 The Parole Board Rules (PBR) 2004 do not apply to recalled determinate sentenced prisoners although the Board treat such recalls in a similar way, with some modifications.[42] The main difference is that recall hearings in relation to determinate sentences prisoners (not including those serving extended sentences) will be heard by a single member rather than a panel of three. The main reason for this is clearly the resource implications,[43] but also a reflection that in *Smith*

42 The draft 2005 rules do apply the same procedures to determine recalls, with provision for hearings by a single member.

43 The *Smith and West* judgment, together with the new statutory requirement to consider all determinate sentence recalls, whether or not the prisoner makes representations, has had huge resource implications for the Board – its Business Plan for 2005/2006 estimated that there would be in the region of 3,500 oral hearings (including lifers) per year, a 600 per cent increase from the 495 held in the year 2002/2003.

and West the Lords did not uphold the absolute right to an oral hearing for determinate sentence recalls.[45]

13.26 Chapter 7 of PSO 6000 does set out a procedure that includes a provisional decision by a panel on the papers similar to the 'sift' procedure for lifers. The aim of this is to ensure that where for example there has been an obvious error in recalling the offender release can be directed without the necessity for a full hearing.

13.27 The recall hearing for a determinate sentence prisoner will be largely the same in terms of procedure as those for lifers, and similar considerations will apply in terms of preparation and evidence, bearing in mind the different test for release that will apply (see below). Although the Home Secretary can be represented at the hearing, in practice this is rare.

The test applied when considering recall

13.28 The Home Secretary has issued standard directions to the Parole Board under section 239(6) of the CJA 2003 (see Appendix 7). These directions were issued to come into operation at the same time as the new CJA 2003 recall procedures in April 2005. As with the previous directions, the key considerations for the Board are the degree to which the offender's continued liberty 'presents an unacceptable risk of a further offence being committed', and whether any licence breaches suggest that the 'objectives of licence supervision have been undermined'.[46]

13.29 However, the new directions do have a different emphasis to those in force previously,[47] which indicated that the type of re-offending that might justify recall did need to involve a risk to public safety, and which also suggested that any licence breaches could justify recall. By contrast, the new directions state that when determining whether to release a prisoner the Board 'should satisfy itself that the prisoner presents an acceptable risk to public safety and that adequate risk management arrangements are in place', and elsewhere 'the assumption is that the Parole Board will seek to re-release the prisoner or set a future release date in all cases where it is satisfied that the risk can be safely managed in the community'.

45 Paras 35, 50, 89.

46 The objectives of supervision being specified as to protect the public, to prevent re-offending and to ensure the prisoner's successful re-integration into the community.

47 From 2002–2005.

13.30 This change of emphasis in the new directions does mean that cases involving challenges to recalls under the old regime should be treated with caution.[48]

13.31 The directions to the Board state that where the Board consider that the initial decision was 'inappropriate, the prisoner should be re-released as soon as it is practicable to do so'. In deciding whether any developments since release justify recall, the Board is not solely concerned with examining the reasons given by the RRS for making the recall decision.[49] Although when determinate sentence prisoners are released automatically (in all cases except where CJA 1991 DCR cases or extended sentence prisoners are released at PED), there does not have to be an assessment by the Board that risk has increased since the initial release to justify recall (as there has to be with lifers, or those previously released on the Board's recommendation), it is implicit in the statutory scheme that there has to be some further behaviour by the offender that gives rise to concern.[50] This is also reflected in current Probation Service guidance, which notes that that a recommendation for recall is based on a judgment that the risk that an offender is assessed as posing has 'increased to the point where recall to custody is necessary to protect the public and prevent further offending'.[51]

13.32 The applicable test in extended sentence cases is dealt with below (see paras 13.37–13.43).

48 For example, *R (on the application of Morecock) v Parole Board* [2004] EWHC (Admin) where the court accepted that recall could be justified where there was no risk to public safety; and *R (on the application of Buxton) v Parole Board* [2004] EWHC 1930 (Admin) which held that in deciding whether there was an 'unacceptable' risk the Board was not required to balance compassionate factors in the prisoner's favour, if these were not relevant to the level of assessed risk. It also held that the Board did not have to consider whether recall would breach the prisoner's Convention rights under articles 3 and 8.

49 See *R (on the application of Jackson) v Parole Board* [2003] EWHC 2437 (Admin), although compare with *Rodgers v Brixton Prison Governor* [2003] EWHC 1923, where a recall was held invalid for failing to give the right reasons at the right time.

50 *R (on the application of Irving) v Parole Board* [2004] EWHC 2863. See also comments of Sedley LJ in *R (on the application of West) v Parole Board* [2002] EWCA Civ 1641 para 43 that recall 'in the case of a short-term prisoner ... results from an assessment of risk to the public in the light of new developments; in the case of the discretionary release of a long-term prisoner it represents a revision in the light of developments of the Board's earlier assessment of risk'.

51 PC 3/2005 para 20.

The Parole Board decision

13.33 Where the Board recommends immediate release on licence, the Home Secretary must give effect to the recommendation.[52] If the Board does not recommend immediate release, and there is 12 months or more before the prisoner's unconditional release date it has the following options:

- it must either fix a future date for the prisoner's release on licence;[53] or
- fix a date for the prisoner's next review by the Board[54] which cannot be more than 12 months from the Board's decision.[55] At subsequent reviews the Board has the same range of powers as on the first referral.[56]

13.34 For CJA 2003 SDS sentence prisoners this obviously gives the Parole Board control over whether the recalled prisoner is released up until the end of the sentence (when, if still detained, the prisoner must be released unconditionally). The position in relation to CJA determinate sentence prisoners is more complicated (see paras 12.36–12.40), as although the statutory framework appears to allow for detention beyond the initial licence expiry date following recall, the guidance to the Board states that they should be released at this point anyway (the three-quarter point of the sentence).

Release on HDC and recall

13.35 The CJA 1991 provides that where a prisoner serving a sentence imposed for an offence committed before 4 April 2005 is released on HDC, where the curfew condition is breached, or where electronic monitoring is no longer possible, the offender can be recalled solely in relation to the curfew condition.[57] This provision is preserved for HDC recalls after 4 April 2005 for CJA 1991 cases.[58] In

52 CJA 2003 s254(4).
53 CJA 2003 s256(1)(a) which must be given effect to by the Home Secretary – s256(4).
54 CJA 2003 s256(1)(b).
55 CJA 2003 s256(2).
56 CJA 2003 s256(5).
57 CJA 1991 s38A.
58 See Criminal Justice Act 2003 (Commencement No 8 and Transitional and Saving Provisions) Order 2005 SI No Sch 2 para 19, and this is of course the only ground of recall for those serving sentences of under 12 months.

these circumstances the recall is reviewed by the Home Secretary[59] and if upheld the prisoner is released at the normal automatic release date.[60] If the offender's behaviour during the HDC licence period was in breach of other licence conditions, recall can be effected in the normal way[61] and the recall referred to the Parole Board.

13.36 The drafting of the CJA 2003 is confusing in that the power to recall those on HDC licence where the offence dates from 4 April 2005 appears to relate to failure to comply with 'any condition' in the licence,[62] not just the curfew condition. This wording makes it unclear whether the Home Secretary also has the power to recall those on HDC under the section 254 powers, which may have the bizarre effect of requiring him to recall those on HDC, even where the grounds raise serious public safety concerns, under provisions that would then necessitate automatic release at the normal halfway point.[63] It is difficult to see this as the Act's intention, which must be, as with the CJA 1991, to enable those on HDC both to be recalled on grounds relating to the curfew condition (which will not affect re-release at the half-way point of the sentence) and for other licence breaches (which will allow detention beyond that point and a review by the Board).[64]

Recall of extended sentence prisoners

Article 5 and extended sentences

13.37 From 4 April 2005 all extended sentence offenders (both under the CJAs 1991 and 2003) are subject to the same statutory framework of recall as other determinate sentence prisoners.[65] However, there are important differences in how the Board has to approach these recalls. This is because the extended sentence is not like a normal determinate sentence, but is rather a hybrid between a determinate and indeterminate sentence.

13.38 The extension period that follows the custodial term is not imposed as punishment, and the statutory presumption is that it will

59 CJA 1991 s38(A)(3).

60 CJA 1991 s33A.

61 Now under CJA 2003 s254.

62 CJA 2003 s255(1)(b).

63 CJA 2003 s244.

64 See PSO 6000 para 7.7.4 which proceeds on this basis.

65 CJA 2003 s254.

be served in the community (as the extension period begins at what would otherwise be the LED for CJA 1991 cases, and at the end of the custodial period in CJA 2003 cases). As the extension period is purely preventative, the legality of detention during it requires the supervision of a court-like body under article 5(4) of the Convention, as the degree to which an offender poses a risk to the public is clearly susceptible to change. Without such supervision there is a risk of arbitrary detention, as whether custody is actually necessary to protect the public during the extension period cannot be anticipated by the sentencing court.[66]

13.39 As article 5 applies to the recall of extended sentence prisoners during the extension period, there must be a causal link between the grounds for recall and the imposition of the sentence. This gives rise to differing tests the Board must apply when considering CJA 1991 cases as against CJA 2003 cases. Extended sentences imposed for offences committed before 4 April 2005 can be imposed for sexual and violent offences where the court is satisfied that the licence period applicable to what would be the commensurate sentence is inadequate to prevent the commission of further offences and to secure rehabilitation.[67] Accordingly, a CJA 1991 extended sentence prisoner's recall can only be in accordance with article 5 by reference to a risk that further sexual or violent offences may be committed.[68]

13.40 By contrast, the CJA 2003 extended sentence is only imposed where the sentencing court makes a finding that the offender poses a risk of 'serious harm'.[69] In these cases the test on recall is therefore a 'serious harm' one as with the indeterminate sentences. Further, recall may be justified where the risk has become unmanageable in the community.

13.41 An important distinction between extended sentences and indeterminate sentences is that, as noted above, the former are released automatically at the end of the custodial period. This means that the Board must also approach these recalls on the basis that the 'default position' is the offender's liberty, and so must be positively satisfied that detention is necessary to protect the public.[70]

66 *R (Sim) v Parole Board* [2004] 2 WLR 1170.

67 Powers of Criminal Courts (Sentencing) Act 2000 (PCC(S)A) 2000 s85.

68 *R (Sim) v Parole Board* [2003] EWHC 152 (Admin) para 44.

69 CJA 2003 ss227(1)(b), 228(1)(b).

70 *R (Sim) v Parole Board* [2004] 2 WLR 1170 para 51 where the Court of Appeal upheld a Human Rights Act 1998 s3 construction of the statutory test to give this effect.

13.42 If extended sentence prisoners are released at the first opportunity by the Board's recommendation (halfway through the custodial term) then they may be on licence for some time before the extension period begins, and so there may be recalls of extended sentence prisoners where the Board is entitled to apply the same test as for other determinate sentence prisoners (however there may be an argument that for CJA 2003 cases, article 5 will be engaged from the half way point of the custodial term in any event (see Chapter 6 above). In any event, in practical terms it may be difficult to apply different tests for recalled extended sentence prisoners depending on when they were recalled. The Board's practice in relation to CJA 1991 cases appears to have been to apply the *Sim* test even if at the date of hearing the custodial term had not expired.

13.43 Where article 5 does apply, the Board is not bound by any directions made by the Home Secretary as to matters to be taken into account in deciding whether to release the prisoner.[71] However, this is not evident from the guidance in PSO 6000 which suggests that in extended sentence recall cases the Board is to apply the same directions as in normal determinate sentence cases.[72] This is also evident by the RRS practice of including a set of the directions in dossiers for extended sentence prisoners. This is misleading for cases involving recalls or detention during the extension period for the reasons outlined above, and the Board should be reminded of this when considering cases.

Extended sentences and the Parole Board Rules

13.44 The procedure for recalls for extended sentence cases is intended to be covered by the Parole Board Rules and so procedure will be the same as for lifers (see below). However, the initial paper consideration is as set out at para 13.22. The test the Parole Board applies in relation to extended sentence prisoners is that release must be directed where it 'is satisfied that it is no longer necessary for the protection of the public that the prisoner should be confined'.[73] Although the equivalent provision in the CJA 1991, section 44A was not saved in the commencement order, the Board will apply the same test, which must be read as requiring the Board to be positively satisfied that the relevant

71 *R (Girling) v Parole Board and Home Secretary* [2005] EWHC 546 (Admin).

72 PSO 6000 para 8.6.2.

73 CJA 2003 s247 – this is expressed as applying to CJA 2003 extended sentence cases only (s247(1).

risk is present (see above). The Home Secretary will normally be represented at the recall hearing by a caseworker from the RRS.

Further annual reviews

13.45 If the Parole Board do not direct release there is an entitlement to further reviews at least annually (see para 13.33 above) if there is sufficient time before the automatic release date (at the end of the extension period for CJA 1991 cases, and at sentence expiry for CJA 2003 cases). The prisoner is entitled to oral hearings at the annual reviews.[75] The process begins 26 weeks after the Board's confirmation of the recall[76] and the prisoner is given a choice of paper review or oral hearing.[77] The procedure is the same as under the Parole Board Rules. The Home Secretary is not normally represented at such hearings.[78]

Recalls and 'return to custody' orders

13.46 Those subject to the provisions of the CJA 1991 (including those serving sentences of less than 12 months for offences committed on or after 4 April 2005)[79] remain 'at risk' of being ordered to return to prison on sentencing for a new offence committed before the sentence expiry date of the first sentence, to a maximum of the period between the commission of the new offence and the sentence expiry of the first.[80] This is a separate power to the recall provisions and the use of one does not preclude the other. However, because of the possible severity of the impact on the prisoner, it has been held that where a prisoner has been recalled, the sentencing court should take this into account when deciding whether and for how long to order a return to prison, and similarly that any order to return should be a relevant factor in deciding whether to recall.[81]

75 For the applicable process see PSO 6000 para 8.12.
76 PSO 6000 para 8.9.1.
77 PSO 6000 para 8.11.
78 PSO 6000 para 8.13.2.
79 Criminal Justice Act 2003 (Commencement No.8 and Transitional and Saving Provisions) Order 2005 SI No 950 Sch 2 para 29.
80 PCC(S)A 2000 s116.
81 *R (on the application of Akhtar (T'Herah)) v Secretary of State for the Home Department* [2001] EWHC Admin 38.

The recall of those serving indeterminate sentences

13.47 As at 30 June 2005 there were 1,362 life licencees in the community under active supervision by the Probation Service. In the period between April 2004 and March 2005, 299 indeterminate sentence prisoners were released on licence and 90 were recalled to prison.[82]

The decision to recall

13.48 LRRS, on behalf of the Home Secretary, can revoke the licence and recall those serving indeterminate sentences in the community either when this is recommended by the Parole Board[83] or in urgent cases, where it is 'expedient in the public interest', without such a referral.[84] There is no procedure to allow the offender to make representations to the Board in relation to initial recommendations for recall under the non-urgent process.

13.49 It is much more usual for indeterminate sentence prisoners to be recalled under the urgent procedure without a prior referral to the Board. However in these circumstances the Home Secretary has adopted an extra-statutory process of referring the decision to the Board for a review, before the 'formal', statutory referral process that leads to an oral hearing is activated (see below). Again this is not a process the offender will play a part in. If as a result of this referral the Board recommend release such a recommendation is not binding on the Secretary of State, unlike a direction under the formal referral process.[85]

13.50 When an indeterminate sentence prisoner is recalled, a hearing is required in accordance with article 5(4) to consider whether the detention is lawful. This does not mean that the statutory scheme whereby the Home Secretary can recall the offender and then refer the matter to the Board for a hearing breaches article 5.[86]

82 LRRS *Lifer News*, Summer 2005 Part 10.

83 Crime (Sentencing) Act (C(S)A) 1997 s32(1).

84 C(S)A 1997 s32(2).

85 *R v Secretary of State for the Home Department, ex p Cummings* [2001] EWCA Civ 45, CA, unreported. Further, this extra-statutory role in the executive decision to recall has been held not compromise the Board's impartiality when considering the formal referral: *R v Parole Board ex p Watson* [1996] 1 WLR 906.

86 *R (Hirst) v Home Secretary and Parole Board* [2005] EWHC 1480 (Admin) – which rejected a claim that in this situation article 5(1)(c) and (3) applied, as these were relevant only where the detention was in anticipation of criminal proceedings.

Further criminal charges/prosecution

13.51 The comments on further criminal charges in relation to determinate sentences (see paras 13.13–13.17 above) also apply to indeterminate sentences. There is a real risk that an approach that endeavours to ignore a further charge, while purporting to make an assessment of risk based upon the behaviour surrounding it, will have unfair results (and may result in a finding that is implicitly taken as a finding of guilt whatever subsequently occurs in relation to the prosecution of the criminal charge). While individual cases may be different, it will often be advisable to seek a deferral pending the disposal of the criminal charge.

The effect of recall

13.52 Once the licence has been revoked, the offender is unlawfully at large until returned to custody.[87] On arrest the offender will be returned to the nearest local prison.[88] Normally lifers will then be transferred to the nearest Category C prison that holds lifers unless there are further charges or risk issues that require them to be held in a local prison.[89]

Referral to the Board

13.53 The recalled prisoner has to be informed of reasons for the recall and of the right to make representations to the Parole Board.[90] Reasons must be given promptly.[91] Although the statute states that only prisoners who make representations or who are recalled under the emergency provisions have their cases referred to the Parole Board[92] for a full review of the recall, the practice is for all recalls to be so referred.

The test for release

13.54 Once the recall is referred to the Parole Board it has the power to direct the prisoner's release, and the Home Secretary has to give

87 C(S)A 1997 s32(6).

88 Prison, Probation and Police Services *Joint protocol on the supervision and recall of offenders* para 9.5 – see PC 3/2005.

89 PSI 8/2004 para 30.

90 C(S)A 1997 s32(3).

91 *Hirst* (fn 86 above) held that the duty in article 5(2) was also applicable in this context and that a failure to give reasons for eight days breached this requirement.

92 C(S)A 1997 s32(4).

effect to that direction.[93] The test for release on recall is the same as for initial release and so the Board will be considering whether the circumstances leading to recall show that the prisoner poses a substantial risk of committing further offences of serious harm.[94]

13.55 The Board in applying this test on recall is not solely bound to consider the validity of the reasons given by the Home Secretary for recall. For example, the Board can uphold a recall, not for the reasons given in the revocation decision, but because of other behaviour that comes to light before the hearing. As those serving indeterminate sentences will previously have satisfied the Board that they were eligible for release, there must be relevant new material to justify the reconsideration of the risk they pose to the public before they can be recalled.[95] If there is no new information of concern and the original reasons for recall are held to be invalid, this would mean that the Board would not lawfully be able to uphold the recall.

13.56 While risk to the public is the issue, if the prisoner's conduct means that supervision arrangements have fundamentally broken down so that the risk to the public is effectively unmanageable in the community, then this may also justify recall.[96]

The recall hearing and the Parole Board Rules

13.57 The PBR 2004 apply to recalled indeterminate sentenced prisoners.[97] However, in recognition of the need to consider recall cases expeditiously, the normal timetable is not applicable and any time limits should be set by the panel chair taking into account both 'the desirability of the Board reaching an early decision in the prisoner's case and the need to ensure fairness'.[98] For the same reason, rules 11–13, which deal with provisional decisions before a single member without a hearing ('sift' decisions), do not apply to recalls.[99]

13.58 The contents of a dossier prepared for a recall hearing is prescribed in Schedule 2 to the PBR. The dossier should specifically contain the Probation Service's reports that led to the revocation of the licence,

93 C(S)A 1997 s32(5).

94 *R v Parole Board ex p Watson* [1996] 1 WLR 906; the grounds for detention must have a 'causal link' with the purpose of the sentence, which is to detain dangerous offenders: *Stafford v UK* (2002) 35 EHHR 32.

95 Ibid p 916D.

96 *R (on the application of Sim) v Parole Board* [2003] EWHC 152 (Admin) para 44.

97 PBR 2004 r2(i).

98 PBR r24(2)(a).

99 PBR r24(1)(a).

the Home Secretary's reasons for recall and details of any Parole Board decisions recommending recall. These will be appended to the dossier prepared for the hearing that directed the prisoner's release, and the Board's decision directing release.

13.59 Often the Probation Service report leading to the recall will rely on unsubstantiated evidence, or multiple hearsay statements, in support of the recall. It will rarely include first-hand evidence of any allegations that have led to the recall, and will often provide very little in the way of detail. However, as noted above (see para 9.13), as the notion of a 'burden of proof' is largely irrelevant in the parole context it is not enough for the prisoner to say that recall has not been justified because of the quality of the evidence.

13.60 Accordingly, it is important for representatives to ensure that, if the allegations in the recall dossier are contested, that LRRS and the Probation Service are required to provide proper evidence to substantiate them, so that this may be properly challenged at the hearing. This may necessitate an early request for directions from the Board[100] requiring LRRS to obtain further documents, witness evidence or to arrange for the attendance of witnesses for cross-examination.[101] However, as with other oral hearings[102] there is no prohibition on hearsay evidence before the Board and the issue will be weight rather than admissibility.

13.61 Recall hearings are likely to involve more contested facts than those considering initial release and this will impact upon the approach the panel will adopt. In most cases, rather than the lifer manager or governor from the holding prison representing the Home Secretary, a representative from LRRS will attend the hearing or in serious cases, counsel instructed by the Treasury Solicitor may attend. Accordingly, recall hearings are often more adversarial and panels should be encouraged to adopt a more exacting approach to evidence (for example, witnesses of contested facts should not be present in the hearing before giving evidence). LRRS will in all cases ask the supervising probation officer to attend the hearing to give evidence as to the circumstances of recall.

13.62 The recall decision may be associated with the breakdown of the release plan, such as the loss of a hostel place. In preparation for the

100 PBR 2004 r8.

101 Including where necessary by securing attendance by witness summons from the court under Civil Procedure Rules (CPR) 34.4 – see *R (on the application of Brooks v Parole Board* [2004] EWCA Civ 80 para 32.

102 See Chapter 10 and *R (on the application of Sim) v Parole Board* [2003] EWCA Civ 1845 para 57.

recall hearing it is important to remember that as well as challenging the basis of recall, the Board will want to know, if minded to direct release, what the release plan will be. If the material in the dossier does not include sufficient details of a release plan, then a direction should be sought from the Board for a further report from the Probation Service. As the supervising probation officer will normally have recommended recall, it can prove difficult to persuade the Probation Service to put a release plan in place. Although a local probation board is under a duty to ensure that there is sufficient provision for providing accommodation in hostels to those on licence[103] this does not impose a duty owed to individual prisoners.[104]

Decisions

13.63 If the Parole Board directs release[105] LRRS, on behalf of the Home Secretary, must give effect to the direction.[106] Decisions, as with those relating to initial release, must be given to the parties within seven days of the end of the hearing. If decision is for release, LRRS aim to make arrangements for release and issue the licence within five working days. If release is refused, it will be for LRRS to decide on the timing of the next review, which cannot be more than two years from the Parole Board decision.[107] It is open to the Board, if it does not direct release, to recommend a transfer to open conditions as with pre-release reviews, but only if the recall referral specifically requests advice on this issue.[108]

103 Criminal Justice and Court Services Act 2000 s5(1)(a).

104 *R (on the application of Irving) v London Probation Board* [2005] EWHC 605 (Admin) – where permission to bring a claim for judicial review was refused in circumstances where the had Board upheld a recall because the Probation Service could not provide accommodation suitable for the offender.

105 C(S)A 1997 s32(5).

106 C(S)A 1997 s32(5) refers to the Board directing 'immediate release' – this means that if release cannot be given effect to *immediately* then the direction may not be binding on the Home Secretary (see *R v Home Secretary ex p Gunnell* [1998] Crim LR 170 and *R v Home Secretary ex p De Lara* (HC 22.3.95, unreported).

107 C(S)A 1997 s28(7)(b).

108 *R (on the application of Mills) v Secretary of State for the Home Department and the Parole Board* [2005] EWHC 2508 (Admin), evidence to the court was that referrals only exceptionally make such requests.

CHAPTER 14

Remedies

Non-judicial remedies

14.1 There may be decisions or failings made during the course of a parole review, that are not decisions of the Board itself, that the prisoner will want to challenge. For example, there may be inclusion in the dossier by the parole clerk of material that should not be there, or an unreasonable delay by the Lifer Review and Recall Section (LRRS) in referring a case to the Board. While decisions and/or failures of the personnel at the individual prison, probation officers and those of the National Offender Management Service (NOMS) officials can ultimately be challenged in judicial review proceedings (see below), there are also complaints procedures that the courts will usually expect to be used before proceeding to litigation.[1]

Prison Service complaints procedure

14.2 Detailed guidance on the Prison Service complaints procedure has been issued.[2] The complaints procedure covers decisions or failings of departments within NOMS, such as LRRS and the Release and Recall Section (RRS). If the complaint is in relation to something that has occurred at the prison, then the prisoner should, in the first instance, submit a COMP 1 form, which should be freely available on the wing, to which there should normally be a response within three days for normal complaints.[3] If the prisoner remains unhappy with the response, then he/she can submit a COMP 1A form within seven days of the first response. This should be responded to by someone at a higher level than issued the first response[4] within seven days for normal complaints. If still dissatisfied, the prisoner can, on the same COMP 1A within seven days, complain to the governor, on whose behalf there should be a response within seven days. Where the matter is particularly 'sensitive or serious', a complaint on COMP 2 can be made directly to the governor.[5]

14.3 If the matter does not relate to a failing at the prison, then the it is a 'reserved subject' and the complaint should be dealt with by the appropriate department at Prison Service Headquarters or NOMS.[6]

1 *R (on the application of Cowl) v Plymouth City Council* [2001] EWCA Civ 1935.

2 PSO 2510.

3 See Chapter 13 of PSO 2510 for time limits.

4 PSO 2510 para 8.4.2.

5 PSO 2510 Chapter 9.

6 See PSO 2510 Chapter 10.

So complaints about the RRS or LRRS should be treated as reserved subjects and forwarded to them for a response.

14.4 Going through the Prison Service complaints procedure is a prerequisite of making a complaint to the Prisons and Probation Ombudsman (see below). However, if a solicitor has raised the issue complained of with the establishment and has received a response on behalf of the governor or on behalf of the relevant decision maker at Prison Service Headquarters, LRRS or RRS, then this will normally be accepted by the Ombudsman as sufficient to trigger the acceptance of a complaint to his office if the matter is otherwise within his remit. (The Ombudsman is currently Stephen Shaw.)

Probation Service complaints

14.5 The Probation Service covers complaints made by those under probation supervision, or the victim of someone under such supervision.[7] Complaints in relation to matters more than a year old will not normally be investigated. The process is started by making a complaint in writing to the relevant Probation Area's Chief Officer. Within five working days of receiving the letter, the Chief Officer should respond to say how the complaint will be dealt with and a timeframe for a response.

14.6 If the complainant is not satisfied with the response, he/she can write within 15 working days to the Secretary of the local Probation Board to appeal. The appeal should be looked at by a panel including at least one Board member, and the outcome will normally be sent within 20 working days of the receipt of the appeal. A complaint can then be made to the Prisons and Probation Ombudsman.

Parole Board complaints procedure

14.7 The Board does have a complaints procedure (available at the Board's website[8]), however this is not for challenging Board decisions,[9] although it appears that it could be used to complain about administrative failings in handling referrals. Complaints should generally be made within six months. If the complaint cannot be dealt with by the person receiving the complaint, it will be treated as a formal complaint and investigated with a response normally within 20 working

7 See Probation Service *Making a complaint*.

8 See www.paroleboard.gov.uk/Complaints%20Procedure.doc.

9 Para 1.5.

days.[10]) If the complainant remains dissatisfied, there is an appeal to the Chief Executive, which should be resolved within three months of the start of the process.[11] If still dissatisfied, the complainant should be informed of his/her right to complain to the Parliamentary Ombudsman,[12] although such complaints need to be referred through a member of parliament.

14.8 Complaints about Parole Board decisions are dealt with by the Post-Panel Team of the Parole Board Secretariat, who will respond to concerns raised directly about decisions, and to letters sent by solicitors on prisoners' behalf.

The Prisons and Probation Ombudsman

14.9 The Prisons and Probation Ombudsman has no jurisdiction over the Parole Board and cannot deal with complaints about its decisions. The Ombudsman will, however, consider complaints where either the Prison or Probation Complaints process has been exhausted.[13] A complaint must be made to the Ombudsman within one calendar month of the final reply in the Prison or Probation Service complaints procedure.

14.10 If the complaint to the Prison or Probation Service has not received a response, the Ombudsman may investigate the complaint when the failure to respond reaches six weeks in relation to the Prison Service, or 45 working days in relation to the Probation Service. Unless the delay is the fault of the Prison or Probation Service (by, for example, failing to respond to a complaint), the Ombudsman will not investigate a complaint where the matter complained of is more than 12 months old.

14.11 The Ombudsman has a target date of 12 weeks for the completion of investigations into complaints (although the office will aim to deal with urgent complaints more quickly). If the complaint is upheld the Ombudsman can make a recommendation to the Director General of the Prison Service, the Director General of the Probation Service or the Home Secretary depending on the subject matter of the complaint. Even though there is no duty to accept Ombudsman recommendations, they are accepted in the vast majority of cases. The

10 Para 12.5.
11 Para 12.5.
12 Para 8.16.
13 For details on which complaints can be investigated and time limits, see the Terms of Reference annexed to the Ombudsman's Annual Report 2004–2005.

Ombudsman does review the merits of decisions not just the fairness of procedures.

14.12 Before the 2005 election a bill was introduced into parliament to put the Prisons and Probation Ombudsman on a statutory footing,[14] and is expected to be re-introduced to parliament.

Judicial remedies

Judicial review

14.13 Decisions of the Parole Board are outside the remit of the Prisons and Probation Ombudsman. If a prisoner tries to submit a complaint about a Parole Board decision under the Prison Service complaints procedure this will be forwarded to the Board, but this will rarely result in the Board agreeing to reconsider the matter or requesting a re-referral by the Home Secretary.[15]

14.14 In practice, the only remedy available to challenge decisions of the Board is judicial review (JR). A detailed analysis of the law and practice relating to JR is outside the scope of this book. However, it is important to note the following:

- In a claim for JR the court is not generally considering an appeal against the merits of a decision, but rather the lawfulness of the decision making process. The court will, to the degree that is appropriate on the facts, come to its own view as to whether there has been a breach of rights under the European Convention on Human Rights (ECHR).[16]
- A consequence of this is that the court will rarely resolve disputed issues of fact and will normally consider cases solely on consideration of the relevant papers (although in exceptional cases witness evidence may be called).
- Remedies in JR claims are discretionary, which means that even where there are good grounds, the court may refuse relief if, for

14 The Management of Offenders and Sentencing Bill, which would have renamed the Ombudsman Her Majesty's Commissioner for Offender Management and Prisons.

15 See Chapter 6 paras 6.49–6.50 for instances where this might happen.

16 *R (on the application of Daly) v Secretary of State for the Home Department* [2001] 2 AC 532, however in Parole Board cases the question as to whether there has a breach of article 5 of the Convention (that is a break in the 'causal link' between the detention and the basis of the sentence) will depend precisely on a factually based assessment of risk that the court will accept is primarily for the Board to consider.

example, the claimant has acted unreasonably (for example by failing to make full and frank disclosure of all material facts), or where relief would be academic, or perhaps most importantly, where the claimant has failed to make use of an adequate alternative remedy (although the court will consider in individual circumstances whether, for example, the applicable complaints procedure is adequate).

- In relation to Parole Board decisions the court will start from the premise that the Board is the expert body set up by statute in order to assess the risk posed to the public by offenders (see below).

Procedure

14.15 JR is governed by Part 54 of the Civil Procedure Rules 1998 (CPR).[17] The pre-action protocol for judicial review requires claimants to send a letter before claim setting out the reasons why it is alleged that the decision is unlawful and giving a time limit for a response (normally 14 days, but this can be less in urgent cases). This is to try to ensure that defendants have an opportunity to respond to claims before they are issued at court so as to avoid unnecessary litigation. Compliance with the pre-action protocol does not affect the time limit for issuing the claim.

14.16 JR claims must be issued in the Administrative Court Office promptly, and in any event within three months of the decision complained of, unless there is good reason for the delay.[18] The claim form (N461) must be served on the defendant and any interested party within seven days of issue.[19] In urgent cases, claimants can ask for expedition by filing, together with the claim form, an urgent consideration form (N463). The defendant, within 21 days of service of the claim form, should serve an acknowledgement of service.[20] A judge will then consider on the papers whether permission for the claim to proceed should be given. If permission is not given, then the claimant can request a hearing to renew the application.[21] If permission is granted, then the defendant should file grounds for resisting the

17 See the DCA CPR homepage for the Rules and pre-action protocols: www.dca.gov.uk/civil/procrules_fin. See also guidance on JR claims on Court Service website: www.hmcourts-service.gov.uk/cms/1220.htm.

18 CPR 54.5.

19 CPR 54.7.

20 CPR 54.8.

21 CPR 54.12.

claim and any evidence in support within 35 days after service of the order giving permission.[22] The claim will then proceed to a full hearing. At the hearing the court has the power to issue:

- *A mandatory order* – An order requiring the public body to do something. For example, where there has been unlawful delay by LRRS in referring a matter to the Parole Board or in arranging the release of a prisoner following the Board's direction, or by the prison in producing the dossier.
- *A prohibiting order* – An order preventing the public body from doing something. For example, to prevent the Board proceeding to determine a matter by use of an unlawful procedure.[23]
- *A quashing order* – An order quashing the public body's decision. This is the most common order sought in Parole Board cases. It has the effect of requiring the Board to make a further decision. The court in JR proceedings will not substitute its own view.
- *A declaration* – Where the court sets out in its decision a principle of law, or what the respective rights of the parties are.
- *Injunctions* – An order prohibiting or requiring a body to do something – normally sought on an interim basis.
- *Damages* – A claim for damages, including damages under the Human Rights Act (HRA) 1998, can be sought in JR claims, although this cannot be the only purpose of the claim. Damages can only be awarded if they could have been awarded in an ordinary claim, so a private law cause of action (such as negligence or false imprisonment) or right to damages under the HRA has to be established.[24]
- *Interim and other relief* – The court has the power to order interim remedies, normally an interim injunction[25] and there is inherent jurisdiction to grant bail, or to grant a stay.[26]

22 CPR 54.14.

23 See, for example, *R (on the application of Roberts) v Parole Board* [2005] UKHL 45, although such challenges will be exceptional as the court will normally want to consider the legality of any procedure in the context of the Board's final decision: see *R (on the application of Hirst) v Parole Board* [2002] EWHC 1592 (Admin).

24 In this context a claim for damages is most likely to arise where there has been a breach of requirement for a speedy review under article 5(4).

25 CPR 25.2.

26 CPR 54.10.

Who is the right defendant?

14.17 If the decision is one of the Board, then as it has its own legal identity, it is the appropriate defendant. If the decision is within the remit of the holding prison (for example, in failing to disclose a dossier) then the defendant will be the governor of the holding prison. If the decision is made by the RRS or LRRS (for example, a refusal to accept the recommendation of the Board to transfer a lifer to an open prison) then, as those bodies make decisions on behalf of the Home Secretary, the correct defendant is the Secretary of State for the Home Department. It will often be the case that there is more than one defendant, for example where there is not only a challenge to the Parole Board decision, but also to LRRS decision on the timing of the subsequent review.

Grounds for seeking judicial review

14.18 This is a large and complex area, but in the parole context a brief outline of the grounds upon which JR might be sought is (although there can be considerable overlap between these broad categories):

- where there is an error of law (for example, where the Board applies the wrong test for release, or acts outside of its statutory powers, takes into account irrelevant matters or fails to consider relevant ones);
- where there is procedural impropriety, that is unfairness in the decision making process (for example, failure to disclose documents to enable representations to be made);
- where the decision is irrational, that is so unreasonable as to be unsustainable, or where there is an abuse of power;
- where the body in question has breached the requirement to act compatibly with rights under the ECHR.[28]

14.19 There is obviously a considerable degree of overlap between these categories.

Particular considerations in Parole Board decisions

The Board as an expert body

14.20 The starting point for the court will be that the Parole Board has been entrusted by parliament to make the sometimes difficult decisions as

28 HRA 1998 s6.

to when prisoners should be released. This means that there will be occasions where, although the court may express a view that the decision in question is not one which it would have made, that the Board's decision will be upheld.

14.21 By way of illustration, in one instance a prisoner serving a ten-year sentence imposed for drug offences challenged a refusal of parole. By the time of his review he was in an open prison, engaged in community work and was supported in his application by both the prison and home probation officers. The Parole Board refused parole on the basis that he had not attended a formal offending behaviour course, notwithstanding the fact that this was not considered necessary by the report writers. The judge, in refusing the claim for judicial review, stated:

> The panel reached a decision which is not the one which I would have reached if I had been in their position. That, however, is nothing to the point. The Parole Board have both experience and expertise in making decisions of this character which judges lack. Furthermore, the decision in question has been entrusted by Parliament to the Parole Board, not the judiciary.[29]

Reasons

14.22 The Board is required to give reasons for its decisions.[30] Where there is a duty to give reasons, the courts require them to be 'proper, adequate and intelligible'.[31] In relation to parole decisions in respect of determinate sentence prisoners where statutory directions have been issued, the courts have held that the reasons given must:

> focus on the question of risk to which their decision is directed. Full account must be taken, as they affect any individual prisoner, of the matters listed in the Secretary of State's directions ... the Board should identify in broad terms the matters judged by the Board as pointing towards and against a continuing risk of offending and the Board's reasons for striking the balance as it does. Needless to say the letter should summarise the considerations which have in fact led to the final decision. It would be wrong to prescribe any standard form of decision letter and it would be wrong to require elaborate or impeccable standards of draftmanship.[32]

29 *R v Parole Board ex p Blake* HC (2000) 23 February, unreported, para 54.

30 See Parole Board Rules r20, and PSO 6000 para 5.19.

31 *In re Poyser and Mills' Arbitration* [1964] 2 QB 467.

32 *R v Parole Board ex p Oyston* (2000) *Independent* 17 April, CA.

How the Board approaches denial of guilt

14.23 This has been the subject of a large amount of litigation, and there is a common misapprehension that those that deny guilt are refused parole for that reason. The courts have held that, as the Board is carrying out an assessment of risk, the fact that the prisoner does not accept guilt of the offence will be a relevant, but not decisive, consideration. The Court of Appeal has approved this summary of the correct approach:

(1) The Parole Board must assume the prisoner's guilt of the offence or offences of which the prisoner has been convicted.

(2) The Board's first duty is to assess the risk to the public that the prisoner might commit further offences if the prisoner is paroled.

(3) It is therefore unlawful for the Board to deny a recommendation for parole *on the ground only* that the prisoner continues to deny his/her guilt.

(4) But in some cases, particularly cases of serious persistent violent of sexual crime, a continued denial of guilt will almost inevitably mean that the risk posed by the prisoner to the public or a section of the public if the prisoner is paroled either remains high or, at least, cannot be objectively assessed. In such cases the Board is entitled (perhaps obliged) to deny a recommendation.[33]

14.24 Denial of guilt does not necessarily prevent the offender completing accredited offending behaviour courses (see Chapter 4), and in any event the prisoner may demonstrate a reduced risk of re-offending in other ways than by completion of courses (for example, a commitment to avoid a lifestyle associated with offending).

Successful challenges

14.25 As challenges to the merits of the decision will rarely be successful, it is in cases where there has been a failure to apply the appropriate test, or procedural failings that claims for judicial review are likely to be more successful. Examples of such cases where there have been successful challenges by way of judicial review of Parole Board decisions are:

- *Where the Board's reasons are inadequate*. For example, by failing to indicate that a significant matter in the prisoner's favour has been taken into account.[34]

33 *R v Parole Board ex p Oyston* (2000) *Independent* 17 April, CA.

34 Ibid.

- *Where the Board misapplies any statutory directions it is required to follow.* For example, when required by directions to balance the risk to the public against the benefits to the prisoner in its decision making, the Board must indicate how competing factors have been balanced.[35]
- *Where the Board makes its decision on the basis of factually inaccurate material in the dossier material to the assessment of risk.*[36]
- *Where the Board has breached the requirements of procedural fairness.* For example, where it considers material as part of the review that was not disclosed to the prisoner.[37]

Timings of reviews and delays

14.26 Where article 5 is engaged (once the minimum term is expired for indeterminate sentence prisoners, or during the extension period for extended sentence prisoners), there is a requirement under article 5(4) for the initial review to be speedy, and where further reviews are necessary for them to be carried out at reasonable intervals.[38] Where this requirement is breached, there is a right to compensation under article 5(5). One of the main issues indeterminate sentence prisoners require advice about is the timing between reviews when release has not been directed. These decisions are made by LRRS, not the Parole Board. Although there is a statutory requirement for a review every two years, the actual review period must be set by reference to what needs to be achieved before a further review would be appropriate. It must be borne in mind that the need for article 5(4) reviews is premised on the fact that levels of dangerousness change over time and so the time between reviews must be tailored to monitor these changes.

14.27 There is a great deal of authority in the European Court of Human Rights and domestically on when delay in the review will breach article 5(4), for example:

- An indeterminate prisoner's review must take place before or on the date of minimum term expiry.[39]

35 *R (on the application of Tinney) v Parole Board* [2005] EWHC 863 (Admin), and in the context of lifers moving to open conditions *R (on the application of Gordon) v Parole Board* [2001] ACD 47, QBD, *R v Parole Board ex p Hart* (2000) 24 May HC.

36 *R v Parole Board ex p Higgins* (1998) 22 September HC – where the offence was wrongly described in the dossier.

37 For example, see *R (AT) v Parole Board* [2004] EWHC 515.

38 *Herczegalvy v Austria* Series A no 244.

39 *R (Noorkoiv) v Home Secretary* [2002] EWCA Civ 770.

- Where after a first review, the Parole Board recommended a 12-month review, but one was not held for 19 months, there was a breach of article 5(4).[40]
- Where a discretionary lifer completed further offending work in eight months, but a review was not held for two years, there was a breach as the interval between reviews needs to be tailored so that the time between reviews can be justified by considerations of 'rehabilitation and monitoring'.[41]
- These decisions do not mean that the 'standard' two-year review between indeterminate sentence reviews will always breach article 5(4), as each case must be considered on its own facts.[42]

14.28 The amount of damages for delays in holding effective hearings under article 5(4) will vary, as there is an obvious distinction between cases where the delay has prolonged the prisoner's release, and those where delay does impact upon release. In the latter cases the court will normally expect there to be contemporaneous evidence of real distress caused by the delay.[43] Delay may be caused by the prison (failing to prepare/disclose dossier), the Home Secretary (delay in disclosure or in referral to the Board), or by the Board itself (delay in listing).

14.29 Where a period of prolonged detention can be directly attributable to a breach of article 5, the courts have held that it is appropriate to look at damages in relation to the comparable tort of false imprisonment when deciding the level of compensation.[44] In one case, LRRS delayed the disclosure of a dossier to a recalled lifer for 14 days without any good reason. The lifer was eventually released after the parole hearing. The entire review process took three months from the date of the recall to release and the lifer received £1,500 compensation for the 14-day delay.[45]

40 *AT v UK* (1995) 20 EHRR CD 59.

41 *Oldham v United Kingdom* (36273/97) (2001) 31 EHRR 34 – see also *Hirst v UK* [2001] Crim LR 919, *Curley v UK* (2001) 31 EHRR 14 and *Waite v United Kingdom* (53236/99) (2003) 36 EHRR 54.

42 *R (on the application of MacNeil) v HMP Lifer Panel* [2001] EWCA Civ 448.

43 See *R (on the application of KB) v Mental Health Review Tribunal (Damages)* [2003] EWHC Admin 193.

44 *KB* above; this approach was the subject of some criticism by House of Lords in *R v Home Secretary ex p Greenfield* [2005] UKHL 14 although that case involved article 6.

45 *R (on the application of Hirst) v Secretary of State for the Home Department* [2005] EWHC 1480 Admin.

APPENDICES

APPENDIX 1

The Parole Board Rules 2004

Made 2004

Coming into force 1st August 2004

ARRANGEMENT OF RULES

The Secretary of State, in exercise of the powers conferred on him by section 32(5) of the Criminal Justice Act 1991, hereby makes the following Rules:

PART I
Introduction

Title, commencement and revocation

1. (1) These Rules may be cited as the Parole Board Rules 2004 and shall come into force on 1st August 2004.
   (2) The Parole Board Rules 1997 are hereby revoked.

Application and interpretation

2. (1) Subject to rule 24, these Rules apply where a prisoner's case is referred to the Board by the Secretary of State under section 28(6)(a), 28(7) or 32(4) of the 1997 Act, or under section 39(4) or 44A(2) of the 1991 Act, at any time after the coming into force of these Rules.
   (2) In these Rules, unless a contrary intention appears –
   'Board' means the Parole Board, continued by section 32(1) of the 1991 Act;
   'Chairman' means the chairman of the Board appointed under paragraph 2 of Schedule 5 to the 1991 Act;
   'chair' means the chairman of a panel appointed under rule 3(5);
   'governor' includes a director of a contracted out prison;
   'panel' means those members of the Board constituted in accordance with rule 3 and having conduct of the case;
   'parties' means the prisoner and the Secretary of State;
   'prison' includes a young offender institution or any other institution where the prisoner is or has been detained;
   'single member panel' means that member of the Board constituted in accordance with rule 3(1);
   'three member paper panel' means those members of the Board constituted in accordance with rule 3(2);

'three member oral panel' means those members of the Board constituted in accordance with rule 3(3);
'the 1991 Act' means the Criminal Justice Act 1991; and
'the 1997 Act' means the Crime (Sentences) Act 1997.

PART II
General

Appointment of panels

3. (1) The Chairman shall appoint one member of the Board for the purpose of conducting proceedings in relation to a prisoner's case without a hearing pursuant to rule 11.
(2) Where consideration of a prisoner's case is required pursuant to rule 13, the Chairman shall appoint three members of the Board to form a panel for the purpose of conducting proceedings without a hearing pursuant to that rule.
(3) Subject to paragraph (6) below, where a hearing is required in relation to a prisoner's case, the Chairman shall appoint three members of the Board to form a panel for the purpose of conducting proceedings with a hearing.
(4) In relation to any prisoner's case, no member shall be appointed to more than one of the panels formed under paragraph (1), (2) or (3) above.
(5) Subject to paragraph (6) below, the Chairman shall appoint one member of each panel to act as chair of that panel.
(6) In relation to cases referred to the Board under section 28(6)(a), 28(7) or 32(4) of the 1997 Act, the members appointed pursuant to paragraph (3) above shall include a person who has a 5 year general qualification, within the meaning of section 71 of the Courts and Legal Services Act 1990, and that person shall act as chairman of the panel.

Listing the case for hearing

4. The Board shall list the case and shall notify the parties of the date when the case was so listed within 5 working days thereafter.

Representation

5. (1) Subject to paragraph (2), a party may be represented by any person who he has authorised for that purpose.
(2) The following are ineligible to act as a representative –
(a) any person liable to be detained under the Mental Health Act 1983,
(b) any person serving a sentence of imprisonment,
(c) any person who is on licence having been released under Part III of the Criminal Justice Act 1967, under Part II of the 1991 Act, under Chapter 6 of Part 12 to the Criminal Justice Act 2003 or under Part II of the 1997 Act, or
(d) any person with a previous conviction for an imprisonable offence which remains unspent under the Rehabilitation of Offenders Act 1974.
(3) Within 5 weeks of the case being listed, a party shall notify the Board and the other party of the name, address and occupation of any person authorised in accordance with paragraph (1).
(4) Where a prisoner does not authorise a person to act as his representative, the Board may, with his agreement, appoint someone to act on his behalf.

Information and reports by the Secretary of State

6. (1) Within 8 weeks of the case being listed, the Secretary of State shall serve on the Board and, subject to paragraph (2), the prisoner or his representative –
(a) the information specified in Part A of Schedule 1 to these Rules,
(b) the reports specified in Part B of that Schedule, and
(c) such further information as the Secretary of State considers to be relevant to the case.

(2) Any part of the information or reports referred to in paragraph (1) which, in the opinion of the Secretary of State, should be withheld from the prisoner on the grounds that its disclosure would adversely affect national security, the prevention of disorder or crime or the health or welfare of the prisoner or others (such withholding being a necessary and proportionate measure in all the circumstances of the case), shall be recorded in a separate document and served only on the Board together with the reasons for believing that its disclosure would have that effect.

(3) Where a document is withheld from the prisoner in accordance with paragraph (2), it shall, unless the chair of the panel directs otherwise, nevertheless be served as soon as practicable on the prisoner's representative if he is –
(a) a barrister or solicitor,
(b) a registered medical practitioner, or
(c) a person whom the chair of the panel directs is suitable by virtue of his experience or professional qualification;

provided that no information disclosed in accordance with this paragraph shall be disclosed either directly or indirectly to the prisoner or to any other person without the consent/authority of the chair of the panel.

Evidence of the prisoner

7. (1) Within 12 weeks of the case being listed, the prisoner shall serve on the Board and the Secretary of State any representations about his case that he wishes to make.

(2) Any other documentary evidence that the prisoner wishes to adduce at a hearing of his case shall be served on the Board and the Secretary of State at least 14 days before the date of the hearing.

Directions

8. (1) Subject to paragraph (4), the chair of the panel may at any time give, vary or revoke such directions as he thinks proper to enable the parties to prepare for the consideration of the prisoner's case or to assist the panel to determine the issues.

(2) Such directions may in particular relate to –
(a) the timetable for the proceedings,
(b) the varying of the time within which or by which an act is required by these Rules to be done,
(c) the service of documents,
(d) as regards any documents which have been received by the Board but which have been withheld from the prisoner in accordance with rule 6(2),

whether withholding such documents is a necessary and proportionate measure in all the circumstances of the case, and

(e) the submission of evidence.

(3) Within 7 days of being notified of a direction under paragraph (2)(d), either party may appeal against it to the Chairman, who shall notify the other party of the appeal; the other party may make representations on the appeal to the Chairman whose decision shall be final.

(4) Directions under paragraph (1) may be given, varied or revoked either –

(a) of the chair of the panel's own motion, or

(b) on the written application of a party which has been served on the other party and which specifies the direction that is sought;

but in either case, both parties shall be given an opportunity to make written representations or, where the chair of the panel thinks it necessary, and subject to paragraph (7)(b), to make oral submissions at a preliminary hearing fixed in accordance with paragraph (5).

(5) Where the chair of the panel decides to hold a preliminary hearing, he shall give the parties at least 14 days' notice of the date, time and place fixed for that hearing.

(6) A preliminary hearing shall be held in private and information about the proceedings and the names of any persons concerned in the proceedings shall not be made public.

(7) Except in so far as the chair of the panel otherwise directs, at a preliminary hearing –

(a) the chair of the panel shall sit alone, and

(b) the prisoner shall not attend unless he is unrepresented.

(8) The power to give directions may be exercised in the absence of the parties.

(9) Notice of any directions given, varied or revoked under this rule shall be served on the parties as soon as practicable thereafter.

Adjournment

9. (1) The panel may at any time adjourn proceedings to obtain further information or for such other purposes as it may think appropriate.

(2) Before adjourning proceedings, the panel may give such directions as it thinks fit to ensure the proceedings can be resumed and the application considered as soon as possible.

(3) Before a three member oral panel resumes any hearing which was adjourned without a further hearing date being fixed, it shall give the parties not less than 3 weeks' notice, or such shorter notice to which all parties may agree, of the date, time and place of the resumed hearing.

Panel decisions

10. (1) Where a panel has been constituted under rule 3(2) or (3), any decision of the majority of the members of the panel shall be the decision of the panel.

(2) For the avoidance of doubt, decisions made pursuant to rule 11(2)(b) or 13(2)(b) are provisional decisions as to the prisoner's suitability for release, a final decision only being made pursuant to rule 12(3) or 13(6) or when the case is determined by a three member oral panel.

PART III
Proceedings without a hearing

Consideration by single member panel

11. (1) Within 14 weeks of the case being listed, a single member panel shall consider the prisoner's case without a hearing.

(2) The single member panel must either –

(a) decide that the case should be considered by a three member oral panel, or

(b) make a provisional decision as to the prisoner's suitability for release.

(3) The decision of the single member panel shall be recorded in writing with reasons, and shall be provided to the parties within a week of the date of the decision.

Provisional decision against release

12. (1) In any case where the single member panel has made a provisional decision under rule 11(2)(b) that the prisoner is unsuitable for release, the prisoner may require a three member oral panel to give consideration to his case with a hearing.

(2) Where the prisoner does so require consideration of his case with a hearing, he must serve notice to that effect on the Board and the Secretary of State within 19 weeks of the case being listed.

(3) If no notice has been served in accordance with paragraph (2) after the expiry of the period permitted by that paragraph, the provisional decision shall become final and shall be provided to the parties within 20 weeks of the case being listed.

Provisional decision in favour of release: consideration by three member paper panel

13. (1) In any case where the single member panel has made a provisional decision under rule 11(2)(b) that the prisoner is suitable for release, consideration of his case must be made by a three member paper panel within 17 weeks of the case being listed.

(2) The three member paper panel must either –

(a) decide that the case should be considered by a three member oral panel, or

(b) uphold the provisional decision of the single member panel that the prisoner is suitable for release.

(3) The decision by the three member paper panel shall be recorded in writing with reasons, and shall be provided to the parties within a week of the date of the decision.

(4) In any case to which paragraph (2)(b) applies, the Secretary of State may require a three member oral panel to give consideration to the prisoner's case with a hearing.

(5) Where the Secretary of State does so require consideration of the case with a hearing, he must serve notice to that effect on the Board and the prisoner within 22 weeks of the case being listed.

(6) If no notice has been served in accordance with paragraph (5) after the expiry of the period permitted by that paragraph, the provisional decision shall

become final and shall be provided to the parties within 23 weeks of the case being listed.

PART IV
Proceedings with a hearing

General provisions

14. (1) This Part of the Rules applies in any case where a decision pursuant to rule 11(2)(a) or 13(2)(a) has been made, or where a notice under rule 12(2) or 13(5) has been served, or in any case referred to the Board under section 32(4) of the 1997 Act or under section 39(4) or 44A(2) of the 1991 Act.
(2) In relation to any case to be given consideration by a three member oral panel by virtue of rule 13(5), rule 15(1) shall have effect as if the reference to 20 weeks was a reference to 23 weeks, and rule 15(2) shall have effect as if the reference to 21 weeks was a reference to 24 weeks.
(3) The prisoner shall, within 23 weeks of the case being listed, notify the Board and the Secretary of State whether he wishes to attend the hearing.
(4) Any reference in this Part of the Rules to a 'panel' is to a three member oral panel.

Witnesses

15. (1) Where a party wishes to call witnesses at the hearing, he shall make a written application to the Board, a copy of which he shall serve on the other party, within 20 weeks of the case being listed, giving the name, address and occupation of the witness he wishes to call and the substance of the evidence he proposes to adduce.
(2) Where the Board wishes to call witnesses at the hearing, the chair of the panel should notify the parties, within 21 weeks of the case being listed, giving the name, address and occupation of the witness it wishes to call and the substance of the evidence it proposes to adduce.
(3) The chair of the panel may grant or refuse an application under paragraph (1) and shall communicate his decision to both parties, giving reasons in writing for his decision in the case of a refusal.
(4) Where a witness is called under paragraphs (1) or (2), it shall be the duty of the person calling the witness to notify the witness at least 2 weeks before the hearing of the date of the hearing and the need to attend.

Observers

16. A party may apply, in accordance with the procedure set out in rule 15(1) and (3), to be accompanied at the hearing by such other persons, in addition to any representative he may have authorised, as he wishes to support him or to observe the proceedings; but before granting any such application the Board shall obtain the agreement of –
(a) the governor where the hearing is held in a prison,
(b) in any other case, the person who has the authority to agree.

Notice of hearing

17. (1) The hearing shall be held within 26 weeks of the case being listed, but when fixing the date of the hearing the Board shall consult the parties.

(2) The Board shall give the parties at least 3 weeks notice of the date, time and place scheduled for the hearing or such shorter notice to which the parties may agree.

Location, privacy of proceedings

18. (1) The hearing shall be held at the prison or other institution where the prisoner is detained, or such other place as the chair of the panel, with the agreement of the Secretary of State, may direct.

(2) The hearing shall be held in private.

(3) In addition to witnesses and observers previously approved pursuant to rules 15 and 16, the chair of the panel may admit to the hearing such other persons on such terms and conditions as he considers appropriate.

(4) The parties may not challenge at the hearing the attendance of any witness or observer whose attendance has previously been approved pursuant to rules 15 and 16.

Hearing procedure

19. (1) At the beginning of the hearing the chair of the panel shall explain the order of proceeding which the panel proposes to adopt, and shall invite each party present to state their view as to the suitability of the prisoner for release.

(2) The panel shall avoid formality in the proceedings and so far as possible shall make its own enquiries in order to satisfy itself of the level of risk of the prisoner; it shall conduct the hearing in such manner as it considers most suitable to the clarification of the issues before it and generally to the just handling of the proceedings it.

(3) The parties shall be entitled to appear and be heard at the hearing and take such part in the proceedings as the panel thinks fit; and the parties may hear each other's evidence, put questions to each other, call any witnesses who the Board has authorised to give evidence in accordance with rule 15, and put questions to any witness or other person appearing before the panel.

(4) The chair of the panel may require any person present at the hearing who is, in his opinion, behaving in a disruptive manner to leave and may permit him to return, if at all, only on such conditions as the chair may specify.

(5) The panel may adduce or receive in evidence any document or information notwithstanding that such document or information would be inadmissible in a court of law, but no person shall be compelled to give any evidence or produce any document which he could not be compelled to give or produce on the trial of an action.

(6) The chair of the panel may require the prisoner, any witness appearing for the prisoner, or any other person present, to leave the hearing where evidence is being examined which the chair of the panel, in accordance with rule 8(2)(d) (subject to any successful appeal under rule 8(2)), previously directed should be withheld from the prisoner as adversely affecting national security, the prevention of disorder or crime or the health or welfare of the prisoner or others.

(7) After all the evidence has been given, the prisoner shall be given a further opportunity to address the panel.

The decision

20. The panel's decision determining a case shall be recorded in writing with reasons, signed by the chair of the panel, and provided in writing to the parties not more than 7 days after the end of the hearing; the recorded decision with reasons shall only make reference to matters which the Secretary of State has referred to the Board.

PART V
Miscellaneous

Time

21. Where the time prescribed by or under these Rules for doing any act expires on a Saturday, Sunday or public holiday, the act shall be in time if done on the next working day.

Transmission of documents etc.

22. Any document required or authorised by these Rules to be served or otherwise transmitted to any person may be transmitted by electronic means, sent by pre-paid post or delivered –
   (a) in the case of a document directed to the Board or the chair of the panel, to the office of the Board;
   (b) in any other case, to the last known address of the person to whom the document is directed.

Irregularities

23. Any irregularity resulting from a failure to comply with these Rules before the panel has determined a case shall not of itself render the proceedings void, but the panel may, and shall, if it considers that the person may have been prejudiced, take such steps as it thinks fit, before determining the case, to cure the irregularity, whether by the amendment of any document, the giving of any notice, the taking of any step or otherwise.

References to the Board following recall

24. (1) Where the Secretary of State refers a prisoner's case to the Board under section 32(4) of the 1997 Act or section 39(4) of the 1991 Act to consider a recall:
   (a) rules 11 to 13 shall not apply; and
   (b) subject to the above, these Rules shall only apply where the prisoner has made representations against recall and subject to the modifications in paragraph (2).

(2) The modifications referred to in paragraph (1) are as follows:
   (a) any references to periods of time set out in these Rules shall apply as if they were references to such period of time as the chair of the panel shall in each case determine, taking into account both the desirability of the Board reaching an early decision in the prisoner's case and the need to ensure fairness to the prisoner; and
   (b) rule 6 shall apply as if the references in paragraph (1)(a) and (b) of that rule to the information and reports specified in Schedule 1 were references to the information and reports set out in Schedule 2.

Transitional provision

25. The revocation by these Rules of the Parole Board Rules 1997 does not affect their operation in relation to any referral of a prisoner's case made to the Board before the coming into force of the revocation.

Home Office
Parliamentary Under-Secretary of State
2004

SCHEDULE 1

Rule 6(1)

INFORMATION AND REPORTS FOR SUBMISSION TO THE BOARD BY THE SECRETARY OF STATE ON A REFERENCE TO THE BOARD UNDER SECTION 28(6)(a) OR (7) OF THE 1997 ACT OR SECTION 44A(2) OF THE 1991 ACT

PART A
INFORMATION RELATING TO THE PRISONER

1. The full name of the prisoner
2. The date of birth of the prisoner.
3. The prison in which the prisoner is detained and details of other prisons in which the prisoner has been detained, the date and reasons for any transfer.
4. The date the prisoner was given the life sentence or extended sentence, details of the offence and any previous convictions.
5. The comments, if available, of the trial judge in passing sentence.
6. Where applicable, the conclusions of the Court of Appeal in respect of any appeal by the prisoner against conviction or sentence.
7. The parole history, if any, of the prisoner, including details of any periods spent on licence during the currency of the life sentence or extended sentence.

PART B
REPORTS RELATING TO THE PRISONER

1. Pre-trial and pre-sentence reports examined by the sentencing court on the circumstances of the offence.
2. Reports on a prisoner while he was subject to a transfer direction under section 47 of the Mental Health Act 1983.
3. Current reports on the prisoner's risk factors, reduction in risk and performance and behaviour in prison, including views on suitability for release on licence as well as compliance with any sentence plan.
4. An up-to-date home circumstances report prepared for the Board by an officer of the supervising local probation board, including information on the following where relevant:
   (a) details of the home address, family circumstances, and family attitudes towards the prisoner;
   (b) alternative options if the offender cannot return home;

(c) the opportunity for employment on release;
(d) the local community's attitude towards the prisoner (if known);
(e) the attitudes and concerns of the victims of the offence (if known);
(f) the prisoner's attitude to the index offence;
(g) the prisoner's response to previous periods of supervision;
(h) the prisoner's behaviour during any temporary leave during the current sentence;
(i) the prisoner's attitude to the prospect of release and the requirements and objectives of supervision;
(j) an assessment of the risk of reoffending;
(k) a programme of supervision;
(l) a view on suitability for release; and
(m) recommendations regarding any non-standard licence conditions.

SCHEDULE 2

Rules 6(1) and 24(2)(b)

INFORMATION AND REPORTS FOR SUBMISSION TO THE BOARD BY THE SECRETARY OF STATE ON A REFERENCE TO THE BOARD UNDER SECTION 32(4) OF THE 1997 ACT OR SECTION 39(4) OF THE 1991 ACT

PART A
INFORMATION RELATING TO THE PRISONER

1. The full name of the prisoner.
2. The date of birth of the prisoner.
3. The prison in which the prisoner is detained and details of other prisons in which the prisoner has been detained, the date and reasons for any transfer.
4. The date the prisoner was given the life sentence or extended sentence, details of the offence and any previous convictions.
5. The parole history, if any, of the prisoner, including details of any periods spent during the currency of the life sentence or extended sentence.
6. In the case of a referral under section 32(4) of the 1997 Act, the details of any life sentence plan prepared for the prisoner which have previously been disclosed to him.
7. The details of any previous recalls of the prisoner including the reasons for such recalls and subsequent re-release on licence.
8. The statement of reasons for the most recent recall which was given to the prisoner under section 32(3)(b) of the 1997 Act or section 39(3)(b) of the 1991 Act.
9. The details of any memorandum which the Board considered prior to making its recommendation for recall under section 32(1) of the 1997 Act or section 39(1) of the 1991 Act, or confirming the Secretary of State's decision to recall under section 32(2) of the 1997 Act or section 39(2) of the 1991 Act, including the reasons why the Secretary of State considered it expedient in the public interest to recall that person before it was practicable to obtain a recommendation from the Board.

PART B
REPORTS RELATING TO THE PRISONER

1. The reports considered by the Board prior to making its recommendation for recall under section 32(1) of the 1997 Act or section 39(1) of the 1991 Act, or its confirmation of the Secretary of State's decision to recall under section 32(2) of the 1997 Act or section 39(2) of the 1991 Act.
2. Any reports considered by the Secretary of State in deciding to recall under section 32(2) of the 1997 Act or section 39(2) of the 1991 Act.
3. In the case of a referral under section 39(4) of the 1991 Act, any pre-sentence report examined by the sentencing court on the circumstances of the offence.
4. Any other relevant reports.

APPENDIX 2

Relevant sections of the Criminal Justice Act 2003

Provisions brought into force from 4 April 2005 – see the Criminal Justice Act 2003 (Commencement No 8 and Transitional and Saving Provisions) Order 2005 SI No 950.

CRIMINAL JUSTICE ACT 2003 ss239, 244–256 AND Sch 19 (AS AMENDED)

NOTES

Information:

Act reference: 2003 c 44. Royal assent: 20 November 2003. Long title: An Act to make provision about criminal justice (including the powers and duties of the police) and about dealing with offenders; to amend the law relating to jury service; to amend Chapter 1 of Part 1 of the Crime and Disorder Act 1998 and Part 5 of the Police Act 1997; to make provision about civil proceedings brought by offenders; and for connected purposes.

239 The Parole Board

(1) The Parole Board is to continue to be, by that name, a body corporate and as such is –

(a) to be constituted in accordance with this Chapter, and

(b) to have the functions conferred on it by this Chapter in respect of fixed-term prisoners and by Chapter 2 of Part 2 of the Crime (Sentences) Act 1997 (c. 43) (in this Chapter referred to as 'the 1997 Act') in respect of life prisoners within the meaning of that Chapter.

(2) It is the duty of the Board to advise the Secretary of State with respect to any matter referred to it by him which is to do with the early release or recall of prisoners.

(3) The Board must, in dealing with cases as respects which it makes recommendations under this Chapter or under Chapter 2 of Part 2 of the 1997 Act, consider –

(a) any documents given to it by the Secretary of State, and

(b) any other oral or written information obtained by it;

and if in any particular case the Board thinks it necessary to interview the person to whom the case relates before reaching a decision, the Board may authorise one of its members to interview him and must consider the report of the interview made by that member.

(4) The Board must deal with cases as respects which it gives directions under

this Chapter or under Chapter 2 of Part 2 of the 1997 Act on consideration of all such evidence as may be adduced before it.

(5) Without prejudice to subsections (3) and (4), the Secretary of State may make rules with respect to the proceedings of the Board, including proceedings authorising cases to be dealt with by a prescribed number of its members or requiring cases to be dealt with at prescribed times.

(6) The Secretary of State may also give to the Board directions as to the matters to be taken into account by it in discharging any functions under this Chapter or under Chapter 2 of Part 2 of the 1997 Act; and in giving any such directions the Secretary of State must have regard to –
   (a) the need to protect the public from serious harm from offenders, and
   (b) the desirability of preventing the commission by them of further offences and of securing their rehabilitation.

(7) Schedule 19 shall have effect with respect to the Board.

NOTES

Initial Commencement:

To be appointed: see s336(3).

Appointment:

For the purposes of the passing of a sentence of imprisonment to which an intermittent custody order relates and the release on licence of a person serving such a sentence): 26 January 2004: see SI 2003 No 3282, article 2, Schedule.

Sub-ss (1)–(4), (7): Appointment (for remaining purposes): 4 April 2005: see SI 2005 No 950, article 2(1), Sch 1 para 19; for transitional provisions see Sch 2 para 16 thereof.

Sub-ss (5), (6): Appointment (for remaining purposes): 7 March 2005: see SI 2005 No 373, article 2(1), (2)(k).

Release on licence

244 Duty to release prisoners

(1) As soon as a fixed-term prisoner, other than a prisoner to whom section 247 applies, has served the requisite custodial period, it is the duty of the Secretary of State to release him on licence under this section.

(2) Subsection (1) is subject to section 245.

(3) In this section 'the requisite custodial period' means –
   (a) in relation to a person serving a sentence of imprisonment for a term of twelve months or more or any determinate sentence of detention under section 91 [or 96] of the Sentencing Act, one-half of his sentence,
   (b) in relation to a person serving a sentence of imprisonment for a term of less than twelve months (other than one to which an intermittent custody order relates), the custodial period within the meaning of section 181,
   (c) in relation to a person serving a sentence of imprisonment to which an intermittent custody order relates, any part of the term [which for the purposes of section 183 (as read with section 263(2) or 264A(2) in the case of concurrent or consecutive sentences) is not a licence period], and
   (d) in relation to a person serving two or more concurrent or consecutive sentences [none of which falls within paragraph (c)], the period determined under sections 263(2) and 264(2).

NOTES

Initial Commencement:

To be appointed: see s336(3).

Appointment:

Sub-ss(1), (2), (3)(c), (d): Appointment (for the purposes of the passing of a sentence of imprisonment to which an intermittent custody order relates and the release on licence of a person serving such a sentence): 26 January 2004: see SI 2003 No 3282, article 2, Schedule.

Sub-ss(1), (2), (3)(d): Appointment (for remaining purposes): 4 April 2005: see SI 2005 No 950, article 2(1), Sch 1 para 19; for transitional provisions see Sch 2 paras 14, 19 thereof.

Sub-s(3)(a): Appointment: 4 April 2005: see SI 2005 No 950, article 2(1), Sch 1 para 19; for transitional provisions see Sch 2, paras 14, 19 thereof.

Amendment:

Sub-s(3)(a): Words inserted (until the coming into force of the Criminal Justice and Court Services Act 2000 s61): SI 2005 No 643, article 3(1), (10), with effect from 4 April 2005 (SI 2005 No 643, article 1(1)).

Sub-s(3)(c): Words substituted: Domestic Violence, Crime and Victims Act 2004 s31, Sch 6 paras 1, 2(a), with effect from 31 March 2005 (SI 2005 No 579, article 3(e)).

Sub-s(3)(d): Words inserted: Domestic Violence, Crime and Victims Act 2004 s31, Sch 6 paras 1, 2(b), with effect from 31 March 2005 (SI 2005 No 579, article 3(e)).

245 Restrictions on operation of section 244(1) in relation to intermittent custody prisoners

(1) Where an intermittent custody prisoner returns to custody after being unlawfully at large within the meaning of section 49 of the Prison Act 1952 (c. 52) at any time during the currency of his sentence, section 244(1) does not apply until –

(a) the relevant time (as defined in subsection (2)), or

(b) if earlier, the date on which he has served in prison the number of custodial days required by the intermittent custody order.

(2) In subsection (1)(a) 'the relevant time' means –

(a) in a case where, within the period of 72 hours beginning with the return to custody of the intermittent custody prisoner, the Secretary of State or the responsible officer has applied to the court for the amendment of the intermittent custody order under paragraph 6(1)(b) of Schedule 10, the date on which the application is withdrawn or determined, and

(b) in any other case, the end of that 72-hour period.

(3) Section 244(1) does not apply in relation to an intermittent custody prisoner at any time after he has been recalled under section 254, unless after his recall the Board has directed his further release on licence.

NOTES

Initial Commencement:

To be appointed: see s336(3).

Appointment:

For the purposes of the passing of a sentence of imprisonment to which an intermittent custody order relates and the release on licence of a person serving such a sentence: 26 January 2004: see SI 2003 No 3282, article 2, Schedule.

246 Power to release prisoners on licence before required to do so

(1) Subject to subsections (2) to (4), the Secretary of State may –
  (a) release on licence under this section a fixed-term prisoner, other than an intermittent custody prisoner, at any time during the period of 135 days ending with the day on which the prisoner will have served the requisite custodial period, and
  (b) release on licence under this section an intermittent custody prisoner when 135 or less of the required custodial days remain to be served.

(2) Subsection (1)(a) does not apply in relation to a prisoner unless –
  (a) the length of the requisite custodial period is at least 6 weeks,
  (b) he has served –
    (i) at least 4 weeks of his sentence, and
    (ii) at least one-half of the requisite custodial period.

(3) Subsection (1)(b) does not apply in relation to a prisoner unless –
  (a) the number of required custodial days is at least 42, and
  (b) the prisoner has served –
    (i) at least 28 of those days, and
    (ii) at least one-half of the total number of those days.

(4) Subsection (1) does not apply where –
  (a) the sentence is imposed under section 227 or 228,
  (b) the sentence is for an offence under section 1 of the Prisoners (Return to Custody) Act 1995 (c. 16),
  (c) the prisoner is subject to a hospital order, hospital direction or transfer direction under section 37, 45A or 47 of the Mental Health Act 1983 (c. 20),
  (d) the sentence was imposed by virtue of paragraph 9(1)(b) or (c) or 10(1)(b) or (c) of Schedule 8 in a case where the prisoner has failed to comply with a curfew requirement of a community order,
  (e) the prisoner is subject to the notification requirements of Part 2 of the Sexual Offences Act 2003 (c. 42),
  (f) the prisoner is liable to removal from the United Kingdom,
  (g) the prisoner has been released on licence under this section during the currency of the sentence, and has been recalled to prison under section 255(1)(a),
  (h) the prisoner has been released on licence under section 248 during the currency of the sentence, and has been recalled to prison under section 254, or
  (i) in the case of a prisoner to whom a direction under section 240 relates, the interval between the date on which the sentence was passed and the date on which the prisoner will have served the requisite custodial period is less than 14 days or, where the sentence is one of intermittent custody, the number of the required custodial days remaining to be served is less than 14.

(5) The Secretary of State may by order –
(a) amend the number of days for the time being specified in subsection (1)(a) or (b), (3) or (4)(i),
(b) amend the number of weeks for the time being specified in subsection (2)(a) or (b)(i), and
(c) amend the fraction for the time being specified in subsection (2)(b)(ii) or (3)(b)(ii).

(6) In this section –
'the required custodial days', in relation to an intermittent custody prisoner, means –
(a) the number of custodial days specified under section 183, or
(b) in the case of two or more sentences of intermittent custody [which are consecutive], the aggregate of the numbers so specified[, or
(c) in the case of two or more sentences of intermittent custody which are wholly or partly concurrent, the aggregate of the numbers so specified less the number of days that are to be served concurrently];
'the requisite custodial period' in relation to a person serving any sentence other than a sentence of intermittent custody, has the meaning given by paragraph (a), (b) or (d) of section 244(3);
'sentence of intermittent custody' means a sentence to which an intermittent custody order relates.

NOTES

Initial Commencement:
To be appointed: see s336(3).
Appointment:
Sub-ss(1)(a), (2), (4)(a): Appointment: 4 April 2005: see SI 2005 No 950, article 2(1), Sch 1 para 19; for transitional provisions see Sch 2 paras 14, 19(a) thereof.
Sub-ss(1)(b), (3), (4)(b)–(i), (5), (6): Appointment (for the purposes of the passing of a sentence of imprisonment to which an intermittent custody order relates and the release on licence of a person serving such a sentence): 26 January 2004: see SI 2003 No 3282, article 2, Schedule.
Sub-ss(1)(b), (3), (4)(b)–(i), (6): Appointment (for remaining purposes): 4 April 2005: see SI 2005 No 950, article 2(1), Sch 1 para 19; for transitional provisions see Sch 2 paras 14, 19(a) thereof.
Sub-s(5): Appointment (for remaining purposes): 7 March 2005: see SI 2005 No 373, article 2(1), (2)(m).
Amendment:
Sub-s(6) 'the required custodial days' (a): Words prospectively repealed by Domestic Violence, Crime and Victims Act 2004 s58(2), Sch 11, from a date to be appointed (Domestic Violence, Crime and Victims Act 2004 s60).
Sub-s(6) 'the required custodial days' (b): Words inserted: Domestic Violence, Crime and Victims Act 2004 s31, Sch 6 paras 1, 3(a), with effect from 31 March 2005 (SI 2005 No 579, article 3(e)).
Sub-s(6) 'the required custodial days' (c): Words inserted: Domestic Violence, Crime and Victims Act 2004 s31, Sch 6 paras 1, 3(b), with effect from 31 March 2005 (SI 2005 No 579, article 3(e)).

247 Release on licence of prisoner serving extended sentence under section 227 or 228

(1) This section applies to a prisoner who is serving an extended sentence imposed under section 227 or 228.

(2) As soon as –

(a) a prisoner to whom this section applies has served one-half of the appropriate custodial term, and

(b) the Parole Board has directed his release under this section,

it is the duty of the Secretary of State to release him on licence.

(3) The Parole Board may not give a direction under subsection (2) unless the Board is satisfied that it is no longer necessary for the protection of the public that the prisoner should be confined.

(4) As soon as a prisoner to whom this section applies has served the appropriate custodial term, it is the duty of the Secretary of State to release him on licence unless the prisoner has previously been recalled under section 254.

(5) Where a prisoner to whom this section applies is released on a licence, the Secretary of State may not by virtue of section 250(4)(b) include, or subsequently insert, a condition in the licence, or vary or cancel a condition in the licence, except after consultation with the Board.

(6) For the purposes of subsection (5), the Secretary of State is to be treated as having consulted the Board about a proposal to include, insert, vary or cancel a condition in any case if he has consulted the Board about the implementation of proposals of that description generally or in that class of case.

(7) In this section 'the appropriate custodial term' means the period determined by the court as the appropriate custodial term under section 227 or 228.

NOTES

Initial Commencement:

To be appointed: see s336(3).

Appointment:

4 April 2005: see SI 2005 No 950, article 2(1), Sch 1 para 19; for transitional provisions see Sch 2 para 14 thereof.

248 Power to release prisoners on compassionate grounds

(1) The Secretary of State may at any time release a fixed-term prisoner on licence if he is satisfied that exceptional circumstances exist which justify the prisoner's release on compassionate grounds.

(2) Before releasing under this section a prisoner to whom section 247 applies, the Secretary of State must consult the Board, unless the circumstances are such as to render such consultation impracticable.

NOTES

Initial Commencement:

To be appointed: see s 336(3).

Appointment:

Sub-s(1): Appointment (for the purposes of the passing of a sentence of imprisonment to which an intermittent custody order relates and the release on licence of a person serving such a sentence): 26 January 2004: see SI 2003 No 3282, article 2, Schedule.

Sub-s(1): Appointment (for remaining purposes): 4 April 2005: see SI 2005 No 950, article 2(1), Sch 1 para 19; for transitional provisions see Sch 2 paras 14, 19(a) thereof.

Sub-s(2): Appointment: 4 April 2005: see SI 2005 No 950, article 2(1), Sch 1 para 19; for transitional provisions see Sch 2 paras 14, 19(a) thereof.

249 Duration of licence

(1) Subject to subsections (2) and (3), where a fixed-term prisoner is released on licence, the licence shall, subject to any revocation under section 254 or 255, remain in force for the remainder of his sentence.

(2) Where an intermittent custody prisoner is released on licence under section 244, the licence shall, subject to any revocation under section 254, remain in force –

(a) until the time when he is required to return to prison at the beginning of the next custodial period of the sentence, or

(b) where it is granted at the end of the last custodial period, for the remainder of his sentence.

(3) Subsection (1) has effect subject to sections 263(2) (concurrent terms) and 264(3) and (4) (consecutive terms) [and subsection (2) has effect subject to section 264A(3) (consecutive terms: intermittent custody)].

(4) In subsection (2) 'custodial period', in relation to a sentence to which an intermittent custody order relates, means any period which is not a licence period as defined by 183(3).

NOTES

Initial Commencement:

To be appointed: see s336(3).

Appointment:

For the purposes of the passing of a sentence of imprisonment to which an intermittent custody order relates and the release on licence of a person serving such a sentence: 26 January 2004: see SI 2003 No 3282, article 2, Schedule.

Appointment (for remaining purposes): 4 April 2005: see SI 2005 No 950, article 2(1), Sch 1 para 19; for transitional provisions see Sch 2 paras 14, 19(a) thereof.

Amendment:

Sub-s (3): Words inserted: Domestic Violence, Crime and Victims Act 2004 s31, Sch 6 paras 1, 4, with effect from 31 March 2005 (SI 2005 No 579, article 3(e)).

250 Licence conditions

(1) In this section –

(a) 'the standard conditions' means such conditions as may be prescribed for the purposes of this section as standard conditions, and

(b) 'prescribed' means prescribed by the Secretary of State by order.

(2) Subject to subsection (6) and section 251, any licence under this Chapter in respect of a prisoner serving one or more sentences of imprisonment of less than twelve months and no sentence of twelve months or more –

(a) must include –
  (i) the conditions required by the relevant court order, and
  (ii) so far as not inconsistent with them, the standard conditions, and
(b) may also include –
  (i) any condition which is authorised by section 62 of the Criminal Justice and Court Services Act 2000 (c. 43) (electronic monitoring) or section 64 of that Act (drug testing requirements) and which is compatible with the conditions required by the relevant court order, and
  (ii) such other conditions of a kind prescribed for the purposes of this paragraph as the Secretary of State may for the time being consider to be necessary for the protection of the public and specify in the licence.

(3) For the purposes of subsection (2)(a)(i), any reference in the relevant court order to the licence period specified in the order is, in relation to a prohibited activity requirement, exclusion requirement, residence requirement or supervision requirement, to be taken to include a reference to any other period during which the prisoner is released on licence under section 246 or 248.

(4) Any licence under this Chapter in respect of a prisoner serving a sentence of imprisonment [or detention in a young offender institution] for a term of twelve months or more (including such a sentence imposed under section 227) or any sentence of detention under section 91 of the Sentencing Act or section 228 of this Act –
(a) must include the standard conditions, and
(b) may include –
  (i) any condition authorised by section 62 or 64 of the Criminal Justice and Court Services Act 2000, and
  (ii) such other conditions of a kind prescribed by the Secretary of State for the purposes of this paragraph as the Secretary of State may for the time being specify in the licence.

(5) A licence under section 246 must also include a curfew condition complying with section 253.

(6) Where –
(a) a licence under section 246 is granted to a prisoner serving one or more sentences of imprisonment of less than 12 months and no sentence of 12 months or more, and
(b) the relevant court order requires the licence to be granted subject to a condition requiring his compliance with a curfew requirement (as defined by section 204),

that condition is not to be included in the licence at any time while a curfew condition required by section 253 is in force.

(7) The preceding provisions of this section have effect subject to section 263(3) (concurrent terms) and section 264(3)[, section 264(3) and (4) (consecutive terms) and section 264A(3) (consecutive terms: intermittent custody)].

(8) In exercising his powers to prescribe standard conditions or the other conditions referred to in subsection (4)(b)(ii), the Secretary of State must have regard to the following purposes of the supervision of offenders while on licence under this Chapter –

(a) the protection of the public,
(b) the prevention of re-offending, and
(c) securing the successful re-integration of the prisoner into the community.

NOTES

Initial Commencement:

To be appointed: see s336(3).

Appointment:

Sub-ss(1)–(3), (5)–(8): Appointment (for the purposes of the passing of a sentence of imprisonment to which an intermittent custody order relates and the release on licence of a person serving such a sentence): 26 January 2004: see SI 2003 No 3282, article 2, Schedule.

Sub-ss(1), (2)(b)(ii), (8): Appointment (for remaining purposes): 7 March 2005: see SI 2005 No 373, article 2(1), (2)(n).

Sub-ss(4)–(7): Appointment: 4 April 2005: see SI 2005 No 950, article 2(1), Sch 1 para 19; for transitional provisions see Sch 2 paras 14, 19 thereof.

Sub-s(4)(b)(ii): Appointment: 7 March 2005: see SI 2005 No 373, article 2(1), (2)(n).

Amendment:

Sub-s(4): Words inserted (until the coming into force of the Criminal Justice and Court Services Act 2000, s 61): SI 2005 No 643, article 3(1), (11), with effect from 4 April 2005 (SI 2005 No 643, article 1(1)).

Sub-s(7): Words substituted: Domestic Violence, Crime and Victims Act 2004 s31, Sch 6 paras 1, 5, with effect from 31 March 2005 (SI 2005 No 579, article 3(e)).

251 Licence conditions on re-release of prisoner serving sentence of less than 12 months

(1) In relation to any licence under this Chapter which is granted to a prisoner serving one or more sentences of imprisonment of less than twelve months and no sentence of twelve months or more on his release in pursuance of a decision of the Board under section 254 or 256, subsections (2) and (3) apply instead of section 250(2).

(2) The licence –
  (a) must include the standard conditions, and
  (b) may include –
    (i) any condition authorised by section 62 or 64 of the Criminal Justice and Court Services Act 2000 (c. 43), and
    (ii) such other conditions of a kind prescribed by the Secretary of State for the purposes of section 250(4)(b)(ii) as the Secretary of State may for the time being specify in the licence.

(3) In exercising his powers under subsection (2)(b)(ii), the Secretary of State must have regard to the terms of the relevant court order.

(4) In this section 'the standard conditions' has the same meaning as in section 250.

NOTES

Initial Commencement:

To be appointed: see s336(3).

Appointment:

For the purposes of the passing of a sentence of imprisonment to which an intermittent custody order relates and the release on licence of a person serving such a sentence: 26 January 2004: see SI 2003 No 3282, article 2, Schedule.

252 Duty to comply with licence conditions

A person subject to a licence under this Chapter must comply with such conditions as may for the time being be specified in the licence.

NOTES

Initial Commencement:

To be appointed: see s336(3).

Appointment:

For the purposes of the passing of a sentence of imprisonment to which an intermittent custody order relates and the release on licence of a person serving such a sentence: 26 January 2004: see SI 2003 No 3282, article 2, Schedule.

For remaining purposes: 4 April 2005: see SI 2005 No 950, article 2(1), Sch 1 para 19; for transitional provisions see Sch 2 para 14 thereof.

253 Curfew condition to be included in licence under section 246

(1) For the purposes of this Chapter, a curfew condition is a condition which –

(a) requires the released person to remain, for periods for the time being specified in the condition, at a place for the time being so specified (which may be premises approved by the Secretary of State under section 9 of the Criminal Justice and Court Services Act 2000 (c. 43)), and

(b) includes requirements for securing the electronic monitoring of his whereabouts during the periods for the time being so specified.

(2) The curfew condition may specify different places or different periods for different days, but may not specify periods which amount to less than 9 hours in any one day (excluding for this purpose the first and last days of the period for which the condition is in force).

(3) The curfew condition is to remain in force until the date when the released person would (but for his release) fall to be released on licence under section 244.

(4) Subsection (3) does not apply in relation to a released person to whom an intermittent custody order relates; and in relation to such a person the curfew condition is to remain in force until the number of days during which it has been in force is equal to the number of the required custodial days, as defined in section 246(6), that remained to be served at the time when he was released under section 246.

(5) The curfew condition must include provision for making a person responsible for monitoring the released person's whereabouts during the periods for the time being specified in the condition; and a person who is made so responsible shall be of a description specified in an order made by the Secretary of State.

(6) Nothing in this section is to be taken to require the Secretary of State to ensure that arrangements are made for the electronic monitoring of released persons' whereabouts in any particular part of England and Wales.

NOTES

Initial Commencement:

To be appointed: see s336(3).

Appointment:

For the purposes of the passing of a sentence of imprisonment to which an intermittent custody order relates and the release on licence of a person serving such a sentence: 26 January 2004: see SI 2003 No 3282, article 2, Schedule.

Sub-ss(1)–(4), (6): Appointment (for remaining purposes): 4 April 2005: see SI 2005 No 950, article 2(1), Sch 1 para 19; for transitional provisions see Sch 2 para 14 thereof.

Sub-s(5): Appointment (for remaining purposes): 7 March 2005: see SI 2005 No 373, article 2(1), (2)(o).

Subordinate Legislation:

Criminal Justice (Sentencing) (Curfew Condition) Order 2005, SI 2005 No 986 (made under sub-s(5)).

Recall after release

254 Recall of prisoners while on licence

(1) The Secretary of State may, in the case of any prisoner who has been released on licence under this Chapter, revoke his licence and recall him to prison.

(2) A person recalled to prison under subsection (1) –

(a) may make representations in writing with respect to his recall, and

(b) on his return to prison, must be informed of the reasons for his recall and of his right to make representations.

(3) The Secretary of State must refer to the Board the case of a person recalled under subsection (1).

(4) Where on a reference under subsection (3) relating to any person the Board recommends his immediate release on licence under this Chapter, the Secretary of State must give effect to the recommendation.

(5) In the case of an intermittent custody prisoner who has not yet served in prison the number of custodial days specified in the intermittent custody order, any recommendation by the Board as to immediate release on licence is to be a recommendation as to his release on licence until the end of one of the licence periods specified by virtue of section 183(1)(b) in the intermittent custody order.

(6) On the revocation of the licence of any person under this section, he shall be liable to be detained in pursuance of his sentence and, if at large, is to be treated as being unlawfully at large.

(7) Nothing in subsections (2) to (6) applies in relation to a person recalled under section 255.

NOTES

Initial Commencement:

To be appointed: see s336(3).

Appointment:

For the purposes of the passing of a sentence of imprisonment to which an intermittent custody order relates and the release on licence of a person serving such a sentence: 26 January 2004: see SI 2003 No 3282, article 2, Schedule.

For remaining purposes: 4 April 2005: see SI 2005 No 950, article 2(1), Sch 1 para 19; for transitional provisions see Sch 2 paras 14, 23(1)(a) thereof (as confirmed by SI 2005 No 2122, article 2).

255 Recall of prisoners released early under section 246

(1) If it appears to the Secretary of State, as regards a person released on licence under section 246 –

(a) that he has failed to comply with any condition included in his licence, or

(b) that his whereabouts can no longer be electronically monitored at the place for the time being specified in the curfew condition included in his licence,

the Secretary of State may, if the curfew condition is still in force, revoke the licence and recall the person to prison under this section.

(2) A person whose licence under section 246 is revoked under this section –

(a) may make representations in writing with respect to the revocation, and

(b) on his return to prison, must be informed of the reasons for the revocation and of his right to make representations.

(3) The Secretary of State, after considering any representations under subsection (2)(b) or any other matters, may cancel a revocation under this section.

(4) Where the revocation of a person's licence is cancelled under subsection (3), the person is to be treated for the purposes of section 246 as if he had not been recalled to prison under this section.

(5) On the revocation of a person's licence under section 246, he is liable to be detained in pursuance of his sentence and, if at large, is to be treated as being unlawfully at large.

NOTES

Initial Commencement:

To be appointed: see s336(3).

Appointment:

For the purposes of the passing of a sentence of imprisonment to which an intermittent custody order relates and the release on licence of a person serving such a sentence: 26 January 2004: see SI 2003 No 3282, article 2, Schedule.

For remaining purposes: 4 April 2005: see SI 2005 No 950, article 2(1), Sch 1 para 19; for transitional provisions see Sch 2 para 14 thereof.

256 Further release after recall

(1) Where on a reference under section 254(3) in relation to any person, the Board does not recommend his immediate release on licence under this Chapter, the Board must either –

(a) fix a date for the person's release on licence, or

(b) fix a date as the date for the next review of the person's case by the Board.

(2) Any date fixed under subsection (1)(a) or (b) must not be later than the first anniversary of the date on which the decision is taken.

(3) The Board need not fix a date under subsection (1)(a) or (b) if the prisoner will fall to be released unconditionally at any time within the next 12 months.

(4) Where the Board has fixed a date under subsection (1)(a), it is the duty of the Secretary of State to release him on licence on that date.

(5) On a review required by subsection (1)(b) in relation to any person, the Board may –

(a) recommend his immediate release on licence, or

(b) fix a date under subsection (1)(a) or (b).

NOTES

Initial Commencement:

To be appointed: see s 336(3).

Appointment:

For the purposes of the passing of a sentence of imprisonment to which an intermittent custody order relates and the release on licence of a person serving such a sentence: 26 January 2004: see SI 2003 No 3282, article 2, Schedule.

For remaining purposes: 4 April 2005: see SI 2005 No 950, article 2(1), Sch 1 para 19; for transitional provisions see Sch 2 para 14 thereof.

SCHEDULE 19
THE PAROLE BOARD: SUPPLEMENTARY PROVISIONS

Section 239(7)

Status and Capacity

1 (1) The Board is not to be regarded as the servant or agent of the Crown or as enjoying any status, immunity or privilege of the Crown; and the Board's property is not to be regarded as property of, or held on behalf of, the Crown.

(2) It is within the capacity of the Board as a statutory corporation to do such things and enter into such transactions as are incidental to or conducive to the discharge of –

(a) its functions under Chapter 6 of Part 12 in respect of fixed-term prisoners, and

(b) its functions under Chapter 2 of Part 2 of the Crime (Sentences) Act 1997 (c. 43) in relation to life prisoners within the meaning of that Chapter.

Membership

2 (1) The Board is to consist of a chairman and not less than four other members appointed by the Secretary of State.

(2) The Board must include among its members –

(a) a person who holds or has held judicial office;

(b) a registered medical practitioner who is a psychiatrist;

(c) a person appearing to the Secretary of State to have knowledge and experience of the supervision or after-care of discharged prisoners; and

(d) a person appearing to the Secretary of State to have made a study of the causes of delinquency or the treatment of offenders.

(3) A member of the Board –

(a) holds and vacates office in accordance with the terms of his appointment;

(b) may resign his office by notice in writing addressed to the Secretary of State;

and a person who ceases to hold office as a member of the Board is eligible for re-appointment.

Payments to members

3 (1) The Board may pay to each member such remuneration and allowances as the Secretary of State may determine.

(2) The Board may pay or make provision for paying to or in respect of any member such sums by way of pension, allowances or gratuities as the Secretary of State may determine.

(3) If a person ceases to be a member otherwise than on the expiry of his term of office and it appears to the Secretary of State that there are special circumstances that make it right that he should receive compensation, the Secretary of State may direct the Board to make to that person a payment of such amount as the Secretary of State may determine.

(4) A determination or direction of the Secretary of State under this paragraph requires the approval of the Treasury.

Proceedings

4 (1) Subject to the provisions of section 239(5), the arrangements relating to meetings of the Board are to be such as the Board may determine.

(2) The arrangements may provide for the discharge, under the general direction of the Board, of any of the Board's functions by a committee or by one or more of the members or employees of the Board.

(3) The validity of the proceedings of the Board are not to be affected by any vacancy among the members or by any defect in the appointment of a member.

Staff

5 (1) The Board may appoint such number of employees as it may determine.

(2) The remuneration and other conditions of service of the persons appointed under this paragraph are to be determined by the Board.

(3) Any determination under sub-paragraph (1) or (2) requires the approval of the Secretary of State given with the consent of the Treasury.

(4) The Employers' Liability (Compulsory Insurance) Act 1969 (c. 57) shall not require insurance to be effected by the Board.

6 (1) Employment with the Board shall continue to be included among the kinds of employment to which a scheme under section 1 of the Superannuation Act 1972 (c. 11) can apply, and accordingly in Schedule 1 to that Act (in which those kinds of employment are listed) at the end of the list of Other Bodies there shall continue to be inserted –

'Parole Board.'.

(2) The Board shall pay to the Treasury, at such times as the Treasury may direct, such sums as the Treasury may determine in respect of the increase attributable to this paragraph in the sums payable under the Superannuation Act 1972 out of money provided by Parliament.

Financial provisions

7 (1) The Secretary of State shall pay to the Board –

(a) any expenses incurred or to be incurred by the Board by virtue of paragraph 3 or 5; and

(b) with the consent of the Treasury, such sums as he thinks fit for enabling the Board to meet other expenses.

(2) Any sums required by the Secretary of State for making payments under sub-paragraph (1) are to be paid out of money provided by Parliament.

Authentication of Board's seal

8 The application of the seal of the Board is to be authenticated by the signature of the Chairman or some other person authorised for the purpose.

Presumption of authenticity of documents issued by Board

9 Any document purporting to be an instrument issued by the Board and to be duly executed under the seal of the Board or to be signed on behalf of the Board shall be received in evidence and shall be deemed to be such an instrument unless the contrary is shown.

Accounts and audit

10 (1) It is the duty of the Board –

(a) to keep proper accounts and proper records in relation to the accounts;

(b) to prepare in respect of each financial year a statement of accounts in such form as the Secretary of State may direct with the approval of the Treasury; and

(c) to send copies of each such statement to the Secretary of State and the Comptroller and Auditor General not later than 31st August next following the end of the financial year to which the statement relates.

(2) The Comptroller and Auditor General shall examine, certify and report on each statement of accounts sent to him by the Board and shall lay a copy of every such statement and of his report before each House of Parliament.

(3) In this paragraph and paragraph 11 'financial year' means a period of 12 months ending with 31st March.

Reports

11 The Board must as soon as practicable after the end of each financial year make to the Secretary of State a report on the performance of its functions during the year; and the Secretary of State must lay a copy of the report before each House of Parliament.

NOTES

Initial Commencement:

To be appointed: see s336(3).

Appointment:

For the purposes of the passing of a sentence of imprisonment to which an intermittent custody order relates and the release on licence of a person serving such a sentence: 26 January 2004: see SI 2003 No 3282, article 2, Schedule.

For remaining purposes: 4 April 2005: see SI 2005 No 950, article 2(1), Sch 1 para 41.

APPENDIX 3

Relevant sections of the Crime (Sentences) Act 1997

These sections relate to the release and recall of indeterminate sentence prisoners.

Crime (Sentences) Act 1997 ss28–32 (as amended)

28 Duty to release certain life prisoners

[(1A) This section applies to a life prisoner in respect of whom a minimum term order has been made; and any reference in this section to the relevant part of such a prisoner's sentence is a reference to the part of the sentence specified in the order].

(1B) But if a life prisoner is serving two or more life sentences –

(a) [this section does not apply to him]s unless [a minimum term order has been made in respect of each of those sentences]e; and

(b) the provisions of subsections (5) to (8) below do not apply in relation to him until he has served the relevant part of each of them.

(5) As soon as –

(a) a life prisoner to whom this section applies has served the relevant part of his sentence,]

(b) the Parole Board has directed his release under this section,

it shall be the duty of the Secretary of State to release him on licence.

(6) The Parole Board shall not give a direction under subsection (5) above with respect to a life prisoner to whom this section applies unless –

(a) the Secretary of State has referred the prisoner's case to the Board; and

(b) the Board is satisfied that it is no longer necessary for the protection of the public that the prisoner should be confined.

(7) A life prisoner to whom this section applies may require the Secretary of State to refer his case to the Parole Board at any time –

(a) after he has served the relevant part of his sentence; and

(b) where there has been a previous reference of his case to the Board, after the end of the period of two years beginning with the disposal of that reference; and

(c) where he is also serving a sentence of imprisonment or detention for a term, after [he has served one-half of that sentence];

and in this subsection 'previous reference' means a reference under subsection (6) above or section 32(4) below.

(8) In determining for the purpose of subsection (5) or (7) above whether a life

prisoner to whom this section applies has served the relevant part of his sentence, no account shall be taken of any time during which he was unlawfully at large within the meaning of section 49 of the Prison Act 1952

[(8A) In this section 'minimum term order' means an order under –

(a) subsection (2) of section 82A of the Powers of Criminal Courts (Sentencing) Act 2000 (determination of minimum term in respect of life sentence that is not fixed by law), or

(b) subsection (2) of section 269 of the Criminal Justice Act 2003 (determination of minimum term in respect of mandatory life sentence).]

(9) . . .

NOTES

Initial Commencement

To be appointed: see s57(2).

Appointment: 1 October 1997: see SI 1997 No 2200 article 2(1)(f).

Extent: This section does not extend to Scotland.

Amendment:

Sub-ss(1A), (1B), (5)(a): substituted, for sub-ss(1)–(5)(a) as originally enacted, by the Criminal Justice and Court Services Act 2000 s74, Sch 7 Pt II paras 135, 136(a), 145, 148, in relation to life sentences passed after 30 November 2000.
Date in force: this amendment came into force on 30 November 2000 (date of royal assent of the Criminal Justice and Court Services Act 2000) in the absence of any specific commencement provision.

Sub-s(1A): further substituted by the Criminal Justice Act 2003 s275(1), (2).
Date in force: 18 December 2003: see the Criminal Justice Act 2003 s336(2).

Sub-s(1B): in para (a) words 'this section does not apply to him' in square brackets substituted by the Criminal Justice Act 2003 s275(1), (3)(a).
Date in force: 18 December 2003: see the Criminal Justice Act 2003 s336(2).

Sub-s(1B): in para (a) words from 'a minimum term' to 'of those sentences' in square brackets substituted by the Criminal Justice Act 2003 s275(1), (3)(b).
Date in force: 18 December 2003: see the Criminal Justice Act 2003 s336(2).

Sub-s(7): in para (c) words 'he has served one-half of that sentence' in square brackets substituted by the Crime and Disorder Act 1998 s119, Sch 8 para 130(2).
Date in force: 30 September 1998: see SI 1998 No 2327 article 2(1)(y), (2)(ll).

Sub-s(8A): inserted by the Criminal Justice Act 2003 s275(1), (4).
Date in force: 18 December 2003: see the Criminal Justice Act 2003 s336(2).

Sub-s(9): repealed by the Criminal Justice and Court Services Act 2000 ss74, 75, Sch 7 Pt II paras 135, 136(b), 145, 148, Sch 8, in relation to life sentences passed after 30 November 2000.
Date in force: this amendment came into force on 30 November 2000 (date of royal assent of the Criminal Justice and Court Services Act 2000) in the absence of any specific commencement provision.

Transitional Modifications: see Sch 5 para 5 hereto.

The Criminal Justice and Court Services Act 2000 s74, Sch 7 Pt II paras 146, 147, 148 provides that sub-s(1B) above has effect as if any reference to a life sentence included a pre-commencement life sentence, any reference to an order or direction in relation to such a life sentence were to an order under sub-s(2)(b) or a direction under section sub-s(4) above (as originally enacted) or a certificate under s33 hereto, and any reference to the relevant part of such a life sentence were to the part specified in the order, direction or certificate, as the case may be, relating to that sentence.

See further: in relation to the disapplication of this section in relation to a person detained in England and Wales in pursuance of a sentence of the International Criminal Court: see the International Criminal Court Act 2001 s42(6), Sch 7 paras 1, 3(1).

See further, in respect of the application of this section (with modifications) in relation to existing prisoners: see the Criminal Justice Act 2003 s276, Sch 22 para 16.

29 . . .

. . .

NOTES

Amendment: Repealed by the Criminal Justice Act 2003 ss303(b)(i), 332, Sch 37 Pt 8.

Date in force: 18 December 2003: see the Criminal Justice Act 2003 s336(2).

30 Power to release life prisoners on compassionate grounds

(1) The Secretary of State may at any time release a life prisoner on licence if he is satisfied that exceptional circumstances exist which justify the prisoner's release on compassionate grounds.

(2) Before releasing a life prisoner under subsection (1) above, the Secretary of State shall consult the Parole Board, unless the circumstances are such as to render such consultation impracticable.

NOTES

Initial Commencement

To be appointed: see s57(2).

Appointment: 1 October 1997: see SI 1997 No 2200 article 2(1)(f).

Extent: This section does not extend to Scotland.

See further: in relation to the disapplication of this section in relation to a person detained in England and Wales in pursuance of a sentence of the International Criminal Court: see the International Criminal Court Act 2001 s42(6), Sch 7 paras 1, 3(1).

31 Duration and conditions of licences

(1) Where a life prisoner[, other than a prisoner to whom section 31A below applies,] is released on licence, the licence shall, unless previously revoked under section 32(1) or (2) below, remain in force until his death.

[(1A) Where a prisoner to whom section 31A below applies is released on licence, the licence shall remain in force until his death unless—

(a) it is previously revoked under section 32(1) or (2) below; or

(b) it ceases to have effect in accordance with an order made by the Secretary of State under section 31A below.]

(2) A life prisoner subject to a licence shall comply with such conditions . . . as may for the time being be specified in the licence; and the Secretary of State may make rules for regulating the supervision of any description of such persons.

[(2A) The conditions so specified shall include on the prisoner's release conditions as to his supervision by –

(a) [an officer of a local probation board] appointed for or assigned to the [local justice area] within which the prisoner resides for the time being;

(b) where the prisoner is under the age of 22, a social worker of the social services department of the local authority within whose area the prisoner resides for the time being; or

(c) where the prisoner is under the age of 18, a member of a youth offending team established by that local authority under section 39 of the Crime and Disorder Act 1998.]

(3) The Secretary of State shall not include on release, or subsequently insert, a condition in the licence of a life prisoner, or vary or cancel any such condition, [except in accordance with recommendations of the Parole Board].

(4) . . .

(5) The power to make rules under this section shall be exercisable by statutory instrument which shall be subject to annulment in pursuance of a resolution of either House of Parliament.

(6) In relation to a life prisoner who is liable to removal from the United Kingdom (within the meaning given by [section 259 of the Criminal Justice Act 2003]), subsection (2) above shall have effect as if [subsection (2A) above] were omitted.

NOTES

Initial Commencement

To be appointed: see s57(2).

Appointment: 1 October 1997: see SI 1997 No 2200 article 2(1)(f).

Extent: This section does not extend to Scotland.

Amendment:

Sub-s(1): words ', other than a prisoner to whom section 31A below applies,' in square brackets inserted by the Criminal Justice Act 2003 s230, Sch 18 para 1(1), (2).

Date in force: 4 April 2005: see SI 2005 No 950 article 2(1), Sch 1 para 40.

Sub-s(1A): inserted by the Criminal Justice Act 2003 s230, Sch 18 para 1(1), (3).

Date in force: 4 April 2005: see SI 2005 No 950 article 2(1), Sch 1 para 40.

Sub-s(2): words omitted repealed by the Crime and Disorder Act 1998, ss 119, 120(2), Sch 8, para 131(1), Sch 10.

Date in force (in relation to certain specified areas): 30 September 1998: see SI 1998/2327, art 3(1)(b), Sch 1.

Date in force (for remaining purposes): 1 April 2000: see SI 2000/924, art 2(c).

Sub-s(2A): inserted by the Crime and Disorder Act 1998, s 119, Sch 8, para 131(2).

Date in force (in relation to certain specified areas): 30 September 1998: see SI 1998/2327, art 3(1)(b), Sch 1.

Date in force (for remaining purposes): 1 April 2000: see SI 2000/924, art 2(c).

Sub-s(2A): in para (a) words 'an officer of a local probation board' in square brackets substituted by the Criminal Justice and Court Services Act 2000, s74, Sch 7, Pt I, para 4(1)(a), (2).

Date in force: 1 April 2001: see SI 2001/919, art 2(f)(i).

Sub-s(2A): in para (a) words 'local justice area' in square brackets substituted by SI 2005 No 886 article 2, Schedule para 53.

Date in force: 1 April 2005: see SI 2005 No 886 article 1.

Sub-s(2A): in para (b) words 'social services department of the' in italics repealed by the Children Act 2004 s64, Sch 5 Pt 4.

Date in force (in relation to England): 1 April 2005: see SI 2005 No 394 article 2(2)(g).

Date in force (in relation to Wales): to be appointed: see the Children Act 2004 s64, Sch 5 Pt 4.

Sub-s(3): words 'except in accordance with recommendations of the Parole Board' in square brackets substituted by the Criminal Justice Act 2003 s304, Sch 32 Pt 1 paras 82, 83(1), (2).

Date in force: 18 December 2003: see the Criminal Justice Act 2003 s336(2).

Sub-s(4): repealed by the Criminal Justice Act 2003 ss304, 332, Sch 32 Pt 1 paras 82, 83(1), (3), Sch 37 Pt 8.

Date in force: 18 December 2003: see the Criminal Justice Act 2003, s336(2).

Sub-s(6): words 'section 46(3) of the 1991 Act' in italics repealed and subsequent words in square brackets substituted by the Criminal Justice Act 2003, s 304, Sch 32, Pt 1, paras 82, 83(1), (4).

Date in force: 4 April 2005: see SI 2005 No 950 article 2(1), Sch 1 para 42(1), (32).

Sub-s(6): words 'subsection (2A) above' in square brackets substituted by the Crime and Disorder Act 1998 s119, Sch 8 para 131(3).

Date in force: 30 September 1998: see SI 1998 No 2327 article 2(1)(y), (2)(mm).

See further: in relation to the disapplication of this section in relation to a person detained in England and Wales in pursuance of a sentence of the International Criminal Court: see the International Criminal Court Act 2001 s42(6), Sch 7 paras 1, 3(1).

31A Imprisonment or detention for public protection: termination of licences]

[(1) This section applies to a prisoner who –
  (a) is serving one or more preventive sentences, and
  (b) is not serving any other life sentence.

(2) Where –
  (a) the prisoner has been released on licence under this Chapter; and
  (b) the qualifying period has expired,

the Secretary of State shall, if directed to do so by the Parole Board, order that the licence is to cease to have effect.

(3) Where –
  (a) the prisoner has been released on licence under this Chapter;
  (b) the qualifying period has expired; and
  (c) if he has made a previous application under this subsection, a period of at least twelve months has expired since the disposal of that application,

the prisoner may make an application to the Parole Board under this subsection.

(4) Where an application is made under subsection (3) above, the Parole Board –

(a) shall, if it is satisfied that it is no longer necessary for the protection of the public that the licence should remain in force, direct the Secretary of State to make an order that the licence is to cease to have effect;

(b) shall otherwise dismiss the application.

(5) In this section –

'preventive sentence' means a sentence of imprisonment for public protection under section 225 of the Criminal Justice Act 2003 or a sentence of detention for public protection under section 226 of that Act;

'the qualifying period', in relation to a prisoner who has been released on licence, means the period of ten years beginning with the date of his release.]

NOTES

Extent: This section does not extend to Scotland: see s57(4).

Amendment:

Inserted by the Criminal Justice Act 2003 s230, Sch 18 para 2 (sub-s(5) further amended (until the coming into force of the Criminal Justice and Court Services Act 2000 s61) by SI 2005 No 643 article 3(1), (17)(a)).

Date in force: 4 April 2005: see SI 2005 No 950 article 2(1), Sch 1 para 40.

32 Recall of life prisoners while on licence

(1) If recommended to do so by the Parole Board in the case of a life prisoner who has been released on licence under this Chapter, the Secretary of State may revoke his licence and recall him to prison.

(2) The Secretary of State may revoke the licence of any life prisoner and recall him to prison without a recommendation by the Parole Board, where it appears to him that it is expedient in the public interest to recall that person before such a recommendation is practicable.

(3) A life prisoner recalled to prison under subsection (1) or (2) above –

(a) may make representations in writing with respect to his recall; and

(b) on his return to prison, shall be informed of the reasons for his recall and of his right to make representations.

(4) The Secretary of State shall refer to the Parole Board –

(a) the case of a life prisoner recalled under subsection (1) above who makes representations under subsection (3) above; and

(b) the case of a life prisoner recalled under subsection (2) above.

[(5) Where on a reference under subsection (4) above the Parole Board directs the immediate release on licence under this section of the life prisoner, the Secretary of State shall give effect to the direction.]

(6) On the revocation of the licence of any life prisoner under this section, he shall be liable to be detained in pursuance of his sentence and, if at large, shall be deemed to be unlawfully at large.

NOTES

Initial Commencement

To be appointed: see s57(2).

Appointment: 1 October 1997: see SI 1997 No 2200 article 2(1)(f).

Extent: This section does not extend to Scotland.

Amendment:
Sub-s(5): substituted by the Criminal Justice Act 2003 s304, Sch 32 Pt 1 paras 82, 84.
Date in force: 18 December 2003: see the Criminal Justice Act 2003 s336(2).
See further: in relation to the disapplication of this section in relation to a person detained in England and Wales in pursuance of a sentence of the International Criminal Court: see the International Criminal Court Act 2001 s42(6), Sch 7 paras 1, 3(1).

APPENDIX 4

Relevant sections of the Criminal Justice Act 1991

Parts of the CJA 1991 saved in relation to the initial release of those sentenced for offences committed before 4 April 2005 – see the Criminal Justice Act 2003 (Commencement No 8 and Transitional and Saving Provisions) Order 2005 SI No 950.

CRIMINAL JUSTICE ACT 1991 ss33, 33A–38A, 40A–44 (AS AMENDED)

NOTES

Information:

Act reference: 2003 c 53. Royal assent: 25 July 1991. Long title: An Act to make further provision with respect to the treatment of offenders and the position of children and young persons and persons having responsibility for them; to make provision with respect to certain services provided or proposed to be provided for purposes connected with the administration of justice or the treatment of offenders; to make financial and other provision with respect to that administration; and for connected purposes.

New arrangements for early release

NOTES

Amendment:

Heading repealed with savings: Criminal Justice Act 2003 ss303(a), 332, Sch 37, Pt 7, with effect from 4 April 2005 (SI 2005 No 950, article 2(1), Sch 1 paras 22, 44(1), (4)(k); for savings see Sch 2 paras 14, 19(c), 23(1) (as confirmed by SI 2005 No 2122, article 2) and para 34 thereof).

33 Duty to release short-term and long-term prisoners

(1) As soon as a short-term prisoner has served one-half of his sentence, it shall be the duty of the Secretary of State –
  (a) to release him unconditionally if that sentence is for a term of less than twelve months; and
  (b) to release him on licence if that sentence is for a term of twelve months or more.

(2) As soon as a long-term prisoner has served two-thirds of his sentence, it shall be the duty of the Secretary of State to release him on licence.

(3) As soon as a short-term or long-term prisoner who –
  (a) has been released on licence under [this Part]; and
  (b) has been recalled to prison under section [39(1) or (2)] below,

would (but for his release) have served three-quarters of his sentence, it shall be the duty of the Secretary of State to release him [on licence].

[(3A) In the case of a prisoner to whom section 44A below applies, it shall be the duty of the Secretary of State to release him on licence at the end of the extension period (within the meaning of [section 85 of the Powers of Criminal Courts (Sentencing) Act 2000].]

(4) ...

(5) In this Part –

'long-term prisoner' means a person serving a sentence of imprisonment for a term of four years or more;

'short-term prisoner' means a person serving a sentence of imprisonment for a term of less than four years.

NOTES

Amendment:

Provision repealed with savings: Criminal Justice Act 2003 ss303(a), 332, Sch 37 Pt 7, with effect from 4 April 2005 (SI 2005 No 950, article 2(1), Sch 1 paras 22, 44(1), (4)(k); for savings see Sch 2 paras 14, 19(c), 23(1) (as confirmed by SI 2005 No 2122, article 2) and para 34 thereof).

Sub-s(3)(a): words in square brackets substituted by Crime and Disorder Act 1998, s119, Sch 8, para 80(1)(a).

Sub-s(3)(b): words in square brackets substituted by Crime and Disorder Act 1998, s119, Sch 8, para 80(1)(b): for savings, see Sch 9, para 12(1), (3).

Sub-s(3): closing paragraph: words in square brackets substituted with savings by Crime and Disorder Act 1998, s104(1): for savings, see Sch 9, para 13.

Sub-s(3A): inserted by Crime and Disorder Act 1998, s119, Sch 8, para 80(2).

Sub-s(3A): words in square brackets substituted by Powers of Criminal Courts (Sentencing) Act 2000, s165(1), Sch 9, para 137.

Sub-s(4): repealed by Crime and Disorder Act 1998, ss199, 120(2), Sch 8, para 80(3), Sch 10.

[33A Duty to release prisoners: special cases

(1) As soon as a prisoner –

(a) whose sentence is for a term of less than twelve months; and

(b) who has been released on licence under section 34A(3) or 36(1) below and recalled to prison under section 38A(1) or 39(1) or (2) below,

would (but for his release) have served one-half of his sentence, it shall be the duty of the Secretary of State to release him unconditionally.

(2) As soon as a prisoner –

(a) whose sentence is for a term of twelve months or more; and

(b) who has been released on licence under section 34A(3) below and recalled to prison under section 38A(1) below,

would (but for his release) have served one-half of his sentence, it shall be the duty of the Secretary of State to release him on licence.

(3) In the case of a prisoner who –

(a) has been released on licence under this Part and recalled to prison under section 39(1) or (2) below; and

(b) has been subsequently released on licence under section 33(3) or (3A) above and recalled to prison under section 39(1) or (2) below, section 33(3) above shall have effect as if for the words 'three-quarters' there were substituted the words 'the whole' and the words 'on licence' were omitted.]

NOTES

Amendment:

Provision inserted: Crime and Disorder Act 1998 s119, Sch 8, para 81, subject ot transitional provisions in Sch 9, para 12(1), (4), with effect from 30 September 1998 (SI 1998 No 2327, article 2(1)(y), (2)(y)).

Provision repealed with savings: Criminal Justice Act 2003 ss303(a), 332, Sch 37 Pt 7, with effect from 4 April 2005 (SI 2005 No 950, article 2(1), Sch 1 paras 22, 44(1), (4)(k); for savings see Sch 2 paras 14, 19(c), 23(1) (as confirmed by SI 2005 No 2122, article 2) and para 34 thereof).

34 ...

NOTES

Amendment:

Provision repealed: Crime (Sentences) Act 1997 s56(2), Schs 5, 6, with effect from 1 October 1997 (SI 1997 No 2200, art 2(1)(p), (2)(a)).

[34A Power to release short-term prisoners on licence

(1) Subject to subsection (2) below, subsection (3) below applies where a short-term prisoner ... is serving a sentence of imprisonment for a term of three months or more.

(2) Subsection (3) below does not apply where –

(a) the sentence is an extended sentence within the meaning of [section 85 of the Powers of Criminal Courts (Sentencing) Act 2000];

(b) the sentence is for an offence under section 1 of the Prisoners (Return to Custody) Act 1995;

(c) the sentence was imposed under [paragraph 4(1)(d) or 5(1)(d) of Schedule 3 to the Powers of Criminal Courts (Sentencing) Act 2000] in a case where the prisoner had failed to comply with a requirement of a curfew order;

(d) the prisoner is subject to a hospital order, hospital direction or transfer direction under section 37, 45A or 47 of the Mental Health Act 1983;

[(da) the prisoner is subject to the notification requirements of [Part 2 of the Sexual Offences Act 2003];]

(e) the prisoner is liable to removal from the United Kingdom for the purposes of section 46 below;

(f) the prisoner has been released on licence under this section at any time and has been recalled to prison under section 38A(1)(a) below;

(g) the prisoner has been released on licence under this section or section 36 below during the currency of the sentence, and has been recalled to prison under section 39(1) or (2) below;

(h) the prisoner has been returned to prison under [section 116 of the Powers of Criminal Courts (Sentencing) Act 2000] at any time; or

(j) the interval between –

(i) the date on which the prisoner will have served the requisite period for the term of the sentence; and

(ii) the date on which he will have served one-half of the sentence,
is less than 14 days.

(3) After the prisoner has served the requisite period for the term of his sentence, the Secretary of State may, subject to section 37A below, release him on licence.

(4) In this section 'the requisite period' means –
(a) for a term of three months or more but less than four months, a period of 30 days;
(b) for a term of four months or more but less than [eighteen months], a period equal to one-quarter of the term;
(c) for a term of [eighteen months] or more, a period that is [135 days] less than one-half of the term.

(5) The Secretary of State may by order made by statutory instrument –
(a) repeal the words 'aged 18 or over' in subsection (1) above;
(b) amend the definition of 'the requisite period' in subsection (4) above; and
(c) make such transitional provision as appears to him necessary or expedient in connection with the repeal or amendment.

(6) No order shall be made under subsection (5) above unless a draft of the order has been laid before and approved by a resolution of each House of Parliament.]

NOTES

Amendment:

Provision inserted: Crime and Disorder Act 1998 s99, with effect from 28 January 1999 (SI 1998 No 3263, article 3).

Provision repealed with savings: Criminal Justice Act 2003 ss303(a), 332, Sch 37 Pt 7, with effect from 4 April 2005 (SI 2005 No 950, article 2(1), Sch 1 paras 22, 44(1), (4)(k); for savings see Sch 2 paras 14, 19(c), 22, 23(1) (as confirmed by SI 2005 No 2122, article 2) and para 34 thereof).

Sub-s(1): words omitted repealed by Release of Short-Term Prisoners on Licence (Repeal of Age Restriction) Order 2003, SI 2003/1681, art 2.

Sub-s(2)(a): words in square brackets substituted by Powers of Criminal Courts (Sentencing) Act 2000, s165(1), Sch 9, para 138(a).

Sub-s(2)(c): words in square brackets substituted by Powers of Criminal Courts (Sentencing) Act 2000, s165(1), Sch 9, para 138(b).

Sub-s(2)(da): inserted by Criminal Justice and Court Services Act 2000, s65.

Sub-s(2)(da): words in square brackets substituted by Sexual Offences Act 2003, s139, Sch 6, para 30.

Sub-s(2)(h): words in square brackets substituted by Powers of Criminal Courts (Sentencing) Act 2000, s165(1), Sch 9, para 138(c).

Sub-s(4)(b): words in square brackets substituted by Release of Short-Term Prisoners on Licence (Amendment of Requisite Period) Order 2003, SI 2003/1602, art 3(1).

Sub-s(4)(c): words in square brackets substituted by Release of Short-Term Prisoners on Licence (Amendment of Requisite Period) Order 2003, SI 2003/1602, art 3(2).

35 Power to release long-term and life prisoners

(1) After a long-term prisoner has served one-half of his sentence, the Secretary of State may, if recommended to do so by the Board, release him on licence.

(2) ...

(3) ...

NOTES

Amendment:

Provision repealed with savings: Criminal Justice Act 2003 ss303(a), 332, Sch 37 Pt 7, with effect from 4 April 2005 (SI 2005 No 950, article 2(1), Sch 1 paras 22, 44(1), (4)(k); for savings see Sch 2 paras 14, 19(c), 22, 23(1) (as confirmed by SI 2005 No 2122, article 2) and para 34 thereof).

Sub-s(2): repealed by Crime (Sentences) Act 1997 s56(2), Schs 5, 6, with effect from 1 October 1997 (SI 1997 No 2200, article 2(1)(p), (3)(b)).

Sub-s(3): repealed by Crime (Sentences) Act 1997 s56(2), Schs 5, 6, with effect from 1 October 1997 (SI 1997 No 2200, article 2(1)(p), (3)(b)).

36 Power to release prisoners on compassionate grounds

(1) The Secretary of State may at any time release a [short-term or long-term prisoner] on licence if he is satisfied that exceptional circumstances exist which justify the prisoner's release on compassionate grounds.

(2) Before releasing a long-term ... prisoner under subsection (1) above, the Secretary of State shall consult the Board, unless the circumstances are such as to render such consultation impracticable.

NOTES

Amendment:

Provision repealed with savings: Criminal Justice Act 2003 ss303(a), 332, Sch 37 Pt 7, with effect from 4 April 2005 (SI 2005 No 950, article 2(1), Sch 1 paras 22, 44(1), (4)(k); for savings see Sch 2 paras 14, 19(c), 23(1) (as confirmed by SI 2005 No 2122, article 2) and para 34 thereof).

Sub-s(1): repealed so far as relating to life prisoners by Crime (Sentences) Act 1997, s56, Schs 5, 6.

Sub-s(1): words in square brackets substituted by Crime and Disorder Act 1998, s119, Sch 8, para 82.

Sub-s(2): words omitted repealed by Crime (Sentences) Act 1997, s56, Schs 5, 6.

37 Duration and conditions of licences

(1) Subject to [subsection (1A), (1B) and (2)] below, where a short-term or long-term prisoner is released on licence, the licence shall, subject to ... any revocation under section 39(1) or (2) below, remain in force until the date on which he would (but for his release) have served three-quarters of his sentence.

[(1A) Where a prisoner is released on licence under section 33(3) or (3A) above, subsection (1) above shall have effect as if for the reference to three-quarters of his sentence there were substituted a reference to the whole of that sentence.]

[(1B) Where a prisoner whose sentence is for a term of twelve months or more is released on licence under section 33A(2) or 34A(3) above, subsection (1) above shall have effect as if for the reference to three-quarters of his sentence there were substituted a reference to the difference between –

(a) that proportion of his sentence; and
(b) the duration of the curfew condition to which he is or was subject.]

(2) Where a prisoner whose sentence is for a term of less than twelve months is released on licence under [section 34A(3) or 36(1) above], subsection (1) above shall have effect as if for the reference to three-quarters of his sentence there were substituted a reference to one-half of that sentence.

(3) ...

(4) A person subject to a licence [under this part] shall comply with such conditions ... as may for the time being be specified in the licence; and the Secretary of State may make rules for regulating the supervision of any description of such persons.

[(4A) The conditions so specified may in the case of a person released on licence under section 34A above whose sentence is for a term or less that twelve months, and shall in any other case, include on the person's release conditions as to his supervision by –
(a) [an officer of a local probation board] appointed for or assigned to the petty sessions area within which the person resides for the time being; or
(b) where the person is under the age of 18 years, a member of a youth offending team established by the local authority within whose area the person resides for the time being.]

[(5) The Secretary of State shall not include on release, or subsequently insert, a condition in the licence of a long-term or life prisoner, or vary or cancel any such condition, except after consultation with the Board.]

(6) For the purposes of subsection (5) above, the Secretary of State shall be treated as having consulted the Board about a proposal to include, insert, vary or cancel a condition in any case if he has consulted the Board about the implementation of proposals of that description generally or in that class of case.

(7) The power to make rules under this section shall be exercisable by statutory instrument which shall be subject to annulment in pursuance of a resolution of either House of Parliament.

NOTES

Amendment:

Provision repealed with savings: Criminal Justice Act 2003 ss303(a), 332, Sch 37 Pt 7, with effect from 4 April 2005 (SI 2005 No 950, article 2(1), Sch 1 paras 22, 44(1), (4)(k); for savings see Sch 2 paras 14, 19(c), 23(1) (as confirmed by SI 2005 No 2122, article 2) and para 34 thereof).

Sub-s(1): words in square brackets substituted by Crime and Disorder Act 1998, s119, Sch 8, para 83(1)(a).

Sub-s(1): words omitted repealed with savings by Crime and Disorder Act 1998, ss119, 120(2), Sch 8, para 83(1)(b), Sch 10 (for savings, see Sch 9, para 12(1), (2)).

Sub-s(1A): inserted with savings by Crime and Disorder Act 1998, s104(2), Sch 8, para 83(1)(b), Sch 10 (for savings, see Sch 9, para 13).

Sub-s(1B): inserted by Crime and Disorder Act 1998, s119, Sch 8, para 83(2).

Sub-s(2): words in square brackets substituted by Crime and Disorder Act 1998, s119, Sch 8, para 83(3).

Sub-s(3): repealed by Crime (Sentences) Act 1997, s56, Schs 5, 6.

Sub-s(4): repealed so far as relating to life prisioners by Crime (Sentences) Act 1997, s56, Schs 5, 6.

Sub-s(4): words in square brackets inserted by Crime and Disorder Act 1998, s119, Sch 8, para 83(4)(a).

Sub-s(4): words omitted repealed by Crime and Disorder Act 1998, ss119, 120(2), Sch 8, para 83(4)(b), Sch 10.

Sub-s(4A): inserted by Crime and Disorder Act 1998, s119, Sch 8, para 83(5).

Sub-s(4A): words in square brackets substituted by Criminal Justice and Court Services Act 2000, s74, Sch 7, Pt I, para 4.

Sub-s(5): repealed so far as relating to life prisioners by Crime (Sentences) Act 1997, s56, Schs 5, 6.

Sub-s(5): substituted by Crime and Disorder Act 1998, s119, Sch 8, para 83(6).

[37A Curfew condition to be included in licence under section 34A

(1) A person shall not be released under section 34A(3) above unless the licence includes a condition ('the curfew condition') which –

(a) requires the released person to remain, for periods for the time being specified in the condition, at a place for the time being so specified (which may be an approved probation hostel); and

(b) includes requirements for securing the electronic monitoring of his whereabouts during the periods for the time being so specified.

(2) The curfew condition may specify different places or different periods for different days, but shall not specify periods which amount to less than 9 hours in any one day (excluding for this purpose the first and last days of the period for which the condition is in force).

(3) The curfew condition shall remain in force until the date when the released person would (but for his release) have served one-half of his sentence.

(4) The curfew condition shall include provision for making a person responsible for monitoring the released person's whereabouts during the periods for the time being specified in the condition; and a person who is made so responsible shall be of a description specified in an order made by the Secretary of State.

(5) The power conferred by subsection (4) above –

(a) shall be exercisable by statutory instrument; and

(b) shall include power to make different provision for different cases or classes of case or for different areas.

(6) Nothing in this section shall be taken to require the Secretary of State to ensure that arrangements are made for the electronic monitoring of released persons' whereabouts in any particular part of England and Wales.

(7) In this section 'approved probation hostel' has the same meaning as in the Probation Service Act 1993.]

NOTES

Amendment:

Provision inserted: Crime and Disorder Act 1998 s100(1), with effect from 30 September 1998 (for certain purposes) (SI 1998 No 2327, article 2(1)(u)); 28 January 1999 (for remaining purposes) (SI 1998 No 3263, article 3).

Provision repealed with savings: Criminal Justice Act 2003 ss303(a), 332, Sch

37 Pt 7, with effect from 1 April 2005 (SI 2005 No 950, article 2(1), Sch 1 paras 22, 44(1), (4)(k); for savings see Sch 2 paras 14, 19(c), 23(1) (as confirmed by SI 2005 No 2122, article 2) and para 34 thereof).

Misbehaviour after release

NOTES

Amendment:

Heading repealed with savings: Criminal Justice Act 2003 ss303(a), 332, Sch 37 Pt 7, with effect from 4 April 2005 (SI 2005 No 950, article 2(1), Sch 1 paras 22, 44(1), (4)(k); for savings see Sch 2 paras 14, 19(c), 23(1) (as confirmed by SI 2005 No 2122, article 2) and para 34 thereof).

38 ...

NOTES

Amendment:

Provision repealed: Crime and Disorder Act 1998 ss103(2), 120(2), Sch 10, with effect from 1 January 1999 (SI 1998 No 3263, article 2(a)).

[38A Breach of curfew condition

(1) If it appears to the Secretary of State, as regards a person released on licence under section 34A(3) above –
 (a) that he has failed to comply with the curfew condition;
 (b) that his whereabouts can no longer be electronically monitored at the place for the time being specified in that condition; or
 (c) that it is necessary to do so in order to protect the public from serious harm from him,

the Secretary of State may, if the curfew condition is still in force, revoke the licence and recall the person to prison.

(2) A person whose licence under section 34A(3) above is revoked under this section –
 (a) may make representations in writing with respect to the revocation;
 (b) on his return to prison, shall be informed of the reasons for the revocation and of his right to make representations.

(3) The Secretary of State, after considering any representations made under subsection (2)(b) above or any other matters, may cancel a revocation under this section.

(4) Where the revocation of a person's licence is cancelled under subsection (3) above, the person shall be treated for the purposes of sections 34A(2)(f) and 37(1B) above as if he had not been recalled to prison under this section.

(5) On the revocation under this section of a person's licence under section 34A(3) above, he shall be liable to be detained in pursuance of his sentence and, if at large, shall be deemed to be unlawfully at large.

(6) In this section 'the curfew condition' has the same meaning as in section 37A above.]

NOTES

Amendment:

Provision inserted: Crime and Disorder Act 1998 s100(2), with effect from 28 January 1999 (SI 1998 No 3263, article 3).

Provision repealed with savings: Criminal Justice Act 2003 ss303(a), 332, Sch 37 Pt 7, with effect from 4 April 2005 (SI 2005 No 950, article 2(1), Sch 1 paras 22, 44(1), (4)(k); for savings see Sch 2 paras 14, 19(c), 23(1) (as confirmed by SI 2005 No 2122, article 2) and para 34 thereof).

[40A Release on licence following return to prison

(1) This section applies (in place of sections 33, 33A, 37(1) and 39 above) where a court passes on a person a sentence of imprisonment which –

(a) includes, or consists of, an order under [section 116 of the Powers of Criminal Courts (Sentencing) Act 2000]; and

(b) is for a term of twelve months or less.

(2) As soon as the person has served one-half of the sentence, it shall be the duty of the Secretary of State to release him on licence.

(3) Where the person is so released, the licence shall remain in force for a period of three months.

(4) If the person fails to comply with such conditions as may for the time being be specified in the licence, he shall be liable on summary conviction –

(a) to a fine not exceeding level 3 on the standard scale; or

(b) to a sentence of imprisonment for a term not exceeding the relevant period,

but not liable to be dealt with in any other way.

(5) In subsection (4) above 'the relevant period' means a period which is equal in length to the period between the date on which the failure occurred or began and the date of the expiry of the licence.

(6) As soon as a person has served one-half of a sentence passed under subsection (4) above, it shall be the duty of the Secretary of State to release him, subject to the licence if it is still subsisting.]

NOTES

Amendment:

Provision inserted with savings: Crime and Disorder Act 1998 s105, with effect from 30 September 1998 (SI 1998 No 2327, article 2(1)(w)) (for savings see Sch 9, paras 12(1), (6), 14).

Provision repealed with savings: Criminal Justice Act 2003 ss303(a), 332, Sch 37 Pt 7, with effect from 4 April 2005 (SI 2005 No 950, article 2(1), Sch 1 paras 22, 44(1), (4)(k); for savings see Sch 2 paras 14, 19(c), 23(1) (as confirmed by SI 2005 No 2122, article 2) and para 34 thereof).

Sub-s(1)(A): words in square brackets substituted by Powers of Criminal Courts (Sentencing) Act 2000, s165(1), Sch 9, para 139.

Remand time and additional days

NOTES

Amendment:

Heading repealed with savings: Criminal Justice Act 2003 ss303(a), 332, Sch 37 Pt 7, with effect from 4 April 2005 (SI 2005 No 950, article 2(1), Sch 1 paras 22, 44(1), (4)(k); for savings see Sch 2 paras 14, 19(c), 23(1) (as confirmed by SI 2005 No 2122, article 2) and para 34 thereof).

41 Remand time to count towards time served

(1) This section applies to any person whose sentence falls to be reduced under section 67 of the Criminal Justice Act 1967 ('the 1967 Act') by any relevant period within the meaning of that section ('the relevant period').

(2) For the purpose of determining for the purposes of this Part –

(a) whether a person to whom this section applies has served one-half or two-thirds of his sentence; or

(b) whether such a person would (but for his release) have served three-quarters of that sentence,

the relevant period shall, subject to subsection (3) below, be treated as having been served by him as part of that sentence.

(3) Nothing in subsection (2) above shall have the effect of reducing the period for which a licence granted under this Part to a short-term or long-term prisoner remains in force to a period which is less than –

(a) one-quarter of his sentence in the case of a short-term prisoner; or

(b) one-twelfth of his sentence in the case of a long-term prisoner.

NOTES

Amendment:

Provision repealed with savings: Criminal Justice Act 2003 ss303(a), 332, Sch 37 Pt 7, with effect from 4 April 2005 (SI 2005 No 950, article 2(1), Sch 1 paras 22, 44(1), (4)(k); for savings see Sch 2 paras 14, 19(c), 23(1) (as confirmed by SI 2005 No 2122, article 2) and para 34 thereof).

42 Additional days for disciplinary offences

(1) Prison rules, that is to say, rules made under section 47 of the 1952 Act, may include provision for the award of additional days –

(a) to short-term or long-term prisoners; or

(b) conditionally on their subsequently becoming such prisoners, to persons on remand,

who (in either case) are guilty of disciplinary offences.

(2) Where additional days are awarded to a short-term or long-term prisoner, or to a person on remand who subsequently becomes such a prisoner, and are not remitted in accordance with prison rules –

(a) any period which he must serve before becoming entitled to or eligible for release under this Part;

[(aa) any period which he must serve before he can be removed under section 46A below;] and

(b) any period for which a licence granted to him under this Part remains in force,

shall be extended by the aggregate of those additional days.

NOTES

Amendment:

Provision repealed with savings: Criminal Justice Act 2003 ss303(a), 332, Sch 37 Pt 7, with effect from 4 April 2005 (SI 2005 No 950, article 2(1), Sch 1 paras 22, 44(1), (4)(k); for savings see Sch 2 paras 14, 19(c), 23(1) (as confirmed by SI 2005 No 2122, article 2) and para 34 thereof).

Sub-s(2)(aa): inserted by Criminal Justice Act 2003, s262, Sch 20, paras 1, 2.

Special cases

NOTES

Amendment:

Heading repealed with savings: Criminal Justice Act 2003 ss303(a), 332, Sch 37 Pt 7, with effect from 4 April 2005 (SI 2005 No 950, article 2(1), Sch 1 paras 22, 44(1), (4)(k); for savings see Sch 2 paras 14, 19(c), 23(1) (as confirmed by SI 2005 No 2122, article 2) and para 34 thereof).

43 Young offenders

(1) Subject to subsections (4) and (5) below, this Part applies to persons serving sentences of detention in a young offender institution, or determinate sentences of detention under [section 91 of the Powers of Criminal Courts (Sentencing) Act 2000], as it applies to persons serving equivalent sentences of imprisonment.

(2) ...

(3) References in this Part to prisoners ..., or to prison or imprisonment, shall be construed in accordance with [subsections (1)] ... above.

(4) In relation to a short-term prisoner under the age of 18 years to whom subsection (1) of section 33 above applies, that subsection shall have effect as if it required the Secretary of State –

(a) to release him unconditionally if his sentence is for a term of twelve months or less; and

(b) to release him on licence if that sentence is for a term of more than twelve months.

(5) In relation to a person under the age of 22 years who is released on licence under this Part, [section 37(4A)] above shall have effect as if the reference to supervision by [an officer of a local probation board] included a reference to supervision by a social worker of a local authority social services department.

NOTES

Amendment:

Provision repealed with savings: Criminal Justice Act 2003 ss303(a), 332, Sch 37 Pt 7, with effect from 4 April 2005 (SI 2005 No 950, article 2(1), Sch 1 paras 22, 44(1), (4)(k); for savings see Sch 2 paras 14, 19(c), 23(1) (as confirmed by SI 2005 No 2122, article 2) and para 34 thereof).

Sub-s(1): words in square brackets substituted by Powers of Criminal Courts (Sentencing) Act 2000, s165(1), Sch 9, para 140.

Sub-s(2): repealed by Crime (Sentences) Act 1997, s56, Schs 5, 6.

Sub-s(3): words omitted in each place repealed by Crime (Sentences) Act 1997, s56, Schs 5, 6.

Sub-s(3): words in square brackets substituted by Crime and Disorder Act 1998, s119, Sch 8, para 87(1).

Sub-s(5): words in first set of square brackets substituted by Crime and Disorder Act 1998, s119, Sch 8, para 87(2).

Sub-s(5): words in second set of square brackets substituted by Criminal Justice and Court Services Act 2000, s74, Sch 7, Pt I, para 4.

[44 Extended sentences for sexual or violent offenders

(1) This section applies to a prisoner serving an extended sentence within the meaning of [section 85 of the Powers of Criminal Courts (Sentencing) Act 2000].

(2) Subject to the provisions of this section and section 51(2D) below, this Part, except [section] 40A, shall have effect as if the term of the extended sentence did not include the extension period.

(3) Where the prisoner is released on licence under this Part, the licence shall, subject to any revocation under section 39(1) or (2) above, remain in force until the end of the extension period.

(4) Where, apart from this subsection, the prisoner would be released unconditionally –
 (a) he shall be released on licence; and
 (b) the licence shall, subject to any revocation under section 39(1) or (2) above, remain in force until the end of the extension period.

(5) The extension period shall be taken to begin as follows –
 (a) for the purposes of subsection (3) above, on the date given by section 37(1) above;
 (b) for the purposes of subsection (4) above, on the date on which, apart from that subsection, the prisoner would have been released unconditionally.

(6) Sections 33(3) and 33A(1) above and section 46 below shall not apply in relation to the prisoner.

(7) For the purposes of sections 37(5) and 39(1) and (2) above the question whether the prisoner is a long-term or short-term prisoner shall be determined by reference to the term of the extended sentence.

(8) In this section 'extension period' has the same meaning as in [section 85 of the Powers of Criminal Courts (Sentencing) Act 2000].]

NOTES

Amendment:

Provision repealed in part in relation to persons sentenced for sexual offences committed before 30 September 1998: Powers of Criminal Courts (Sentencing) Act 2000, s165(4), Sch 12 Pt I; for remaining purposes with savings: Criminal Justice Act 2003 ss303(a), 332, Sch 37 Pt 7, with effect from 4 April 2005 (SI 2005 No 950, article 2(1), Sch 1 paras 22, 44(1), (4)(k); for savings see Sch 2 paras 14, 19(c), 23(1) (as confirmed by SI 2005 No 2122, article 2) and para 34 thereof).

Provision substituted with savings: Crime and Disorder Act 1998, s59, with effect from 30 September 1998, except in relation to a person who is sentenced for a sexual offence which was committed before that date (Crime and Disorder Act 1998 (Commencement No 2 and Transitional Provisions) Order 1998, SI 1998/2327, arts 2(1)(n), 8(1)) (for savings, see Sch 9, para 12(1), (7), Crime and Disorder Act 1998).

Sub-s(1): words in square brackets substituted by Powers of Criminal Courts (Sentencing) Act 2000, s165(1), Sch 9, para 141(1), (2).

Sub-s(2): words in square brackets substituted by Powers of Criminal Courts (Sentencing) Act 2000, s165(1), Sch 9, para 141(1), (3).

Sub-s(8): words in square brackets substituted by Powers of Criminal Courts (Sentencing) Act 2000, s165(1), Sch 9, para 141(1), (2).

APPENDIX 5

Directions to the Parole Board on the release of determinate sentence prisoners

Issued May 2004.

Directions issued under section 32(6) CJA to the Parole Board on initial release of DCR Prisoners

1 In deciding whether or not to recommend release on license, the Parole Board shall consider primarily the risk to the public of a further offence being committed at a time when the prisoner would otherwise be in prison and whether any such risk is acceptable. This must be balanced against the benefit, both to the public and the offender, of early release back into the community under a degree of supervision which might help rehabilitation and so lessen the risk of re-offending in the future. The Board shall take into account that safeguarding the public may often outweigh the benefits to the offender of early release.

2 Before recommending release on parole licence, the Parole Board shall consider:

a) whether the safety of the public would be placed unacceptably at risk. In assessing such risk, the Board shall take into account:

i) the nature and circumstances of the index offence including any information provided in relation to its impact on the victim or victim's family;

ii) the offender's background, including the nature, circumstances and pattern of any previous offending;

iii) whether the prisoner has shown by his attitude and behaviour in custody that he is willing to address his offending behaviour by participating in programmes or activities designed to address his risk, and has made positive effort and progress in doing so;

iv) behaviour during any temporary release or other outside activities;

v) any risk to other persons, including the victim, their family and friends;

vi) any medical, psychiatric or psychological considerations relevant to risk (particularly where there is a history of mental instability);

vii) if available, the indication of predicted risk as determined by a validated actuarial risk predictor;

viii) that a risk of violent or sexual offending is more serious than a risk of other types of offending;

b) the content of the resettlement plan;
c) whether the longer period of supervision that parole would provide is likely to reduce the risk of further offences being committed;
d) whether the prisoner is likely to comply with the conditions of his licence and the requirements of supervision, taking into account occasions where he has breached trust in the past;
e) the suitability of home circumstances;
f) the relationship with the supervising probation officer;
g) the attitude of the local community in cases where it may have a detrimental affect upon compliance; and
h) representations on behalf of the victim in respect of licence conditions.

3 Each individual case shall be considered on its merits, without discrimination on any grounds.

APPENDIX 6

Criteria for the release of determinate sentence prisoners facing deportation

Following are the criteria applied by the Home Secretary when considering release on licence for deportees under the enhanced assessment for the early release scheme, or on parole licence for CJA 1991 DCR prisoners.

Criteria for the release of those long-term prisoners liable to deportation or removal from the UK

1 The decision whether to release before NPD a prisoner liable to deportation or removal from the UK should focus primarily on the need to protect the public from serious harm and the prevention of further offending.

2 Each case should be considered on its individual merits, without discrimination on any grounds.

3 Before deciding whether or not to release a deportee in advance of automatic release at the two-thirds point of sentence, the following factors – the weight and relevance of which may vary according to the circumstances of the case – should be taken into account:–

a. the offender's background, including any previous convictions and their pattern;

b. the nature and circumstances of the original offence;

c. where available, the sentencing judge's comments and probation and medical reports prepared for the court;

d. any risk to the victim or other persons, including persons outside the jurisdiction;

e. attitude and behaviour in custody including offences against prison discipline;

f. attitude to other inmates and positive contributions made to prison life;

g. remorse, insight into offending behaviour and steps taken, within available resources, to address offending and to achieve any treatment or training objectives set out in a sentence plan;

h. any medical or psychiatric considerations;

i. any other information, including representations by or on behalf of the offender, which may have a bearing on risk assessment.

APPENDIX 7

Directions to the Parole Board on the recall of determinate sentence prisoners

Directions to the Parole Board under Section 239(6) of the Criminal Justice Act 2003 on recall of determinate sentence prisoners – applicable from 4 April 2005

Where an offender is subject to a custodial sentence, the licence period is an integral part of the sentence, and compliance with licence conditions is required. In most cases the licences are combined with supervision by a probation officer, social worker or member of the Youth Offending Team (the exception to this is the use of Home Detention Curfew licences for adult prisoners serving a sentence of less than 12 months).

The objects of supervision are:

- to protect the public;
- to prevent reoffending;
- to ensure the prisoner's successful reintegration into the community

Review of a Decision Taken by the Secretary of State to Recall an Offender

Section 254 of the Criminal Justice Act 2003 requires the Parole Board to review any decision taken by the Secretary of State to recall an offender to prison. The review will take place once the offender has been returned to custody. In determining whether the recall was appropriate, the Parole Board is entitled to take into account the information available at the time the recall decision was taken, together with any subsequent information, including representations made by or on behalf of the offender. The Parole Board should consider whether:

(a) The prisoner's continued liberty presents an unacceptable risk of a further offence being committed; or

(b) The prisoner has failed to comply with one or more of his or her licence conditions; and that failure suggests that the objectives of probation supervision have been undermined.

In cases where the Parole Board believes that the initial decision to recall was inappropriate, the prisoner should be re-released as soon as it is practicable to do so. In determining when to re-release the prisoner, the Parole Board should satisfy itself that the prisoner presents an acceptable risk to public safety and that adequate risk management arrangements are in place.

Where a prisoner has been charged for an offence committed whilst subject to Home Detention Curfew licence, the Board shall additionally take into account that it is desirable for such a prisoner to be recalled to custody, unless it is clearly apparent that the conduct that has led the prisoner to being charged does not merit recall.

The Board's decision to re-release

The Board has powers to:

- release immediately;
- release at a specified future date;
- review the case again; and
- decline to release (only in cases where the prisoner has less than 12 months to serve before the sentence expires).

The assumption is that the Parole Board will seek to re-release the prisoner or set a future re-release date in all cases where it is satisfied that the risk be safely managed in the community. In making this assessment, the Board should take into account that a risk of sexual or violent offending is more serious than a risk of other types of offending.

In determining whether to set a re-release or review date, the Parole Board shall consider:

(a) Whether the risk management plan, prepared by the Probation Service is adequate to address any potential risk of harm or reoffending presented by the prisoner during the licence period.

(b) The likelihood, of the offender complying with the requirements of probation supervision should he or she be re-released during the licence period. In assessing the likelihood of compliance, the Board should consider the conduct of the offender during the licence period to date and the extent to which previous enforcement has influenced such conduct.

(c) The availability of a suitable release plan, the availability and timing of any offending behaviour work either in custody or in the community.

(d) The date on which the outcome of any pending prosecution will be known.

(e) Whether in the interests of public protection the prisoner's long term rehabilitation would be better served if the offender were re-released whilst subject to probation supervision.

The Parole Board shall take into account the fact that prisoners who have been sentenced under the provisions of the Criminal Justice Act 1991 cannot be disadvantaged by the recall provisions of the Criminal Justice Act 2003.

Each individual case shall be considered on its own merits, without any discrimination on any unlawful grounds.

APPENDIX 8

Directions to the Parole Board on the release and recall of life sentence prisoners

Issued in 2004.

NB The Parole Board is not required to follow the directions, but they have been considered by the court to consist of matters that are properly to be taken into account (see *Girling v Parole Board* [2005] EWHC 546 (QBD)).

DIRECTIONS TO THE PAROLE BOARD UNDER SECTION 32(6) OF THE CRIMINAL JUSTICE ACT 1991 RELEASE AND RECALL OF LIFE SENTENCE PRISONERS

INTRODUCTION

1 The Secretary of State may refer to, and seek advice from, the Parole Board on any matters relating to the early release and recall to custody of those prisoners sentenced to imprisonment for life, custody for life, detention during Her Majesty's pleasure, and detention for life.

2 The Parole Board is empowered to direct the release, or re-release following recall to custody, of those life sentence prisoners (lifers) who have served the period of imprisonment necessary to satisfy the requirements of retribution and deterrence

3 The Parole Board cannot direct the release of any lifer unless the following conditions are met:–

a) the Secretary of State has referred the case to the Parole Board for consideration of the prisoner's suitability for release;

b) the Parole Board is satisfied that it is no longer necessary for the protection of the public that the prisoner should be confined.

4 The test to be applied by the Parole Board in satisfying itself that it is no longer necessary for the protection of the public that the prisoner should be confined, is whether the lifer's level of risk to the life and limb of others is considered to be more than minimal.

DIRECTIONS

5 Before directing a lifer's release under supervision on life licence, the Parole Board must consider:–

a) all information before it, including any written or oral evidence obtained by the Board;

b) each case on its merits, without discrimination on any grounds;

c) whether the release of the lifer is consistent with the general requirements and objectives of supervision in the community, namely;
   - protecting the public by ensuring that their safety would not be placed unacceptably at risk;
   - securing the lifer's successful re-integration into the community.

6 In assessing the level of risk to life and limb presented by a lifer, the Parole Board shall consider the following information, where relevant and where available, before directing the lifer's release, recognising that the weight and relevance attached to particular information may vary according to the circumstances of each case:

a) the lifer's background, including the nature, circumstances and pattern of any previous offending;

b) the nature and circumstances of the index offence, including any information provided in relation to its impact on the victim or victim's family;

c) the trial judge's sentencing comments or report to the Secretary of State, and any probation, medical, or other relevant reports or material prepared for the court;

d) whether the lifer has made positive and successful efforts to address the attitudes and behavioural problems which led to the commission of the index offence;

e) the nature of any offences against prison discipline committed by the lifer;

f) the lifer's attitude and behaviour to other prisoners and staff,

g) the category of security in which the lifer is held and any reasons or reports provided by the Prison Service for such categorisation, particularly in relation to those lifers held in Category A conditions of security;

h) the lifer's awareness of the impact of the index offence, particularly in relation to the victim or victim's family, and the extent of any demonstrable insight into his /her attitudes and behavioural problems and whether he/she has taken steps to reduce risk through the achievement of life sentence plan targets;

i) any medical, psychiatric or psychological considerations (particularly if there is a history of mental instability);

j) the lifer's response when placed in positions of trust, including any absconds, escapes, past breaches of temporary release or life licence conditions and life licence revocations;

k) any indication of predicted risk as determined by a validated actuarial risk predictor model, or any other structured assessments of the lifer's risk and treatment needs

l) whether the lifer is likely to comply with the conditions attached to his or her life licence and the requirements of supervision, including any additional non-standard conditions;

m) any risk to other persons, including the victim, their family and friends.

7 Before directing release on life licence, the Parole Board shall also consider:–

a) the lifer's relationship with probation staff (in particular the supervising probation officer), and other outside support such as family and friends;

b) the content of the resettlement plan and the suitability of the release address;
c) the attitude of the local community in cases where it may have a detrimental effect upon compliance;
d) representations on behalf of the victim or victim's relatives in relation to licence conditions.

APPENDIX 9

Directions to the Parole Board on the transfer of life sentence prisoners to open conditions

A period in open conditions is essential for most life sentence prisoners ('lifers'). It allows the testing of areas of concern in conditions which are nearer to those in the community than can be found in closed prisons. Lifers have the opportunity to take home leave from open prisons and, more generally, open conditions require them to take more responsibility for their actions.

In considering whether a lifer should be transferred to open conditions, the Parole Board should balance the risks against the benefits to be gained from such a move. Such consideration is, thus, somewhat different from the judgment to be made when deciding if a lifer should be released: in those cases, the Parole Board is asked only to consider risk.

The principal factors which the Parole Board should take into account when evaluating the risks of transfer against the benefits are:

a) whether the lifer has made sufficient progress towards tackling offending behavior to minimize the risk and gravity of re-offending and whether the benefits suggest that a transfer to open conditions is worthwhile at that stage;

and

b) whether the lifer is trustworthy enough not to abscond or to commit further offences (either inside or outside the prison).

Each case should be considered on its individual merits.

Before recommending transfer to open conditions, the Parole Board should consider whether:

a) the extent to which the risk that the lifer will abscond or commit further offences while in an open prison is minimal.
b) the lifer has shown by his performance in closed conditions that he has made positive efforts to address his attitudes and behavioral problems and the extent to which significant progress has been made in doing so.
c) the lifer is likely to derive benefit from being able to continue to address areas of concern in an open prison and to be tested in a more realistic environment.

Before deciding whether or not to recommend transfer to open conditions, the Parole Board must take into account all of the papers submitted to it.

APPENDIX 10

Useful addresses and contact details

Lifer Review and Recall Section
Abell House
John Islip Street
London SW1P 4LH
Tel: 020 7210 3000

Team 1 – Surnames beginning with the letters B, K, R, V, Q, Y
  Fax: 020 7217 2183
Team 2 – E, H, L, N, Z
  Fax: 020 7217 1916
Team 3 – All post release casework (licences, recalls etc)
  Fax: 020 7217 5283
Team 4 – D, S, T
  Fax: 020 7217 5517
Team 5 – A, J, M, U, X
  Fax: 020 7217 5517
Team 6 – F, I, O, W; and all female lifers and young offenders
  Fax: 020 7217 5892
Team 7 – C,G,P
  Fax: 020 7217 1915

National Offender Management Service
Home Office
3rd Floor
Peel Building
2 Marsham Street
London SW1P 4DF
Tel: 0207 035 1530

National Probation Directorate
Horseferry House
Dean Ryle Street
London SW1P 2AW
Tel: 020 7217 0659
Fax: 020 7217 0660
Website: www.probation.homeoffice.gov.uk (which provides access to Probation Circulars online, and contact details for regional probation boards)

The Parole Board
Grenadier House
99–105 Horseferry House
London SW1P 2DD

General enquiries:
Tel: 0870 420 3505
Fax: 0870 420 3506
Website: www.paroleboard.gov.uk

The Secretariat is divided up into an Oral Hearings Team, a Pre-Hearings Team, a Representations against Recall Team, a Paper Hearings Team and the Post-Panel Team that deals with legal challenges to Parole Board decisions.

Prison and Probation Ombudsman
Ashley House
2 Monck Street
London SW1P 2BQ
Tel: 020 7035 2876 or 0845 010 7938
Fax: 020 7035 2860
Website: www.ppo.gov.uk

HM Prison Service Headquarters
Cleland House
Page Street
London SW1P 4LN
Tel: 020 7210 3000
Website: www.hmprisonservice.gov.uk (includes contact details for all prisons in England and Wales, and access to PSOs and PSIs online)

Release and Recall Section
Abell House
John Islip Street
London SW1P 4LH
and
7th Floor, Amp House
Croydon CR0 2LX

Head of Section is located in the London Office. The London Office contains:

The Public Protection Team (MAPPP level 3 and extended sentence recalls)
Fax: 020 7217 5223

Oral Hearings and Review Team
Fax: 020 7217 2119

Pre-release Casework Team
Dealing with decisions relating to deportees, and cases where the Home Secretary has to approve release decisions (such as DCR 1991 cases where the sentence is 15 or more years)

HDC Breach Team
Fax: 020 7217 2139

ACR and DCR caseworking teams are located in the Croydon Office, as are Recall casework teams which are divided up by reference to the probation area making the recall recommendation:

Recall Team 1 – Responsible for Humberside, London and Yorkshire probation regions
Fax: 020 8774 0268
Recall Team 2 – Responsible for North West and South West probation regions
Fax: 020 8760 1766
Recall Team 3 – Responsible for North East, South East and East Midlands probation regions
Fax: 020 8760 1746
Recall Team 4 – Responsible for East of England, Wales and West Midlands probation areas
Fax: 020 8760 1781

Index